Preston

AUTHOR

Handbook of Clinical

TITLE

Handbook of Clinical
Psychopharmacology
for Therapists

Third Edition

John D. Preston, Psy.D.
John H. O'Neal, M.D.
Mary C. Talaga, R.Ph., M.A.

New Harbinger Publications, Inc.

Figures 6-A, 6-B, 6-E, 8-D, 8-E, 9-B, and 15-F have been previously published in *Clinical Psychopharmacology Made Ridiculously Simple*, 1994, MedMaster Inc., Miami, and are reproduced here with the permission of the copyright holder.

Handbook of Clinical Psychopharmacology for Therapists, Third Edition
Copyright © 2004 by John Preston, Psy.D., John H. O'Neal, M.D., and
                  Mary C. Talaga, B.S., Pharm., R.Ph., M.A.
                  New Harbinger Publications, Inc.
                  5674 Shattuck Avenue
                  Oakland, CA 94609

ISBN 1-57224-269-8 Hardcover

Cover design by SHELBY DESIGNS & ILLUSTRATES.
Text design by Tracy Marie Carlson.
Indexed by James Minkin.

All rights reserved. Printed in the United States of America using recycled paper.

New Harbinger Publication's Web site address: www.newharbinger.com

First edition printed from June 1994 to December 1996.

Second edition printed from September 1997 to March 2001.

Third Edition

06   05   04

15   14   13   12   11   10   9   8   7

To my boys, Matt and David
—J.P.

To Wendy, Sean, and Matthew for their loving support through the writing of this book
—J.O.

To my parents for opening my mind . . . and to my sons for opening my heart
—M.T.

What is paraded as scientific fact is simply the current belief of some scientists. We are accustomed to regard science as truth with a capital "T." What scientific knowledge is, in fact, is the best available approximation of truth in the judgment of the majority of scientists who work in the particular specialty involved. Truth is not something that we possess, it is a goal towards which we hopefully strive ... the current opinion of the scientific establishment is only the latest and never the last word.

—M. Scott Peck, M.D.,
author of *The Road Less Traveled*

Contents

Acknowledgments   ix

Part One
Understanding Psychopharmacology: The Basics

1   Introduction   3

2   Integrated Models   15

3   Neurobiology   27

4   Pharmacology   43

Part Two
Clinical Syndromes: Etiology, Diagnosis, and Treatment Implications

5   Preliminary Diagnostic Considerations   57

6   Depressive Disorders   69

7   Bipolar Disorders   85

8   Anxiety Disorders   97

9   Obsessive-Compulsive Disorder   113

10   Psychotic Disorders   119

11   Post-Traumatic Stress Disorder   131

12   Borderline Personality Disorders   139

13   Substance-Related Disorders   145

14   Other Miscellaneous Disorders   153

Part Three
Medications

15	Antidepressant Medications	163
16	Mood Stabilizers	181
17	Antianxiety Medications	193
18	Antipsychotic Medications	201
19	Over-the-Counter Products	209
20	Red Flags: When to Reevaluate	213
Epilogue: On the Horizon		221

Appendixes

A	Pharmacokinetics	223
B	Pharmacotherapy in Special Populations	229
C	Psychotropic Drug Interactions	239
D	Differentiating Psychotropic Side Effects from Psychiatric Symptoms	247
E	Neurocognitive Mental Status Exam	251
F	Trade Versus Generic Drug Names: A Quick Reference	255
G	Books for Patients About Medication Treatment	259
References		261
Index		271

Acknowledgments

Many thanks to our publisher, Dr. Matthew McKay, and our editors, Leslie Tilley and Kayla Sussell, for helping our ideas to take form.

To our families and friends, with deep appreciation, for their patience and encouragement throughout this project.

Finally, heartfelt thanks to our students and our patients. May this book reach many and hopefully contribute to our ongoing struggle to reduce emotional suffering.

Part One

Understanding Psychopharmacology: The Basics

Part one of this book briefly covers the development of psychopharmacology from an historical and sociological perspective and then goes on to provide an overview of neurobiology and pharmacology. The purpose of these chapters is not to provide a comprehensive discussion of the fields of pharmacology or neurophysiology, but is simply to familiarize you with the basic terminology and models of pharmacokinetics.

1

Introduction

This book is intended primarily for mental health professionals and those in graduate training in psychology, social work, and counseling. The professional goal of most readers will be to provide services that aim to reduce emotional pain, to promote psychological growth and healing, and to foster the development of personal autonomy. To this end, we in the field are trained in various theoretical approaches that attempt to explain the development of maladaptive lifestyles and subjectively painful psychiatric symptoms. These theories serve to give meaning and coherence to what we do in clinical practice and, most importantly, lay a foundation of understanding so that interventions make sense and further the goal of reducing suffering in ways that are effective.

Many schools of thought exist regarding the origins of mental health problems. As has been well documented in the history of psychiatry, as schools of thought evolve, controversy, dogma, and empassioned belief systems emerge. It may be inherent to the development and maturation of science that these emotionally toned belief systems and the resulting debates occur.

From the mid-sixties through the seventies, polarization occurred within psychiatry between those advocating psychological theories (primarily psychodynamic and behavioral models) and those on the other side of the fence using biological and medical models. The disagreements that emerged were more than differences of opinion or dry debate. Each school attracted followers who had strong emotional investments in their perspective.

For many years this division resulted in the development of barriers between groups of mental health clinicians—and at times in fragmentation in care. Fortunately, during the past decade something has changed. We are beginning to witness a shift in thinking, as increasing numbers of practitioners and training institutes move away from egocentric and dogmatic positions and begin to embrace a more integrated approach with regard to both theories of etiology and methods of treatment.

New discoveries in the neurosciences, refined technical advances in psychotherapy, and a large number of outcome studies in both pharmacotherapy and psychotherapy have made it abundantly clear: People are complex. Mental health problems spring from many sources; and reductionist, unidimensional models are simply inadequate to explain the wide array of mental and emotional problems people experience. Likewise, no single approach to treatment works for all problems. Certain disorders clearly respond better to certain interventions, whereas others require alternative approaches.

In writing this book, although our primary focus is on psychopharmacology, we share a strong respect for what will be termed *integrative approaches* to treatment: recognition of the importance of varied treatments and collaboration among professionals from different disciplines.

We hope that you will find this book helpful as you engage in this most important profession and work toward the goal of reducing emotional pain.

History of Biological Psychiatry

In understanding psychopharmacology, it may be helpful if you are able to place it in a historical context. Let's take a brief look at this history as it unfolded.

In the late 1800s psychiatry was clearly rooted in the medical model and the neurology of the day. Psychiatrists believed, almost exclusively, that mental illness could be attributed to some sort of biologic disturbance. The earliest attempts to approach the understanding of mental illness in this era involved two main areas of investigation.

On one front was the development of the first systematic nosologic system by Emil Kraepelin. This pioneering work laid the foundation for all later diagnostic schema (such as the *Diagnostic and Statistical Manual of Mental Disorders*, or *DSM*). And many of Kraepelin's original notions about the classification of major mental illness have stood the test of time. He was a brilliant investigator and the one most responsible for ushering in descriptive clinical psychiatry. However, his endeavors must have been accompanied by a good deal of frustration and impotence, since, despite the development of a systematic approach to diagnosis, Kraepelin and other psychiatrists of his time had few if any methods of treatment.

At the same time, the hunt was on for evidence of brain pathology, which was presumed to underlie mental illness. Research was conducted in neuroanatomy labs but yielded few concrete results. For example, the famous French neurologist Jean-Martin Charcot believed that hysterical conversation symptoms were undoubtedly due to some type of central nervous system lesion. He explained the fact that no demonstrable pathology could be isolated on autopsy by saying it simply suggested that somehow the lesion mysteriously disappeared at the time of death. We must bear in mind, however, that in all likelihood, these researchers and clinicians were desperate to find causes and cures and went at it by the means best known to them (biology) and using the scant technology available at the time.

Biological psychiatry got a shot in the arm in the late 1800s, as two discoveries were made. At the time, probably one half of those housed in asylums suffered from a type of psychotic-organic brain syndrome which ultimately was found to be caused by the *Treponema pallidum* bacteria (a central nervous system infection seen in the late stages of syphilis). It was also eventually discovered that some organic mental syndromes were due to pellagra (a disease associated with niacin and protein deficiency). These were important discoveries, and they fueled enthusiasm in biological psychiatry. It was just a matter of time, they felt, before other biologic causes would be isolated and medical treatments developed. However, such discoveries did not occur until the middle of the twentieth century. For practical purposes, biological psychiatry came to a halt as it entered the 1900s.

The disappointments stemming from medical research on mental illness and the failure to develop any effective treatment probably increased the receptivity of psychiatry to divergent approaches. At this same time Sigmund Freud was assembling the basic notions of psychoanalysis. Freud's initial theory was strongly influenced by his own medical and neurological training (for example, his "Project for a Scientific Psychology," 1895), and many of his prevailing ideas continued to have their roots in biology, including drive theory, instincts, and psychosexual development. However, his newly emerging theory and techniques of treatment sparked interest in the use of novel, nonmedical approaches to treatment.

By the 1920s psychological (rather than biological) explanations for the development and treatment of psychopathology had found their place in clinical psychiatry, and by the 1940s psychodynamic thinking had permeated American psychiatry and become the dominant theoretical model. Yet these newly developed approaches proved to be inadequate in the treatment of the more serious forms of mental illness, such as schizophrenia and manic-depressive psychosis. In one of his last manuscripts, Freud himself admitted his disappointment in psychoanalytic methods for treating schizophrenia. He hypothesized that eventually it would be discovered that these grave mental disorders were due to some form of biologic abnormality, and that perhaps drugs would eventually be found to treat these illnesses.

Somatic Therapies

In the days of Kraepelin, pharmaceuticals were used to treat mentally ill patients. Generally, the drugs were prescribed to sedate wildly agitated psychotic patients. For example, Kraepelin listed in one of his textbooks the following group of recommended medications (Spiegel and Aebi 1989):

For Agitation	**To Produce Sleep**
Opium	Chloral Hydrate
Morphine	Ether
Scopolamine	Alcohol
Hashish	Chloroform
	Bromides

Kraepelin noted, however, that none of these preparations cured mental illness, that they were for short-term use, and that a number of them could lead to problems with addiction. All of these drugs achieved behavioral control by sedating patients; none really affected psychotic symptoms per se, nor did they have any impact on activating patients who were stuporous or clinically depressed.

Other somatic therapies were developed in the first half of the twentieth century, with variable results. Malaria therapy was conceived in 1917, insulin shock in 1927, psychosurgery in 1936, and electroconvulsive treatment (ECT) in 1938. All of these methods, as originally conceived, carried serious risks, and most demonstrated marginal effectiveness. Psychosurgeries were carried out by the thousands in the 1940s, resulting in rather effective behavioral control over agitated psychotic patients but at great human cost. Many, if not most, lobotomized patients were reduced to anergic, passive, and emotionally dead human beings.

Electroconvulsive treatment, conversely, was quite effective in certain groups of patients, such as those with psychotic depressive disorders. However, early methods of administration were fraught with dangerous complications and side effects, and ECT was used on a widespread basis, indiscriminately. Many patients were treated with it inappropriately and did not respond. (As shall be discussed later, in recent years significant advances have been made in ECT, and it now affords a highly effective, safe treatment for selected types of patients.)

Most severely ill patients in the late nineteenth and early twentieth centuries continued to be housed in overcrowded state mental hospitals and were "treated" using tried and true methods of the day: seclusion, restraint, and wet sheet packs. Although seemingly inhumane procedures were employed, it may be important to consider that the psychiatrists of that era were relatively helpless in the face of very severe mental illnesses and that these approaches (although certainly misused at times) reflected their attempt to reduce the horrendous human suffering seen in thousands of severely ill people.

New Discoveries

In the 1950s, three new discoveries heralded the beginnings of a new interest in biological psychiatry. Interestingly, these three areas of investigation were conducted by separate groups of researchers, each with little knowledge of the work being done by their colleagues (Kety 1975).

Thorazine and other early psychotropic drugs

Immediately after World War II, medical researchers and chemists working for pharmaceutical companies were trying to develop a drug that would reduce the complications associated with shock following major surgery. In early 1951, a compound initially labeled #4560 RP was developed and testing with surgical patients was begun (Spiegel and Aebi 1989). The initial results were encouraging. Given preoperatively, it was able to relax patients, somewhat reduced postoperative shock, and proved to be a good antiemetic (preventing postsurgical nausea). The finding that it produced noticeable sedation came as a surprise. In the aftermath of field trials with surgical patients, the pharmaceutical company Laborit decided to try this medication with restless, agitated psychiatric patients to help improve sleep, totally unaware that the drug would prove to have more widespread effects on the psychiatric patients who were tested.

Initial clinical trials first reported in 1952 resulted in marked behavioral changes when given to manic and schizophrenic patients. Not only did it produce a calming effect, but after a period of time it actually appeared to reduce psychotic symptoms such as delusions and hallucinations. Additional studies were carried out the following year, and by 1954 the drug was approved for use. The new medication was given the generic name chlorpromazine; in the United States it was marketed under the brand name Thorazine. It received immediate acceptance, and by the end of 1954, for the first time ever, there was a marked decrease in the number of patients incarcerated in state mental hospitals: the first major breakthrough in psychopharmacology.

Other psychotropic medications were discovered during the fifties. The first antidepressant was developed in 1952 (iproniazid, an MAO inhibitor), although clinical studies in humans did not take place until 1956. The first tricyclic antidepressant, imipramine (Tofranil), was developed in 1954 and entered the market in 1957. The first minor tranquilizer, meprobamate, was released in 1955, followed shortly by the safer benzodiazepine, chlordiazepoxide (Librium), in 1958. Finally, lithium carbonate, originally used as a sedative by J. Cade in 1948, began to be used to treat manic-depressive illness in the early 1960s.

It is interesting to note that most of these psychopharmacological discoveries were accidental; that is, the drug companies were developing medications to treat other, medical illnesses, and just happened to find that the drugs could affect psychiatric symptoms. Also, these discoveries were made empirically; they were not developed as an outgrowth of a particular theory of neurochemical dysfunction, nor was the mechanism of action at all known. What was evident was that the medications worked and were far superior to any previous treatments for severe mental illness.

The synapse and neurochemical transmission

Although C. S. Sherrington inferred the existence of the synapse (the small space separating individual nerve cells) as early as 1906, the specific details of synaptic transmission were not fully understood for many decades thereafter. Sherrington's ideas involved a sort of telephone switchboard model of the nervous system, and neuronal messages were assumed to be transmitted via electrical stimulation. It was not until the 1950s that neuroscientists realized that communication between nerve cells, although partially electrochemical in nature, is largely due to the release of chemical substances. These chemicals, which transmit messages from one nerve cell to another, are referred to as neurotransmitters; other chemicals that play an indirect role in neurotransmission are called neuromodulators.

With this discovery, it became possible to imagine that certain neurologic dysfunctions might be caused by chemical irregularities, and that therefore it might be possible to develop drugs that could influence or alter neurotransmitter function.

Genetic studies

The third line of investigation involved both genetics and studies of familial patterns of mental illness. The earliest research in this direction was ultimately criticized for numerous methodological flaws. Yet some of the basic findings proved to be fundamentally correct. There is a strong genetic loading for certain mental illnesses, in particular for schizophrenia and manic-depressive illness. (In recent times evidence has been obtained revealing genetic loadings for a number of mental disorders, although clearly the strongest evidence exists for bipolar disorder and some types of schizophrenia.)

Controversy

By the early sixties then, it had been discovered that synaptic activation is chemical in nature; certain illnesses seem to be genetically passed on from generation to generation (and genetic factors are expressed biochemically); and newer drugs could significantly reduce psychiatric symptoms. The triangulation of this data provided rather strong support for a renewed interest in biological psychiatry. There was new hope for the millions of patients suffering from serious mental illness, and psychiatry had begun to step back into "real medicine" again.

However, despite the advances, these new treatments were plagued by a host of side effects—some unpleasant, some actually dangerous. These potent drugs were also often overused or were misused in certain treatment settings. Consequently, controversy began to arise, both among professionals, and in the lay public and mass media.

Medications and the Media

Research studies and clinical experience certainly influence prescribing practices. However, in recent years the media has had a profound effect on public opinion and ultimately on clinical practice.

In the late 1980s negative attention was focused on the drug Ritalin (methylphenidate), a widely prescribed stimulant used in the treatment of hyperactivity and attention deficit disorder (ADD). Andrew Brotman, summarizing the work of Safer and Krager (1992), states, "The media attack was led by major national television talk show hosts and in the opinion of the authors, allowed anecdotal and unsubstantiated allegations concerning Ritalin to be aired. There were also over twenty lawsuits initiated throughout the country, most by a lawyer linked to the Church of Scientology" (Brotman 1992).

In a study of the effects of this negative media and litigation blitz conducted in Baltimore County, Maryland, Safer and Krager (1992) found that the use of Ritalin had dropped significantly. From 1981 through 1987, the use of Ritalin had increased fivefold. However, in the two-year period during and just following the negative media attention, there was a 40 percent decrease in prescriptions for Ritalin. And this decrease occurred at a time when research on ADD and stimulant treatment continued to strongly support the safety and efficacy of such medications. The authors go on to state that 36 percent of children who discontinued Ritalin experienced major academic maladjustment (such as failing grades or being suspended), and an additional 47 percent who discontinued encountered mild to moderate

continued

Professional dissention

Within professional ranks, debate issued from two fairly discrete theoretical camps: those who were pro-medication and those who were pro-psychotherapy. Each group amassed impassioned arguments not only in favor of their own point of view, but also against the other school of thought, as set out below.

Pro-medication (anti-psychotherapy) — arguments in favor of medication treatment, as the treatment of choice:

- Because of its quantifiable nature—that is, the ability to monitor dosage—medication treatment can be studied much more systematically than psychotherapy.

- Medications act quickly to reduce painful and debilitating symptoms.

- The quicker response seen with medications can help to restore hope and reduce demoralization.

- Treatment with medications can be conducted in a much more systematic and standardized fashion, whereas psychotherapy relies heavily on the individual skill of the psychotherapist.

- Rapid and effective symptom relief can potentially reduce suffering to such an extent that the patient is better able to engage productively in psychotherapy. Likewise, the reductions of drive strength afforded by some psychotropic medications may operate to free up more psychic energy, which could then be channeled into adaptive ego functions.

- Medications can provide help to patients who have limited intellectual capacity, poor ego strength, or both; that is, drugs may be effective with people for whom psychotherapy is inappropriate.

- Psychotherapy is often prolonged and expensive, may be unavailable to many people, and is of unproven effectiveness (this was the case especially in light of the very limited psychotherapy outcome studies available in the 1950s and 1960s). Thus medications are much more cost-effective and more readily available to the general public.

Finally, those strongly wedded to a biochemical model of psychopathology contended that social, behavioral, and psychological approaches simply could not correct the underlying biologic abnormality responsible for major mental illnesses. Recent studies, however, have cast doubt on this hypothesis.

Pro-psychotherapy (anti-medication) — arguments in favor of psychotherapy as the treatment of choice:

- Only psychotherapy, not medications, can address the complexity of human psychological functioning. Medications only treat symptoms, whereas psychotherapy focuses on the whole person or psyche.

- Psychotherapy aims toward personal growth and autonomy, whereas drugs are likely to foster dependency, either on the doctor or on the drug itself.

- Drugs can interfere with autonomy and expressions of free will, whereas psychotherapy honors these processes. The prescription of medications may, at least at an unconscious level, communicate the message that the drug will do the work, you don't have to. (Numerous documented instances of overuse of tranquilizing medications to achieve behavioral control provided fodder for this argument.)

- Medications may reduce anxiety and other forms of suffering to such an extent that people will be less motivated to engage in psychotherapy.

- Many drugs have undesirable or dangerous side effects, and some can lead to dependence and abuse.

- Medications ultimately do not solve problems, teach adaptive coping skills, mend broken hearts, or fill empty lives (Menninger 1963).

Although this debate continued throughout the 1960s and 1970s, clearly there were also a number of what G. L. Klerman (Beitman and Klerman 1991) calls "pragmatic practitioners"—those mental health professionals who used whatever approaches seemed to work. Certainly it was, and is, reasonable to consider that some disorders are best treated by psychotropic medications, others by psychotherapy, and it often makes sense to use a combination of both modalities.

academic problems. Concurrently, as Ritalin use (especially new prescriptions) decreased, there was a significant (fourfold) increase in the prescription of tricyclic antidepressants among ADD children. It is important to note that tricyclics, although often used to treat ADD, tend to have more troublesome side effects than Ritalin, and have been implicated in six reports of cardiac fatalities. Brotman (1992) concludes, "When there are reports in the media that lead to stigmatization of a certain drug . . . there tends to be a move to other medications which have less notoriety, even if they may, in fact, be more problematic."

More recently, following wide acclaim as a new "breakthrough drug for depression" (Cowley et al. 1990), Prozac (fluoxetine) came under attack by consumer groups and, again, the Church of Scientology. The negative attention was sparked by a single article (Teicher, Glod, and Cole 1990) documenting the emergence or reemergence of suicidal ideas in six patients treated with Prozac. The six patients had been diagnosed as suffering from severe depressive disorders, and in no case were there actual suicide attempts following the onset of treatment with Prozac. But suddenly Prozac was thrust into a very unfavorable light and was the next drug in line to find itself the topic of television talk shows.

Subsequent studies have failed to find any evidence that Prozac is more likely to be associated with suicidal feelings than any other antidepressant (Fava and Rosenbaum 1991; Beasley and Dornseif 1991). In fact, in one study the incidence of suicidal ideations was greater in patients treated by placebo or imipramine

continued

(a tricyclic antidepressant) than by Prozac (Beasley and Dornseif 1991).

The Church of Scientology attempted to convince the Federal Drug Administration (FDA) to pull Prozac from the market. However, the FDA ruled against taking such action because there was no scientific evidence to support the claims made by the Church of Scientology (Burton 1991).

All medications produce some side effects. Reports of adverse effects, even if very infrequent, must be taken seriously and investigated systematically. There is a place for skepticism and scrutiny. However, one must consider the negative effect of unsubstantiated reports in the lay press. For example, the risk of Prozac-induced suicide appears to be *extremely* low, and the suicide rate in untreated major depression is reported to be 9 percent. Clearly, failure to treat carries the graver risk.

It is very likely that many seriously depressed people and parents of ADD children have been understandably, and unnecessarily, frightened by negative, sensationalistic reports in the media. To quote Brotman (1992) again, "Pharmacotherapy does not exist in a social and political vacuum."

Public opinion

A parallel to the professional debate began to occur within the general public. In institutes of higher education, the humanistic movement began to permeate not only departments of psychology but the global academic community as well. The post-McCarthy social climate was ripe for new attitudes that challenged political and social control and applauded the expression of free will, self-expression, and self-actualization. Reports began to surface regarding the abuse of psychiatric medication by the medical profession. Opponents to drug treatment accused the psychiatrists of using medications to achieve control. The term "chemical straitjacket" became popularized.

The 1970s saw the proliferation of new tranquilizers, and pharmaceutical companies reaped fortunes from the sale of well-known pills such as Valium and Librium. The vast majority of prescriptions written for minor tranquilizers (more than 90 percent) were written by family practice doctors, not psychiatric specialists. The "drugged state" was the fastest growing state in the union (Bly 1990). The inappropriate use and abuse of tranquilizers gained increasing public attention and even found its way into popular songs (the Rolling Stones' "Mother's Little Helper") and movies (*I'm Dancing As Fast As I Can*).

In the 1960s, the Church of Scientology was successfully sued by the American Psychiatric Association. In retaliation, it began a long, embittered assault on American psychiatry. Initially the Church of Scientology launched a negative campaign against the use of Ritalin, a psychotropic medication used to treat attention-deficit disorder. More recently it has orchestrated a move to shed negative light on the antidepressant Prozac (see sidebar on page 8).

Biological psychiatry was under attack. Although clearly there was a good deal of abuse and misuse of psychoactive drugs, there also continued to be decreasing numbers of people living in mental hospitals, and drug companies were at work developing newer and "cleaner" psychotropic medications, medications with fewer side effects.

Rapprochement: Biological and Psychological Perspectives

During the 1980s, a shift began in which increasing numbers of mental health practitioners and researchers widened their previously narrow views on etiology and treatment of mental illness. Increasingly, it became recognized that unidimensional models, whether psychological or biological, fell short of explaining the tremendous complexities of human psychological functioning and psychopathology. This

Who Writes Prescriptions for Psychotropic Medications

Class of Medications	Psychiatrists (%)	Nonpsychiatric M.D.s (%)
Antipsychotics	40	60
Antidepressants	31	69
Antianxiety	10	90
Hypnotics	11	89
Lithium	62	38

Source: Beardsley et al. 1988

Figure 1-A

transition to more complimentary and integrated views of cause and cure can be attributed to several new developments:

- The side effects of medications historically resulted in very poor compliance rates among psychiatric patients, and the most effective medication available is useless if the patient doesn't take the drug as prescribed. Newly discovered compounds introduced in the 1980s and early '90s have yielded effective medications with much more "user-friendly" side effect profiles.

- Discoveries have been made in which new medications and newer uses for existing medications provide very good results in treating certain types of mental illnesses, such as panic disorder and obsessive-compulsive disorder. This greatly increases the psychiatrist's arsenal of effective medications.

- A growing body of well-controlled research studies (double-blind, randomized, placebo controlled) lend convincing support to the efficacy of psychotropic drugs.

- Newly developed neuro-imaging techniques, such as PET and SPECT scans, allow researchers to view metabolic activity in the living brain. These technologies have been able to isolate localized brain abnormalities in certain mental disorders, including panic disorder, schizophrenia, ADD, and obsessive-compulsive disorder. They can provide data on particular sites of drug action or binding and can illustrate changes between the pre- and post- treatment status of particular brain

Psychopharmacology and the "Managed Care" Dilemma

Since the advent of newer generation psychotropic medication, many millions of people are receiving more effective treatment for a host of psychiatric conditions. For this we are grateful. However, it also has become abundantly clear that the effects of psychiatric drugs are limited. Under the best of all circumstances such treatments do not have an impact on all aspects of psychological suffering.

In our view, successful psychiatric treatment should always include psychotherapy. Only in the context of a healing relationship may many aspects of psychological dysfunction be adequately addressed. Numerous interpersonal, intrapsychic, spiritual, and existential dimensions of human functioning simply are not amenable to pharmacologic treatment.

In this book we acknowledge the many benefits of drug treatment; however, we must also share a concern: In these days of cost containment and managed care, individual human lives and quality-of-life issues are often ignored. It is a real concern that an automatic, knee-jerk reaction

continued

will be just to prescribe pills, when so much more is needed. We are treating people, not just nerve cells.

However, given the rising cost of pharmaceuticals, the most recent cost containment strategies are as likely to focus on the use of psychiatric medication as well as on psychotherapeutic interventions. Paradoxically, perhaps as psychotropic drugs begin to account for an ever-increasing percentage of total health care expenditures, we will see best-practice guidelines influenced in a way that will support psychotherapy.

We hope that critical questions will be raised. Are medication treatment failures completely an effect of the drugs not working? Or could the relative lack of psychotherapeutic modalities be a contributing factor? Similarly, as the prescribing of psychotropics has become the first step in treatment, has that first step been taken before an accurate diagnosis was made? Are we medicating out of habit, when it is not really indicated? If the patient would benefit more from psychotherapy, are we doing more harm than good?

We remain hopeful that the pendulum will swing back to support what most practicing clinicians know to be true—the best outcomes result from appropriately balanced treatment that includes therapy and medications.

Human beings and their life problems are enormously complex. And it is the highly trained clinician who must ultimately decide which combinations of treatments are best suited for each individual client (*not* insurance companies, treatment manuals, or untrained technicians)!

structures. Imaging techniques have added considerable "hard data" to various theories of biochemical etiology in selected mental illnesses.

• Neuro-imaging techniques have been accompanied by a host of new laboratory procedures that allow neuroscientists to assay the neurochemical by-products found in spinal fluid. Although early psychopharmacology was implemented without any real knowledge of the underlying pathophysiology, in the past decade biochemical theories have gained tremendous scientific support.

These new developments in psychiatry and the neurosciences have been hard to ignore. Many formerly hard-line psychotherapists have been won over by the flood of research findings and their personal experiences in treating people with psychoactive drugs.

During this same period, important advances were made in the theory and practice of psychotherapy. During the late seventies and the eighties the first truly well-controlled psychotherapy studies emerged (including the now popular meta-analyses). The results of these studies cast doubt on the findings of early research that had suggested that psychotherapy was ineffective (Eysenck 1965, for example). Of the many forms of psychotherapy that have been developed, the meta-analyses suggest that no single school of therapy is clearly superior and that psychotherapies across the board are often much more effective than no treatment.

Also during this time we witnessed the development of novel treatment approaches, such as cognitive-behavioral psychotherapy (Beck 1976) and inter-personal psychotherapy (Klerman et al. 1984) as a treatment for particular disorders, such as depression and panic disorder. These approaches have appeal, in that they can be somewhat systematically applied (some even provide "canned" formats or "cookbooks"). Also, the methodology is a *bit* less reliant on the personal characteristics of the therapist. These approaches then lend themselves to a short-term format and can often be conducted in groups. And, finally, these psychotherapies can be more easily studied. Both cognitive-behavioral and interpersonal psychotherapies have a solid track record of effectiveness (as is discussed further in the next chapter).

Finally, both clinical-anecdotal and research studies have emerged that support the combined use of pharmacotherapy and psychotherapy in the treatment of particular disorders. At times, the combined treatments have been shown to be superior to either single treatment alone.

For many in the mental health community, the writing on the wall has become far more legible: A single model for understanding and treating mental disorders is too narrow and is simply inadequate. As we shall be discussing in subsequent chapters, current evidence suggests that particular disorders do respond best to certain medical treatments, and for these, medications are the treatment of choice. Other disorders have little to do with biochemical dysfunction, and medications play little or no role in their treatment. And still other disorders require the skillful integration of biological and psychotherapies.

As the saying goes, when you only have a hammer, every problem looks like a nail. Fortunately, at the present time mental health professionals have access to a "toolbox" of approaches that can, if employed appropriately, dramatically increase our effectiveness in reducing emotional suffering and promoting mental health.

Why Learn About Psychopharmacology?

In the United States, the majority of mental health services are provided by nonmedical therapists. Likewise, the majority of prescriptions for psychotropic medications are written by family practice and primary care physicians (see figure 1-A). Thus, even though psychiatrists represent the branch of medicine that specializes in psychopharmacology, they are directly responsible for providing only a fraction of professional services to the mentally ill. Consequently, it is becoming increasingly important for all mental health clinicians to have a basic familiarity with psychiatric medication treatment.

Many nonmedical psychotherapists are or will become strongly and rather directly involved in medication treatment. In some settings psychologists and social workers assume a major role in monitoring client responses to psychotropic medications. As primary therapist, these practitioners are in most frequent contact with clients and are in the best position to observe symptomatic improvement, side effect problems, and issues involving medication compliance. When consulting with primary care physicians, or as a staff member in some HMO settings, nonmedical therapists who are well-versed in the use of psychiatric medications can play an active (albeit collaborative) role in recommending particular medications and dosage adjustments. In addition, the Department of Defense, in response to an inadequate number of psychiatrists available in the military, has recently implemented a program to train a small number of psychologists so that they are able to prescribe a limited formulary of psychiatric medications. These various activities reflect quite direct involvement in medication treatment by nonmedical therapists.

In contrast, many nonmedical therapists have little to do with drug treatment. In some cases this may be due to the nature of their position in a particular treatment setting, in others it may have more to do with their own preferences and biases, such as opposition to medication treatment. However, we believe that, regardless of the degree of involvement and interest in medication treatment, it is increasingly important that *all* mental health therapists become acquainted with some basic notions regarding psychopharmacology.

Convincing evidence now exists that certain mental disorders are either caused or accompanied by neurochemical abnormalities. The failure to appropriately diagnose and medically treat such conditions can result in the use of ineffective or only partially effective treatments and hence in prolonged suffering. Aside from the obvious cost in human terms, prolonged inappropriate treatment results in excessive financial burdens for clients, their families, and the health care system.

In addition, to date there have been successful malpractice suits brought against therapists who failed to treat or refer for treatment patients suffering from particular disorders known to be generally responsive to medication.

All mental health professionals must be able to, at the very least, diagnose mental disorders that require psychotropic medication treatment so that appropriate referrals can be made. Differential diagnosis will be discussed in detail in this book.

In many cases, clients may not choose to see a psychiatrist, even when told by their therapist that medication treatment is indicated. This may be due to financial concerns or to the negative stigma some people believe is attached to psychiatric treatment. A viable alternative, in some cases, is referral to the family practice doctor. Many people suffering from emotional distress see their family physician first. This doctor may begin treatment with psychotropic medications and may also refer the patient for psychotherapy. In such cases, the nonmedical therapist may be in a key position to supply information regarding diagnosis and treatment response. Increasingly, family practice physicians and nonmedical therapists become partners collaborating on the treatment of many clients—especially those suffering from fairly uncomplicated depressive and anxiety disorders.

Effective consultation with family practice doctors and psychiatrists alike is enhanced by the nonmedical therapist's ability to accurately communicate and discuss diagnosis, target symptoms, presumed etiology, and possible treatments. We are hopeful that this book will provide a solid grounding in basic issues to help improve communication and cooperation between professionals.

Mental health treatment has moved increasingly toward greater acceptance of multidisciplinary and integrated treatment modalities. As sophistication in the diagnosis and medical treatment of mental disorders continues to develop, it will be important that mental health professionals not take a step backward. The polarization of models and professional "turf battles" of the sixties and seventies may have sparked useful and lively debate, but they also often resulted in a fragmentation of care. Ongoing knowledge of and respect for diverse models and collaborative involvement hold promise for increasingly effective efforts in treating mental illness.

2

Integrated Models

The decision about whether to use psychotropic medications in the treatment of psychiatric disorders is influenced by a number of factors. Unfortunately, often the decision is based largely on the clinician's a priori view toward treatment, deriving from his or her theoretical perspective. As we shall argue, the critical variable in this decision is more appropriately based on the diagnosis, and in particular on the presence or absence of key target symptoms that suggest the patient is experiencing some form of neurochemical disorder.

In broad and extremely heterogeneous groups of disorders, such as mood disorders, *some* may be largely or exclusively caused by biological factors. Other disorders in such groups share *some* symptoms with biologic-based mental illness, yet their etiology stems largely or exclusively from nonbiologic sources, for example, emotional, psychosocial, or cognitive sources. Thus a very important question to address when making a diagnosis and subsequent decisions about treatment is, "Is there any evidence to suggest that this person's problems are due to some form of biologic disturbance?" However, all too often this question is framed overly simplistically: "Is the disorder biological or is it psychological?"

The distinction between what is psyche and what is soma is ambiguous at best. Invariably, there is a complex interaction between psychological and biological factors in all cases of emotional disorder. This complexity will be the focus of this chapter.

Psychology and Biology:
A Two-Way Street

A comprehensive discussion of the classic philosophical issue, mind-brain dualism, is beyond the scope of this book. (The reader is referred to Goodman 1991; Young 1987.) However, we would like to highlight a small number of cases and research studies that illustrate the interactive effects of biologic and psychologic factors.

Biological Factors, Impact on Psychological Functioning

Men ought to know that from the brain, and from the brain only, arise our pleasures, joys, laughter, and jests, as well as our sorrows, pains, griefs, and fears ... It is the same thing which makes us mad or delirious, inspires us with dread and fear, whether by night or by day, brings sleeplessness, inopportune mistakes, aimless anxieties, absentmindedness, and acts that are contrary to habit.

—Hippocrates

For the past two thousand plus years, there has been at least rudimentary recognition of the brain as the site of reasoning and emotions.

Early physicians were keen to note that brain injuries could result in profound changes in personality, cognition, and emotional control. And, as noted in chapter 1, in the earliest days of modern psychiatry the field was grounded in biological sciences and the medical model.

Two fairly common clinical examples serve as illustrations of how disordered brain functioning can lead to marked psychiatric symptomatology.

Case 1

Robert B. is a 42-year-old stockbroker. He has always been an ambitious, bright, energetic man. Despite normal stresses of daily life, he never experienced major psychiatric problems until a month ago. For no apparent reason he began gradually to slip into a state of lethargy, fatigue, and low motivation. His normal zest for life diminished, his usual sharpness of wit became dull, and his sense of enthusiasm gave way to increasing blandness and emptiness. He was totally perplexed as he searched his recent life experiences to find the cause for his malady. None was to be found.

In the ensuing weeks he lost weight, frequently woke at 3:00 A.M. and was unable to go back to sleep, and lost all sexual desire for his wife.

Upon close investigation by his family physician, it was eventually discovered that the depressive symptoms began several weeks after he had started taking an antihypertensive drug to treat his high blood pressure. The medication was suspect and was eventually changed. Within a couple of weeks, the depression vanished.

This case illustrates how a medication can, at times, dramatically alter a person's brain chemistry, resulting in major psychiatric symptoms. In Robert's case, there was no evidence of long-standing psychological problems and no clear psychological stressors.

The brain can be seen, in a sense, as a tremendously complex biological ecosystem. As in other ecosystems, global functioning and survival depend on a large number of interrelated variables. At times, small changes in one aspect of the system influence a number of other variables—in essence, sending a ripple effect throughout the entire system. In the brain, often certain delicately balanced neurochemical systems can be altered (the term often used is *dysregulated*), resulting in a cascade of alterations affecting many other neurochemicals and the functioning of a host of brain structures. A drug, as in the example above, is but one of many variables that can result in neurochemical dysregulation and resulting psychiatric symptoms. (More will be said about other causes later in the chapter.)

Case 2

Elizabeth M. is a 68-year-old retired accountant whose passion is gardening. However, during the past three months she became unable to tend her garden for more than a few minutes at a time. She was almost constantly seized by tremendous restlessness and agitation, fretting, wringing her hands, and pacing about her house. "I feel like I am going to crawl out of my skin," she said.

Elizabeth lost 25 pounds over this three-month period and suffered fitful sleep. She also began to contemplate suicide. Her hopes for a well-deserved, peaceful retirement seemed to have been erased, as if she were plagued by some kind of curse. She could pinpoint absolutely no painful life events that might give meaning to her condition.

Fortunately, ultimately it was discovered that she was suffering from hyperthyroidism. Following successful treatment, she has been able to return to her garden and her life.

In this case, a metabolic disorder was the culprit. In the cases of both Robert and Elizabeth, neurochemical and hormonal factors grossly interfered with brain functioning. In both cases, the people were radically changed. Their perceptions were altered (pessimism, hopelessness), their sense of self was shaken, their emotions were out of control, and their physiological functioning had been derailed. Certainly they had strong emotional reactions to these changes (a phenomenon sometimes referred to as secondary emotional symptoms); however, in both cases the *primary* etiology was biological.

All mental health clinicians will encounter clients who present for treatment with presumed psychological problems but who in fact are suffering from biologically based disorders. Such disorders fall into three categories:

- Due to medical illnesses (such as hyperthyroidism)

- Due to drugs (prescribed, over-the-counter, or recreational)

- Endogenous mental illnesses[1]

Psychological Factors' Impact on Biological Functioning

For a very long time there has been some vague notion that emotional stress can affect physiology. For example, for hundreds of years it has been noted that severe stress can lead to disease. Family physicians have long noted that in the wake of tragic losses, the bereaved easily fall prey to illness. Yet not until this century did the psychology-biology interaction begin to be explored. Psychosomatic medicine was ushered in by the pioneering work of Franz Alexander in the 1940s. And an explosion of interest and research has been seen in the eighties and nineties in the

---

1. The term *endogenous* means "arises from within." Certain psychiatric disorders have been found to be largely endogenous; that is, they arise spontaneously in the absence of provoking psychosocial stressors. The disorders can be attributed to a biological abnormality or a predisposition or vulnerability to dysfunction. Many of the so-called endogenous disorders appear to carry a genetic loading: are passed from generation to generation and presumably can be linked to certain genetic factors. More will be said about endogenous psychiatric disorders in subsequent chapters.

emerging field of psycho-neuro-immunology—the study of the effects of emotional factors on disease susceptibility and disease resistance.

It would require several textbooks to even begin to review the literature in psychosomatics and psycho-neuro-immunology. We would, however, like to briefly discuss a few studies that shed some light on the issue of the interaction of psychology and biology and its relationship to mental illnesses. The first two of these studies involved experimentation with animals.

- E. Kandel and colleagues have studied the effects of environmental experiences and learning on the nervous system in the *Aplysia* (a marine mollusk). This animal is well suited for such a study because its nerve cells are quite large and easy to visualize. Also it does respond well to learning experiments such as habituation, sensitization, and classical conditioning (Pinsker et al. 1970).

  The researchers were able to trace neural pathways from touch receptors in the mollusk's gill and siphon, through its primitive nervous system, and out into corresponding motor neurons. Using repeated exposures to mild aversive stimuli, the investigators were able to document specific biochemical changes at the synapse, as well as structural changes in specific nerve cells. Conclusion: Environmental events and learning are actually accompanied by measurable changes in nerve cells; the animal's biology is altered.

- Neurologic changes have similarly been demonstrated in studies of learned helplessness in rats. In these classic studies, animals are exposed to extremely aversive conditions, from which they have no escape. After a period of exposure, the animals begin to exhibit marked behavioral changes: They become passive and immobile. And they fail to mount coping responses (escape) from later aversive situations from which escape *is* possible. In many respects, the animals have learned that they are helpless to respond, and then they come to take on characteristics that resemble major depression in humans. Interestingly, not only do these helpless rats behave in a depressed manner, but their biochemical functioning is altered. Measures of brain chemistry reveal neurochemical alterations that are identical to those seen in humans suffering from severe grief reactions or clinical depression. Again, environmental experiences have modified brain functioning (Weiss, Glazer, and Pohorecky 1976).

- In very similar ways, in numerous studies the biochemistry of people with reactive depressions has been shown to be markedly altered. For example, emotionally healthy individuals without a personal or family history of depression who encounter major psychosocial stressors (especially losses) can become depressed. Presumably such people are not especially at risk (biologically or psychologically) for depression, but nonetheless they become depressed in response to significant stressful events. Further, in the course of their reaction, *some* patients develop not only emotional symptoms (sadness, pessimism, low self-esteem) but also a host of biologic symptoms, such as sleep disturbances, and marked biochemical abnormalities. The chemical dysfunctions include dysregulation of both neurotransmitters in the brain and hormones (for instance, adrenal hormones such as cortisol). Metabolic by-products of neurotransmitters have been measured in assays of spinal fluid, and by way of brain-imaging techniques such as PET and SPECT scanning.

- Baxter et al. (1992) have convincingly demonstrated that psychotherapy can affect brain functioning. PET scans allow researchers to directly image living brain tissue and thus provide data on metabolic activity of specific areas of the brain. Studies using PET scans in severe obsessive-compulsive disorder reveal a localized brain abnormality: a metabolic disturbance in the head of the candate nucleus, a brain structure that is part of the basal ganglia. In obsessive-compulsive disorder, when individuals are symptomatic this abnormality is visible on PET scans. Yet following successful *behavioral* treatment (exposure and response-prevention treatments) the functioning of this brain area normalizes.

- Evidence also exists supporting the theory that the earliest episodes of affective illnesses in bipolar patients are often "reactive" in nature; that is, the initial episode is not an endogenous, biologic event but rather is evoked by psychological stressors. As a consequence of the initial episode, neurons in key areas of the limbic system may undergo a process of modification (neurochemically and even structurally), whereby the brain is changed more or less permanently. The result of this is that, following the first one or two episodes, the altered brain functioning leaves the nervous system at much greater risk for subsequent episodes and sets in motion an endogenous process whereby affective episodes can then occur spontaneously, even in the absence of psychological stress. From that point on, if the disorder is not controlled, each episode further affects the nervous system; the threshold for recurring episodes becomes progressively lower. This process is known as *kindling*. It begins as a response to external stressors and evolves into a largely biological illness.

These are but a few of many studies and clinical findings that collectively provide strong support for the idea that environmental and psychological factors can significantly affect biologic and neurologic functioning.

Biological-Psychological Interactions

It is very likely that complex, interactive effects exist between biological and psychological factors. It's never a question of all or none. In the case of Robert B., he was suffering from an endogenous depression and experiencing marked lethargy, poor concentration, and low motivation. This eventually led to performance problems at work, and a number of critical remarks from his boss. These events began to fuel the flame of low self-esteem. Low self-esteem is generally not felt to be a primary symptom of biologically based depressive disorders, but it is almost universally seen to emerge as patients live with ongoing clinical depression.

Biologic effects may secondarily affect psychological functioning in a number of ways, among them:

- Altered perception. Biologic effects can contribute to the pessimistic thinking seen in depressive disorders and the tendency to anticipate fearful outcomes often seen in anxiety disorders.

- Increased emotional sensitivity and reduced emotional controls. Increased emotional arousal or pain may motivate a person to become more socially withdrawn and can often lead to a host of negative conclusions regarding personal competency, as in, "What's wrong with me? I'm crying like a baby."

- Decreased energy and arousal, poor concentration, and lowered motivation, which often leads to impaired performance in school and work.

- Sexual dysfunction, which can translate into interpersonal problems in intimate relationships.

- Bizarre behavior enacted during a psychotic episode. Such behavior can continue to be a source of tremendous personal embarrassment and shame long after the psychotic episode is resolved.

These consequences of a primarily biologically based mental disorder have an impact on the individual's sense of self-worth and competency in the world. Conversely, this increased level of despair can, in itself, operate to intensify the underlying biological abnormality.

Practical Implications

As previously mentioned, the question "Is this disorder psychological or is it biological?" is too simplistic. The more appropriate question is "To what extent is there evidence that biochemical factors may be contributing to a patient's current symptomatology?" This is much more than an academic question. To the extent that we can determine biologic etiology (or at least a degree of biologic dysfunction as a part of the more global disorder), pharmacologic treatments may be indicated. (How a biologic etiology and the need for medication are determined is addressed in detail in later chapters.)

Stimulus-Response Specificity

Stimulus-response specificity is a concept describing conditions where a very specific response can be predicted with tremendous regularity when a stimulus is applied. One example would be that an electrical shock to muscle tissue evokes a contraction. This model is appropriate for some types of medical interventions. For example, for acute cardiac and respiratory arrest, the techniques of cardiopulmonary resuscitation (CPR) can be used with most victims, regardless of their age, socioeconomic status, sex, or religious beliefs. When there is an obstructed airway, performing an emergency tracheotomy is appropriate for victims regardless of their emotional status, personality style, or level of psychosocial maturity. Likewise, some medications have fairly universal effects on all people; for instance, sodium pentothal produces unconsciousness (Deckert 1985).

Medical treatments in psychiatry generally *do not* follow the rule of stimulus-response specificity. Although the particular mechanism of drug action may be identified, the same medication given to two depressed patients, for example, may affect them very differently. Some of these differences may be traced to variations in metabolism from individual to individual (see chapter 4). Or the underlying biochemical abnormality in one depressed patient may be different than the abnormality in another depressed patient, and thus the medications affect different underlying disorders.

Beyond these physiological differences, however, the patients' responses may be influenced to a significant degree by a host of social, cognitive, and personality factors that have little or nothing to do with biology. In the realm of psychiatric medication treatment, sociocultural experiences and beliefs, personality style, and a vast number of personal psychodynamic factors can, and do, dramatically influence patient response. Psychological functioning cannot be understood using the simple, reductionist notions implied in stimulus-response specificity.

The good clinician *always* treats the person, not just the disorder. We may choose to influence nerve cells with psychotropic drugs, but the response will always be woven into the complex fabric of highly idiosyncratic personality factors. Therefore, successful pharmacologic treatment *always* requires a thorough knowledge of not only the diagnosis and pathology and the medications used, but the unique meaning of the treatment to the individual patient. Assembly-line psychotropic treatment often fails, not because medications are ineffective, but because clinicians do not take time to understand their patients.

Unfortunately, in many overcrowded mental health clinics, some clinicians act as if stimulus-response specificity is appropriate. The result is that often these attempts at treatment efficiency and cost containment backfire. Many patients don't respond well and either must demand further outpatient services or continue to decompensate until they require hospitalization. And, of course, there is the human cost associated with prolonged suffering.

In the remainder of the chapter, we explore a number of ideas regarding psychological factors that have direct bearing on the outcome of medication treatment.

The Psychodynamics of Pharmacologic Treatment

When a prescription is written and a pill is taken, the effects of the medication are almost always influenced by a number of psychological factors. Some of these factors have to do with the commonly held beliefs regarding "drugs" and "illness" that are etched into the experience of most people in our culture. Other factors spring from highly personal, idiosyncratic sources, either in conscious awareness or buried deeply in the unconscious mind.

The astute clinician should continually ask the questions, "If medications are suggested or prescribed, how will this be perceived by my patient?" and "What personal meaning might be attached to this form of intervention?" Prescribing and recommending medication always occurs in an interpersonal context. It is not like a landscaper recommending and applying a particular fertilizer to your lawn. Rather, it can be a highly personalized communication between therapist and client, a communication ripe for all sorts of transference distortions and a type of interaction that *may* alter the nature of the therapeutic relationship.

In addressing these issues, we will first speak about rather common, generic themes, and then go on to describe more unique, personal concerns. Let's consider some of the possible consequences.

Generic Meanings

In our culture, certain themes are evident in our cliches and language that link the taking of medicine with badness and punishment. The saying "Give him a taste of his own medicine" is but one example. One of the classic scenes from the "Our Gang" movie shorts has the wicked stepmother punishing Spanky and Alfalfa by making them swallow castor oil. Hearing bad news or carrying out unpleasant tasks is sometimes referred to as having to "swallow a bitter pill." Even in mature adults, these connections between "taking your medicine" and punishment may echo at unconscious levels.

Probably more common are notions regarding medication and "being sick." Many psychiatric patients may be able to view their difficulties honorably, as "problems in living," and yet feel shamed and humiliated by a suggestion that they take psychotropic medications. The unspoken meaning they perceive may be, "You need medications, thus you are *sick*." And being sick, in psychological terms, often carries its own assortment of negative connotations: weak, inadequate, crazy, deranged, and so on.

A common underlying concern sparked by the recommendation for psychotropics is, "The therapist must think I can't handle things on my own—thinks I need a crutch." This can not only be wounding to the client's self-image, but may undermine the client's belief that the therapist is hopeful regarding his or her capacity for growth and healing.

Morality pervades many beliefs about the taking of drugs for emotional problems. Some people erroneously assume that all psychiatric drugs are alike. They conclude that all psychotropics are "tranquilizers," that all can lead to drug addiction, and that such dependence on drugs is little different than alcoholism. Thus, if you take drugs, you are bad, or at the very least, weak willed. This view of drugs as evil, or at least as dangerously addictive, is adopted by some twelve-step chemical dependency programs. The lay leaders of some twelve-step groups are understandably skeptical and afraid of drugs that can lead to abuse, but may be ignorant of the fact that most psychotropic medications are not addictive at all. It is all too common for someone who has received a dual diagnosis of, for example, alcohol abuse and major depression to encounter tremendous pressure in his or her twelve-step recovery program to discontinue antidepressant medication. Fortunately, many recovery programs are learning about the appropriate use of some psychiatric medications, and understand their role in treating dual-diagnosis clients.

Finally, psychiatric drugs are seen by some as an assault on free will and autonomy. Certainly this idea has been brought to our attention by media reports of instances in which psychotropic drugs have been used solely to achieve behavioral control. "Chemical straitjackets" and other forms of biological restraint, such as lobotomies, have been the subject of popular film and television productions (for example *One Flew Over the Cuckoo's Nest, Frances,* and *Will There Really Be a Morning?*). And clearly these abuses have and do occur. However, appropriately used medical interventions oftentimes work to free people and promote autonomy.

Case 3

Sara M. is a 34-year-old housewife. Over the past two years she has been plagued by devastating panic attacks and unable to leave her home or to be alone. Her husband must have relatives stay with Sara or hire a "babysitter" to be with her when he goes to work. Sara is frightened, and she feels humiliated.

Sara initially balked at the suggestion that she take psychiatric medications. She saw the recommendation as an attack on her sense of adequacy and worth. However, after a period of psychotherapy, she did agree to take the medications. After eight weeks of treatment with paroxetine and clonazepam she was free from panic attacks and began to venture out of her home for the first time in two years. Six months later she was reentering the mainstream of life and had just attended a performance of the local symphony. One of her greatest personal losses had been her inability to attend the symphony.

For Sara, the medication played a key role in reducing panic symptoms. But it was her own courage that enabled her to resume normal living, as she gradually chose to go outside her home or to spend time alone. In Sara's case, medications played *a part* in restoring her autonomy and bringing her back to life.

Case 4

One of the authors treated a young woman, Ellen G., who came for her first appointment at the mental health clinic with this opening line: "I'm starting to fall apart again. I guessed it was time to come in and start taking my Thorazine again." She had been treated with this antipsychotic drug off and on for the past three years and was now consulting with a new therapist. The therapist commented, "Well, maybe you're right about needing the medication again. But let's take some time to talk and see if we can understand what's going on for you."

As her story unfolded, it became clear that she was experiencing symptoms of a serious, delayed-onset post-traumatic stress disorder. In prior treatments, her therapists had never explored her circumstances beyond observing her feelings of panic, depersonalization, and confusion. They were quick to medicate her and seal over her distress.

In the current treatment, medications were not used. Months later this woman remarked, "That first day when you didn't just give me meds, but said 'Let's talk' . . . It was the first time I started to feel hopeful about therapy."

When medications are given, especially if they are offered or recommended early on in treatment, many clients' perception is, "They just want to drug me. They don't want to talk . . . They don't want to hear my pain." Patients may feel they are being treated as a "case" (as in stimulus-response specificity) and the result can be a serious warp in the developing therapeutic alliance or even premature termination of therapy.

At times when therapists feel stuck with a client, their own sense of futility or impotence may lead to the decision to try medications. This feeling of pessimism may be picked up on by the client. As Jerome Frank (1973) and others have argued, one of the most important roles therapists can play is to help maintain realistic hopefulness, especially during times when clients are feeling especially demoralized. Certainly, psychotropic medications may be indicated and can be crucial interventions with *some* "stuck" psychotherapy clients. However, the choice to medicate should be based on thorough consideration of diagnostic issues, and not be simply a response to the therapist's own pessimism.

Personal Meanings

Just like any other type of intervention or communication in therapy, the therapist's behaviors and interactions can certainly be perceived in particular, unique ways by the client—ways that make sense when the client's psychodynamics are understood. Although such personal dynamics vary tremendously from person to person, we would like to address several fairly common examples that can be seen in clinical practice.

Dependent patients

The request for medications (explicit or implicit) by dependent patients, often conveys a need to be fed. Aside from direct medication effects, the gratification experienced by the patient when given drugs may account for symptomatic improvement. It is also important to note that once the therapist prescribes medications (however appropriate this may be) in some way he or she has strayed from a position of neutrality, and this may have consequences for the therapeutic relationship. Conversely, the choice not to prescribe or recommend medications may be seen as "withholding." The symbolic-dynamic issues discussed here are also important concerns in the treatment of clients with borderline personality disorders.

Obsessive-compulsive patients

People with obsessive-compulsive personality styles value control and precise intellectual scrutiny. Thus, when medications are prescribed, the therapist will often be confronted with (1) a request for detailed information about the medication and its side effects, (2) frequent discussions regarding medication response and side effects (even *very* minor side effect problems), and (3) worries centering around loss of control experiences that may result from even very minimal side effects, such as slight degree of sedation or dizziness.

Case 5

Albert K. is a 54-year-old engineer, receiving treatment for a major depression. This rigid, obsessional man came for his appointment a week after being started on antidepressants. During the past week he had written a computer program to track medication side effects on a daily basis, and he brought a data sheet with him to the session. The program addressed fifteen different side effects (which he had gleaned from the *Physicians' Desk Reference*); each one was rated daily on a scale of 1 to 10, and results were displayed in terms of daily scores and weekly averages and on bar graphs. This was Albert's style, his way of approaching medication treatment. The therapist thought it was a classic for obsessional patients and was impressed with Albert's program and charts.

Anxious patients

Individuals who suffer from severe anxiety disorders and, in particular, phobias and panic disorder, already experience a significant amount of fearfulness in their daily life. Oftentimes when medications are prescribed, the medication itself becomes a new source of fear for these patients. This is frequently seen when such individuals are started on antidepressant medications. These medications may present some side effects, such as a rapid heart rate, and these are quickly interpreted by the anxious patient as a sign of increased anxiety and loss of control. This may lead to patients quickly discontinuing the medication or even therapy itself.

Paranoid patients

The issues encountered with paranoid patients often surround struggles over control and autonomy. These people are especially frightened by others assuming a position of control over them, and being "medicated" often touches on this theme. In more psychotic paranoid patients, this issue not uncommonly takes the form of delusions in which the patient feels the therapist is trying to poison him or her.

Depressed patients

Frequently, seriously depressed patients, when encountering very minor side effect problems, complain bitterly about these difficulties or abruptly discontinue antidepressant medication treatment. It may be difficult to understand why a profoundly depressed person would abandon treatment when all he or she has encountered is a slightly dry mouth or minor degree of sedation. Yet it bears keeping in mind that such people are already exquisitely sensitive to discomfort, overwhelmed by psychological pain, and prone to tremendous pessimism. Although the therapist hopes for significant benefit from the antidepressant, the patient's experience is often focused on a here-and-now awareness of added discomfort and probably persistently bleak view of the future.

Narcissistic patients

The never-ending search for the perfect relationship, the perfect job, and the perfect life that narcissistic patients pursue may extend to the demand for the perfect medication—which pharmaceutical companies have not as yet developed.

Medication as a tool for resistance

Across diagnostic groups, a common experience is for the patient to bring up medication and medication problems as a form of resistance. It is, of course, important to track medication responses and encourage patient-therapist dialogue regarding effects. However, when this topic comes to dominate too much of the therapy hour, it may be an indication that the subject is being used in the service of resistance. That is, the focus is shifted away from inner thoughts and feelings to symptoms and side effects. In addition, arguments or complaints regarding medication issues may also become an arena for struggles over control.

Countertransference issues

Medications are sometimes given to patients in a sort of "rescue response," when the therapist either fears the therapy is ineffective or worried about the patient experiencing excessive emotional pain. Although certainly this may be appropriate at times, it can also be a countertransference problem that interferes with treatment.

A therapist will sometimes give medications to a patient to soften the blow of termination or to assuage the therapist's guilt over stopping treatment—a problem seen more commonly these days in short-term therapy clinics. Some clinics offer only limited psychotherapy, but will allow patients to continue some form of contact with therapists if they are on medications. So prescribing medications can be a way to "legitimize" continued contact and avoid the losses associated with termination.

It is not our goal to recommend specific solutions to these various client dynamics or countertransference problems but rather to highlight them as particular concerns. The well-trained therapist never views medication treatment in a vacuum or as a stimulus-response specific intervention. Alertness to these issues and a willingness to inquire about personal interpretation of the recommendation for medication are our best hedge against problems that can potentially derail treatment or contribute to poor medication compliance.

3

Neurobiology

The Nervous System on a Cellular Level

This chapter provides an overview of neurobiology in order to create a foundation for subsequent chapters that address biologic etiologies and pharmacology. For the interested reader, sidebars contain more technical and detailed discussions.

The Nerve Cell

The human brain contains approximately 100 billion nerve cells (also referred to as *neurons*). Although there are numerous types of nerve cells, most function in a similar fashion. The proper functioning of the nervous system depends on communication between the neurons. Structurally, all neurons are composed of a cell body, dendrites, axon, and terminal boutons (see figure 3-A). *Dendrites* are short, branched structures projecting out from the cell body. They receive and conduct information to the cell body; there may be one or many dendrites on each cell. Extremely fine projections on the dendrites are called *dendritic spines*. Spines are common locations for synapses. The *axon* is a long fiber that ends in enlarged structures called *terminal boutons*. The axon serves to conduct impulses away from the cell body.

Within the cell body lie a number of tiny structures responsible for moment-to-moment operation and survival of the cell. Each neuron receives oxygen, glucose, and a host of other molecules from capillaries that lie adjacent to the cell. Some of the more important molecules delivered to the nerve cells via the bloodstream are amino acids, which serve as the building blocks for proteins.

Each cell must manufacture a multitude of proteins, which are then used for many different purposes including the production of receptors, enzymes that regulate intracellular biochemical processes, growth factors, and structural elements of the cell. Each cell also produces its own messenger molecules (*neurotransmitters*), which are secreted by the cell and which then may influence the functioning of

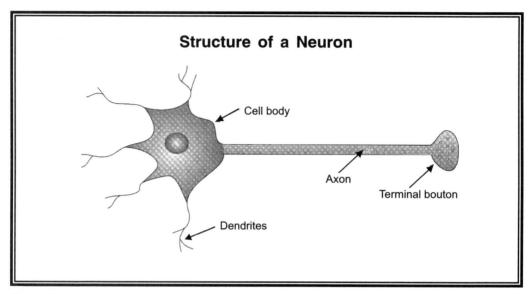

Figure 3-A

adjacent neurons. Because of this influence on adjacent neurons, neurotransmitters are sometimes referred to as *first messenger* molecules.

Intercellular Communication

When nerve cells are activated and produce a nerve impulse, the resulting surge of electrochemical energy begins in the cell body and is rapidly passed along the axon (i.e., away from the cell body) ending in the terminal bouton. Here, the impulse causes the release of neurotransmitter molecules into the tiny space between nerve cells referred to as the *synapse*. The human brain's 100 billion nerve cells are richly interconnected, making approximately 100 trillion synapses. Yet in almost all instances, the nerve cells do not actually touch one another; they are separated by this tiny space. Communication between nerve cells requires the action of neuro-transmitting molecules which deliver stimulation (and thus information) across the synapse. Let's see how this works and also how it can malfunction.

Conduction and Transmission

The process of nerve activity begins with stimulation of the cell. A variety of molecules, called *ligands*, may be able to bind to and activate receptors. Such mole-cules include neurotransmitters, hormones, and certain drugs. The activation of excitatory receptors on the dendrites or the cell body results in a brief change in elec-trical potential from the cell's resting state. This change is called an *action potential*. The action potential is converted into a nerve impulse as it spreads throughout the dendrites, cell body, and ultimately down the axon. At the nerve ending, the nerve impulse performs the critical function of causing the release of neurotransmitting chemicals into the synapse. The neuron that releases the neurotransmitters is called the *presynaptic* neuron, the neuron that receives the neurotransmitters is called the *postsynaptic* neuron. The process of impulse movement along the axon is referred to as *conduction; transmission* refers to the passage of the impulse across the synaptic space.

Neurotransmitter molecules are manufactured in the cell body and are then transported down the axon for storage in tiny containers (*vesicles*). While enclosed in vesicles, the neurotransmitters are protected from destruction by enzymes that reside in the fluid within the presynaptic terminal bouton. Upon receiving stimulation from the action potential, the vesicles migrate toward the cell membrane, fuse with it, and for a microsecond create a pore (a tiny gateway in the cell membrane), discharging

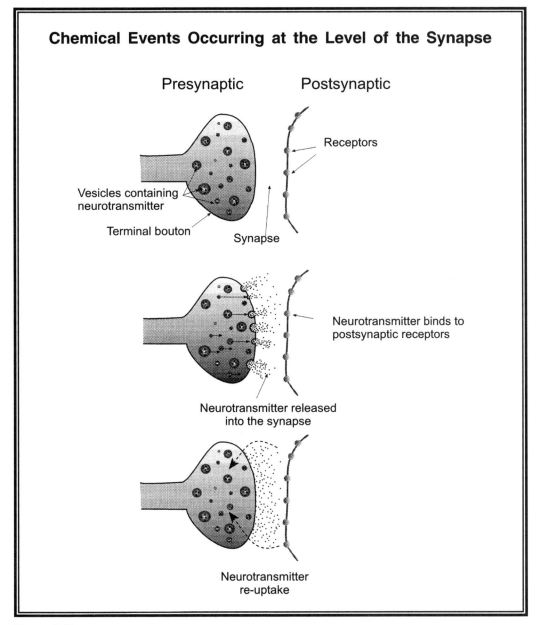

Figure 3-B

Messenger Molecules

In detailed discussions of neuro-transmission, distinctions are often made in describing specific types of neurotrans-mitters, also referred to as neuromodulators. Categorization models are based on properties such as the size of type of molecule, or the location of synthesis within the neuron.

These models undergo nearly continuous revision as new information is discovered. Regardless of classification criteria, there are two very important and basic properties common to most neurotrans-mitters. The first is that these chemicals are found within neu-rons, and released as a result of the nerve impulse. The second is the ability of all neurotrans-mitters to produce a physio-logical effect on a neuron. A neurotransmitter classification system that includes the biogenic amines, the neuropep-tides, and the amino acids is useful for understanding psychopharmacology. Within each category there are numerous specific chemicals.

When narrowly defined, the *biogenic amines* comprise only epinephrine, norepinephrine, and dopamine. However, in a broader and more practical sense, serotonin, histamine, and acetylcholine are often also included.

Endorphins and *enkephalins* are examples of neuropeptides. They are sometimes called natu-rally occurring opioid peptides because of their ability to bind to the same receptors as mor-phine. Other important peptides that will be discussed in this book are cortico-tropin releasing factor (CRF) and substance P. In this family of neuropeptides, there are numerous substances with purported effects on such diverse physiological systems as

continued

their contents into the synapse. Receptors are on the adjacent, postsynaptic membrane (see figure 3-B).

The Effects of Receptor Binding

Neurotransmitter molecules, when released into the synapse, are capable of binding to specific recep-tors (for example, dopamine molecules bind only to dopamine receptors, and have no direct impact on other receptors). *The binding of neurotransmitters to receptors is the primary means by which one nerve cell can influence the functioning of other neurons.*

The effects of receptor binding vary tremen-dously depending on which type of receptor is involved. Functionally, some neurotransmitters are excitatory, since they activate adjacent neurons, and others are inhibitory (i.e., acting like a brake when turned on; they have the impact of reducing nerve cell excitability). One notable exception is seen with the serotonin system in the brain. The molecule, serotonin, is not itself inherently excitatory or inhibitory. It all depends on which type of seroto-nin receptor is activated. Currently fourteen sub-types of serotonin receptors have been discovered. Most are inhibitory, although some are excitatory. Thus, if serotonin levels are increased in the entire brain, it will have multiple effects (Barnes and Sharp 1999).

When neurotransmitters are released into the synapse, some molecules bind to receptors, some are chemically destroyed by enzymes found in the extra-cellular fluid, and many are rapidly reabsorbed into the presynaptic neurons. The reabsorption is accom-plished by way of a *reuptake transporter pump* (see figure 3-B). This is a protein structure in the cell mem-brane. Neurotransmitter molecules re-enter the nerve cell and are repackaged in the vesicles. This is a sort of molecular recycling that allows neurotransmitters to be used again and again.

Many of the currently available antidepressants operate via reuptake inhibition, where the drug molecule enters the reuptake pore and blocks it. The result is that the neurotransmitters released into the synapse stay there longer and thus may have a greater effect on the postsynaptic neuron. Ultimately, neurotransmitters die off and disappear due to enzymatic degradation, thus making it essential for nerve cells to continuously manufacture new neuro-transmitters to replenish those that have been lost.

Across the Synapse: Receptors and Intracellular Actions

Receptors are protein molecules that have been produced in the neuron and are embedded in the cell membrane. A portion of the molecule is exposed on the surface of the neuron membrane, and the other end penetrates into the cell. The exposed portion has certain binding sites where messenger molecules are able to attach themselves, and thus activate the receptor.

Most nerve cells have between 2,000 to 3,000 receptors on the surface of the cell body and dendrites. Any given cell may have dozens of receptor subtypes on its surface (e.g., a dopamine cell may have dopamine receptors, but it may also have serotonin receptors, opiate receptors, and so forth, allowing it to be influenced by a host of neurotransmitters and hormonal molecules). Most receptors are on the surface of the cell, although some reside within the cell body.

The absolute number of receptors and the ratio of inhibitory-to-excitatory receptors (brakes and accelerators), which ultimately help determine sensitivity/excitability levels of the cell, are partially determined by genetics, the inherent nature and makeup of the cell. However, it is important to note that populations of receptors are significantly influenced by external factors (such as the impact of stressors or drugs). (See the sidebar entitled "Impact of Stress on Receptors.")

The life span of receptors is between twelve and twenty-four hours. After this period of time, they wear out or are reabsorbed into the cell. Thus, throughout an individual's lifespan, nerve cells must be capable of continuously monitoring receptor populations and replacing lost receptors. Also, the cell must be able to adjust receptor populations in accord with environmental demands (see sidebar entitled "Impact of Stress on Receptors"). Thus, nerve cells are by no means static. In order to handle stressors they are ever-changing, and it is remarkable how the nervous system is able to do this so effectively (at least, most of the time).

One way to categorize receptors is from a *functional* standpoint based on the end result of neurotransmitter-receptor coupling. The most basic distinction is inhibitory versus excitatory. That is, when activated by a messenger molecule, will the impact on the cell be in the direction of increased or decreased neuronal excitation?

pain response, memory and learning, appetite, and temperature regulation.

Amino acid neurotransmission is pervasive throughout the brain. Quantitatively, amino acids constitute the majority of all transmitters in the brain. There are several amino acid neurotransmitters with relevance in neuropsychiatry. Glutamate, which is highly concentrated in the brain, and aspartate, which is localized in the spinal cord, are excitatory. Gamma amino butyric acid (GABA), heavily distributed in the brain, and glycine, primarily found in the spinal cord, are inhibitory. The neurotransmission of amino acids is a major focus of neuropsychiatric disease state research and drug development.

Advances in neurotransmitter research have challenged the classic criteria for neurotransmitter typology (Snyder and Ferris 2000). The gases nitric oxide and carbon dioxide are identified as atypical neurotransmitters. They are distinct from typical neurotransmitters in that they are not stored in presynaptic vesicles and do not interact via a postsynaptic receptor complex. Mirror image amino acids, known as *enantiomers*, are also being studied to determine if they possess the requisite properties to be considered neurotransmitters. One such molecule, D-serine, may prove to have a role in the etiology and treatment of schizophrenia.

It has been proposed that D-serine and glutamate combine to activate NMDA receptors. The atypical feature of D-serine is that it resides in glia (the supporting cells surrounding neurons), rather than in neurons. Another proposed novel neurotransmitter is adenosine, which has neuroactive properties, yet is neither a biogenic amine nor an amino acid.

Impact of Stress on Receptors

Many biological systems are said to be "regulated systems." This means that organisms, organ systems, tissues, or individual cells, to assure survival may alter their functioning (chemical functioning and even structure/morphology) to accommodate to changing environmental circumstances. However, there is also an inherent tendency to return to baseline or "homeostasis" after an environmental disturbance has ended. Should such disturbance last a long time (such as is the case with chronic stress or drug abuse) cells can react in a number of ways (e.g., by developing tolerance, adjusting excitability levels, etc.).

Neuronal adaptations take place via the mechanisms of *up-regulation* or *down-regulation*. Chronic exposure to high levels of stress causes a bombardment by certain excitatory neurotransmitters. This often leads to a down-regulation (reduction in the number and density) of excitatory receptors. Conversely, abnormally low levels of certain neurotransmitters or hormones may spur the up-regulation of excitatory receptors as an attempt of the cells to normalize the activity/firing rates of neurons. This is but one form of biological flexibility and adaptation seen in response to changes in the external environment (Post, Weiss, and Leverich 1994; Post and Weiss 1997).

Assessing the status of receptor density in certain brain regions is one way to identify particular types of pathology (e.g., depression) and/or psychotropic medication effects.

Typically, the terms *up-regulation* and *down-regulation* refer to changes in the number of receptors. However, the terms are used sometimes to refer to changes in overall neurotransmitter systems (e.g., *up-regulating brain serotonin* may refer to an increase in global central nervous system (CNS) serotonin activity).

Another way to consider receptors is from a *mechanistic* standpoint. In other words, how does the ligand-receptor activity occur? The majority of receptor activities can be categorized into five basic types, which are often referred to as *signaling mechanisms*. Signaling mechanism research has become increasingly important for understanding biological functioning (and malfunctioning) and provides an expanding platform for new drug development. In neuropsychiatry, two of the most relevant types of signaling mechanisms are the *ion-channel mediated process* and the *G-protein mediated second messenger system* described in the sidebar called "Into the Neuron: Second Messenger Systems and Gene Expression." These two mechanisms are also known as *ionic* or *metabolic*, respectively.

Ionic actions take place when receptors are associated with ion channels. Ion channels are tiny pores on the surface of nerve cell membranes. When neurotransmitters, drugs, or other ligands bind to these receptors, it causes the ion channel to open transiently, thus allowing certain ions (electrically charged molecules, e.g., chloride or sodium) to pass throughout the membrane. (During the momentary opening of channels, the membrane is said to be *permeable* to certain molecules.) Ionic actions are responsible for rapid and transient changes in nerve cell activity, e.g., as occurs with neuronal firing underlying sensory perception or voluntary muscle action.

Most psychiatric medications do not operate via ionic receptors. One exception are the minor tranquilizer/benzodiazepine drugs that facilitate the opening of chloride-ion channels. Once these drugs enter the central nervous system (CNS), they are able to produce a rapid onset of actions (i.e., tranquilization).

Metabolic actions, in contrast, are not rapidly occurring, rather, they involve gradual changes in neuronal functioning that take place over hours, days, weeks, or even months. When ligands bind to these receptors, they operate by activating what are referred to as *second messenger systems* within the cytoplasm of the cell. This process is said to involve a cascade of chemical actions that ignite a number of intra-cellular biochemical events. These alterations in the cell's inner chemical microenvironment operate to change or regulate cellular activity, partly by influencing gene expression. For details see the sidebar called "Into the Neuron: Second Messenger Systems and Gene Expression."

Most psychiatric medications operate by acting on metabolic receptors and this explains, in part, why most of these drugs require several weeks of administration before the onset of noticeable symptomatic improvement.

Neuronal Malfunction

A number of things can go amiss at the cellular level in the brain, with consequent psychiatric symptoms. Most of the time, these pathologic cellular changes take place after a period of time during which particular neurons are bombarded by extreme amounts of excitation spurred by psychological stresses or drug abuse. Gradually the internal chemistry and even the structure of key nerve cells develop abnormalities leading to neuronal malfunctions. Let's take a look at several common dysfunctions that are believed to underlie major mental illness (these abnormalities will be explored in greater detail in later chapters).

- The initial synthesis (production) of neurotransmitters may be inhibited, thus little neurotransmitter is available for release.

- Neurotransmitters may be subject to excessive degradation by enzymes (such as MAO, monoamine oxidase).

- Certain biologically based disorders or drugs may either facilitate or inhibit the release of neurotransmitters by the presynaptic bouton.

- The process of reuptake absorption may be altered. For example, cocaine abuse leads to a blocking of dopamine reuptake pores. In clinical major depression, reuptake of serotonin, norepinephrine, and/or dopamine may become accelerated.

- Receptors may be either abnormally up-regulated or down-regulated (see sidebar "Impact of Stress on Receptors") causing neurons to malfunction.

- Pathological alterations can occur in gene expression due to marked changes in second messengers (see sidebar

Into the Neuron: Second Messenger Systems and Gene Expression

Through metabolic receptor action (also referred to as "G-protein-linked receptors"), drug molecules and other ligands are able to activate G-proteins (tiny protein molecules that lie adjacent to the interior surface of the cell membrane). The activation of G-proteins is the starting point for a diverse array of biochemical changes that can then take place within the cell. G-proteins act like molecular switches activating enzymes in the cytoplasm. G-protein activation also can have an impact on ion channels (not opening them per se, but rather, altering their intrinsic excitability). But their more common role is the activation of a number of enzymes, collectively referred to as *second messengers*. Seconds messengers are usually small, water soluble molecules found in the cytoplasm.

The primary means of second messenger activation is by way of a biochemical reaction referred to as protein phosphorylation. Second messengers regulate enzymes referred to as protein kinases, which transfer phosphate groups from adenosine triphosphate (ATP) onto specific protein substrates, while protein phosphatases basically do the opposite (i.e., they remove phosphates). Altered proteins then are "activated" and capable of bringing about several different changes in cellular functioning including (Hyman and Nestler 1996; Post, Weiss, and Leverich 1994; Post and Weiss 1997):

1. Inactivation of ion channels or, conversely, activation of other ion channels

2. Turning on the production of neurotransmitters

3. Effects on gene expression (i.e., turning on genes)

Gene Expression: Within the nucleus of all human cells are 23 pairs of chromosomes. Each chromosome is comprised of long, double-stranded DNA molecules. Embedded in the DNA are genes (sequences of

continued

nucleotides). Each cell contains all the genes for the entire human body (i.e., the *human genome*), although each cell accesses and expresses only those gene sequences responsible for the functioning of that particular cell. Gene sequences are the molecular blueprints for the production of proteins (which are subsequently manufactured in the cell, and yield a host of molecules that have numerous important functions, e.g., receptors, growth factors, enzymes, etc.).

For genes to have an effect on cellular functioning, they first must be accessed and activated (i.e., gene expression). Specific gene expression may be an endogenous process, but may also be influenced by environmental stimulation (e.g., activated by stressors and by certain drugs, which can turn genes on or off, and can thus influence the rate of protein synthesis). Gene expression involves several steps. Transcription factors activated by second messengers attach to specific areas of the DNA molecule (promoter sites) and, in turn, activate genes (expose them and initiate the process of gene transcription onto messenger RNA molecules). Messenger RNA molecules (mRNA; also proteins) align alongside the DNA and make a copy of the gene sequence (much as a floppy disk is used to copy data from a computer hard drive). Then the mRNA exits the nucleus and travels to a part of the cell known as the *endoplasmic reticulum*. Here it attaches to ribosomes, where proteins are constructed.

Next, transfer RNA (tRNA) collects amino acids from the cytoplasm and helps to arrange them in the particular sequence encoded on the mRNA. The result is a chain of amino acids that, when complete, forms a protein. The final molecules are referred to as a "gene product." Second messengers either may facilitate or interfere with gene expression. And, ultimately, stimulation by neurotransmitters influenced by stressors or drugs will thus have an impact on second messengers. Additionally, stress hormones such as glucocorticoids, thyroid, and sex hormones also can influence the rate of gene expression.

entitled "Into the Neuron: Second Messenger Systems and Gene Expression") and may result in numerous abnormal cellular responses including: cell growth, altered receptor sensitivity, dendrite retraction, loss of dendrite spines, and/or cell death (apoptosis).

The Impact of Neuronal Malfunction

Nerve cells in the three critical neurotransmitter systems (dopamine, serotonin, and norepinephrine) in total represent less than 1 percent of total brain neurons. Yet malfunctions in any of these systems can result in marked dysregulation of the brain, and at times, in catastrophic psychiatric symptoms. Sometimes the changes in the nervous system are relatively transient; for example, as those that occur with certain adjustment disorders. At other times, the impact is greater and more long-lasting, but it is also subject to eventual spontaneous remission, as is the case in some types of major depression. However, in many psychiatric disorders, the underlying biological changes can, without treatment, be more or less permanent and often progressive (e.g., bipolar disorder).

Neuroanatomy

Advances in the neurosciences, especially newer neuro-imaging techniques (such as functional MRI, PET, and SPECT scanning), have allowed researchers to identify more precisely which brain structures are implicated in the cognitive, perceptual, and emotional aspects of brain functioning. Likewise, such techniques have made possible the delineation of the brain structures and neurotransmitter systems that appear to malfunction in cases of primary brain pathology and in neurochemically mediated psychopathologies.

Although volumes have been written about neuroanatomy and brain functioning, in this discussion we will touch only on those brain structures believed to be relevant to the study of psychiatric disorders. What follows represents a very brief overview of functional neuroanatomy, which will lay the groundwork for specific material presented in the chapters that follow.

Brain Structures

For practical purposes, the brain can be divided into three basic units: the brain stem and adjacent structures, the central core of the brain (including the limbic system, diencephalon, and basal ganglia), and the cerebral cortex (see figure 3-C). Clearly, the highest area of the brain, the cerebral cortex, is responsible for much of what is termed human: perception, complex cognitive processes, reality testing, and initiation of behavior, judgment, and so forth. Interestingly, however, the major biological dysfunctions seen in psychiatric disorders are thought to take place primarily outside of the cortex proper.

Major mental illnesses appear to involve neurochemical dysfunctions occurring in various subcortical areas: the limbic system, basal ganglia, reticular system, and brain stem. These brain structures are complexly interconnected and play critical roles in mediating primary affective states and a host of biological rhythms and drives (such as sleep, sex, and hunger).

Figure 3-D outlines the basic structures found in these important areas of the CNS, with reference to their various normal functions and the hypothesized psychopathology associated with each brain structure. However, it is important to note that few if any psychiatric disorders have been associated with pathology or dysfunction of any single brain structure, although clearly specific neuro-anatomical areas have been implicated in playing a special role in certain mental disorders.

Every region of the brain is activated and controlled by specific nerve cells. Billions of interconnecting nerve cells orchestrate the complex interactions necessary to carry out a host of functions ranging from basic instincts, reflexes, and life support, such as regulation of blood pressure, to highly developed abilities, such as abstract thought. When all is working as it should, people are able to respond to physiological and psychological demands in a normal and adaptive fashion.

However, brain functioning can be derailed by damage to brain tissue, via trauma, toxins, or disease, or by malfunction occurring in nerve cells. At times, such dysfunctions may affect only a tiny percentage of brain neurons. Yet the results can be devastating. The specific nature and location of brain dysfunctions will be revisited in later chapters as the physiological bases of major mental disorders is explored. Here, an overview of functional neuroanatomy is presented (see figure 3-E). It focuses only on those brain structures and systems currently believed to underlie psychiatric disorders.

The Hypothalamus

This primitive brain center is about the size of a pea and lies at the base of the brain. It is a complex structure and is responsible for regulating a host of biologic functions including the following: the circadian rhythm, sleep cycles, appetite, sex drive, and regulation of both the autonomic nervous system and almost all of the endocrine glands. The now familiar neurotransmitters, serotonin, norepinephrine, and dopamine are thought to be crucial in regulating certain aspects of hypothalamic functioning. The hypothalamus is intimately connected to the structures of the limbic system and to the pituitary gland.

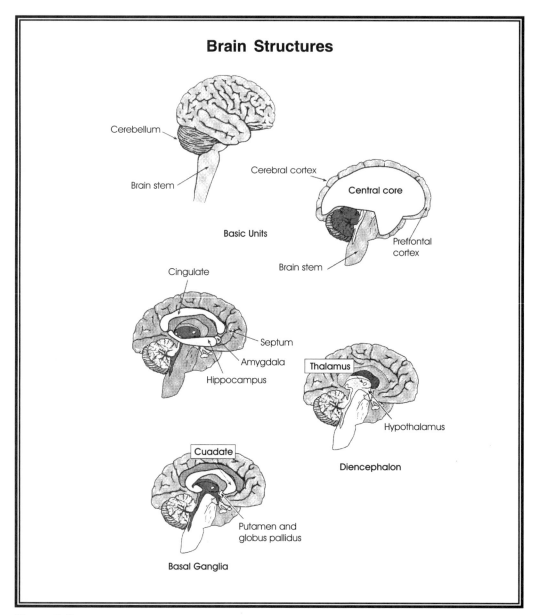

Figure 3-C

The Limbic System: The "Emotional Brain"

The structures of the limbic system (amygdala, septum, cingulate, and hippocampus) are common to all mammals (see figure 3-C). The limbic system is involved in three primary functions: the appraisal of emotional stimuli, initiation of emotional responses (e.g., the "fight-or-flight" response), and, finally, shutting down reactivity after external stressors subside (and restoring the nervous system and body to a state of homeostasis).

A highly detailed discussion of the limbic system is beyond the scope of this book, although we will address several basic issues here.

Neuroanatomy, Psychological Functions, and Psychopathology

Brain Structure	Functions	Psychopathology
Cortex	Higher cognitive processing	Dementia, confusional states
Prefrontal cortex	Impulse control, attention, behavior monitoring, organization of complex information	Attention deficit disorder, schizophrenia, obsessive-compulsive disorder, depression
Diencephalon		
thalamus	Many nerves pass through this brain structure	Not implicated in major psychiatric disorders
hypothalamus	Regulates sleep cycles, hunger, sex drive; controls endocrine and autonomic nervous system; influences immune system	Depression, anxiety disorders, sleep disorders
Limbic system		
amygdala	Elicits and controls aggression, primitive threat appraisal	Impulse control disorders, depression, borderline personality disorder*, anxiety disorders
septum	Emotional and stimulus "gate," pleasure centers	Schizophrenia, impulse control disorders, addictive disorders
cingulate	Neuronal pathways connecting limbic system structures and prefrontal lobes, affect regulation	Obsessive-compulsive disorder
hippocampus	Recent memory, new learning, impulse and emotional control	Alzheimer's disease, postconcussion syndrome, depression
Basal ganglia	Controls aspects of motor behavior	Parkinson's disease, antipsychotic medication side effects (extrapyramidal symptoms [EPS])
	Neuronal pathways connecting limbic system and prefrontal lobes	Obsessive-compulsive disorder
Brain stem reticular system	Stimulus filter or "gate"	Attention deficit disorder, schizophrenia

* Likely, but not proven

Figure 3-D

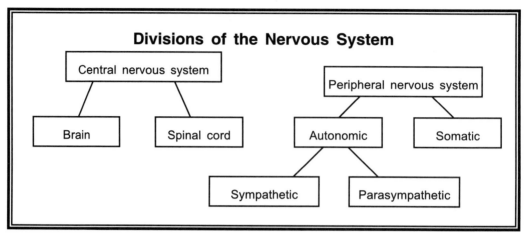

Figure 3-E

Information Processing

Incoming sensory information is appraised by way of two main processing centers in the brain. The cerebral cortex (the most highly evolved part of the brain) is capable of complex information processing and critical thinking. A parallel system exists subcortically. The amygdala (there are two amygdalae in the brain; one in each temporal lobe) has the capacity to register, perceive, and analyze sensory data also. However, the appraisal of environmental stressors, at the level of the amygdala, is crude. This brain structure is able to engage in gross pattern recognition, and if such patterns resemble objects or events previously associated with danger, neuronal impulses exiting the amygdala elicit a fight-or-flight response (independent of the cerebral cortex). Since perception at the amygdala level is often rapid, crude, and inexact, there are many false alarms (for example, misperceiving a piece of rope for a snake). However, this primitive fear appraisal system is believed to be adaptive and ultimately aids or facilitates survival (Le Doux 1996).

Igniting the Fight-or-Flight Response

When a person is confronted with a stressor, as noted above, this is perceived and interpreted on two levels (cortical and subcortical) and an emotional response is initiated. The main pathway for this involves neuronal activation of the hypothalamus by the amygdala.

At the level of the hypothalamus, three primary stress response pathways are activated (these are illustrated in more detail in figures 8-B and 8-C in chapter 8). The first, and most immediately felt response to a perceived danger, is evoked by the sympathetic nervous system (SNS). Nerves of the SNS go to almost all areas of the body and immediately release norepinephrine. This readily activates adrenergic receptors and causes increased heart rate, increased blood pressure, and sweating. SNS nerves also penetrate to the core of the adrenal gland (the adrenal medulla), which then discharges norepinephrine and adrenaline into the bloodstream.

The two additional pathways are termed neuro-endocrine (i.e., brain activation of endocrine glands). The hypothalamic-pituitary-adrenal pathway (commonly called the HPA axis) results in the release of steroid hormones from the adrenal gland (this class of hormones includes glucocorticoids, which facilitate the release of glucose into circulation). In humans, the main glucocorticoid is cortisol.

The second neuro-endocrine pathway is the hypothalamic-pituitary-thyroid axis. When activated, it causes the release of the two thyroid hormones: thyroxine (T4) and triiodothyronine (T3). The combined effect of these primary stress hormones along with SNS activation is to quickly mobilize the body to take action to avoid danger (fight or flight).

Return to Baseline

Finally, the various stress hormones, which are circulated throughout the bloodstream, re-enter the brain and trigger a shutting down of the stress response. This process of hormonal feedback allows the nervous system to regulate itself, and when danger subsides, to return to a state of homeostasis.

The hippocampus is one of the most important limbic structures that reduce arousal; in a sense, it turns off the stress response (specifically, it shuts off the HPA axis). The hippocampi (again, one in each temporal lobe) are densely populated with glucocorticoid receptors (GR). When cortisol molecules reach the hippocampus and bind to the GRs, that activates the hippocampus which then exerts inhibitory control over the hypothalamus and thus deactivates the stress response. Feedback and inhibition also take place at the levels of the hypothalamus and pituitary. Additionally, some evidence exists suggesting that the anterior (i.e., most frontal aspect) cingulate gyrus may also play a role in reducing emotional arousal (Mayberg 1997).

Peripheral Nervous System

As figure 3-E indicates, in addition to the CNS (brain and spinal cord) the nervous system contains a further division, the peripheral nervous system (PNS). Within the PNS is the somatic division, which controls voluntary action of the skeletal muscles and carries information from sensory organs to the CNS.

A second branch of the peripheral nervous system is the autonomic nervous system (ANS). The ANS innervates involuntary organs, such as the heart, smooth muscles, and glands. Further divisions of the peripheral ANS are the sympathetic and parasympathetic systems. These systems generally can be thought of as antagonistic, although this is not absolute for every activity. Most organs are innervated by both systems, and regulation is established through opposing functions.

The sympathetic nervous system (SNS) plays a role in the fight-or-flight response. Set in motion by activity in the limbic system and hypothalamus, the SNS mobilizes the body to take action in response to dangerous situations. Conversely, the parasympathetic system, which is activated at times of relaxation and quiescence, acts to reduce heart rate and blood pressure in an overall attempt to conserve energy (see figure 3-F).

Many psychotropic medications can, unfortunately, affect the parasympathetic and sympathetic nervous systems, thus producing side effects. The parasympathetic system is mediated by the chemical acetylcholine. As we shall see in subsequent chapters, many psychiatric medications have anticholinergic effects (that is, they block acetylcholine) with resulting side effects (see figure 3-G).

The sympathetic system is mediated primarily by norepinephrine. (Nerve cells activated by norepinephrine, epinephrine, and related compounds are called adrenergic nerves.) Certain psychotropic medications either block or activate adrenergic neurons in the SNS, again producing undesirable effects.

Pathways to Psychopathology

Certainly a number of psychiatric disorders do not appear to involve gross dysfunction in underlying neurobiology or neurochemistry. Such disorders may aptly be seen primarily as either psychological reactions to psychosocial stressors and/or characterological difficulties. However, an increasing number of psychiatric disorders are being found to have neurobiologic aspects; either a primary biological problem is the sole cause or brain changes have resulted from encounters with stressful life events.

Effects of SNS and PNS Activity on Target Organs

Organ or Gland	Sympathetic Actions	Parasympathetic Actions
Pupils	Dilate	Constrict
Salivary glands	Reduce secretions	Secrete
Lungs (bronchi)	Dilate	Constrict
Heart	Increase rate	Slow rate
GI tract	Interrupt digestion	Digest
Adrenal gland	Secrete	—
Bladder	—	Empty fluids
Arteries	Constrict	Relax

Figure 3-F

Side Effects Affecting Autonomic Nervous System

Parasympathetic System— Anticholinergic Effects	Sympathetic System— Adrenergic Effects
Blurry vision	Hypotension (low norepinephrine)
Dry mouth	Rapid heart rate (elevated norepinephrine)
Constipation	
Urine retention	

Figure 3-G

Among those disorders that have a biologic element, let us consider the following:

- Genetically transmitted vulnerability, which may manifest in psychiatric disorder. This includes disorders such as schizophrenia, bipolar disorder, major depression, and attention deficit disorder. Other conditions that may be related to genetic factors include these: obsessive-compulsive disorder, panic disorder, and some substance abuse disorders.

- Nonneurologic medical illnesses that ultimately affect neurochemistry (e.g., thyroid disease).

- Acquired brain dysfunction; due to multiple causes such as brain trauma, toxins, chronic effects of substance abuse, primary brain diseases (e.g., brain tumors, Alzheimer's disease, etc.), pre-natal factors that have caused abnormal brain development, etc.

- Abnormal brain development due to excessive stress: Considerable research strongly suggests that very severe stress can alter brain functioning in more or less permanent ways. Most notable are the effects of severe neglect or abuse early in life (this will be explored in greater detail in chapter 11 on post-traumatic stress disorder) (Nemeroff 1997; Lewis, Amini, and Lennon 2000).

- Brain damage caused by exposure to excessively high levels of stress hormones (e.g., abnormally high levels of cortisol, often seen in major depression, may damage nerve cells in the hippocampus). For details see chapter 6 on depression (Sapolksy 1996).

What has become abundantly clear is that the older and more categorical model of *"either* biological *or* psychological" etiology is no longer a relevant schema. Primary biological disorders do exist, but whether or not they become manifest may be highly dependent on the effects of psychological stress. Conversely, severe and prolonged stress can often transform a rather pure "psychological disorder" after weeks or months, until we see changes in brain chemistry and stress hormones emerge.

Psychological treatments are often effective in treating many psychiatric illnesses, and (as some research is beginning to show) may in fact alter/improve underlying neurobiology (Gabbard 2000). However, when significant abnormalities in brain functioning exist, biologic interventions such as pharmacotherapy may be necessary.

4

Pharmacology

Psychiatry, perhaps uniquely in health care, operates from an established multi-disciplinary approach. The opportunity, as well as the responsibility, exists for all clinicians to be involved in medication decisions as appropriate to their discipline. As treatment approaches in mental health continue to evolve, it is likely that current practices will expand and demand participation from knowledgeable therapists.

From a practical standpoint, possessing fundamental knowledge is critical in the rapidly changing field of psychopharmacology, along with the attendant challenge of understanding emerging treatments, new applications of existing medications, and multiple drug regimens. Additionally, medical comorbidity in psychiatric patients (coexisting medical illness and psychiatric disorder) mandates at least a familiarity with psychotropics' potential actions and interactions with various nonpsychotropic therapeutic agents.

In your practice as a psychotherapist, it is not essential to become an expert in the area of physiology, pharmacology, or biochemistry. However, it is important to become generally familiar with a few preliminary concepts, which will lay a groundwork for the clinical chapters which follow. This chapter presents basic pharmacologic principles, defines terminologies commonly found in later chapters of this book (and in standard medical or medication texts), and integrates factual information about medication effects on organ systems and at the cellular level.

Basic Principles of Pharmacokinetics

The broad definition of a drug as "any substance that brings about a change in biologic function through its chemical actions" (Katzung 2001) is helpful in understanding the relationship between the body and administered medications. This is a fluid and interactive process, composed of two elements: *pharmacodynamics* and *pharmacokinetics*.

Pharmacodynamics can be viewed as the drug's effect on the body (discussed in detail for specific drugs in part three of this book). Conversely, pharmacokinetics can be considered the body's effect on the drug. There are four basic pharmacokinetic factors: *absorption, distribution, biotransformation,* and *excretion* (see figure 4-A). Every drug will exhibit a unique kinetic profile (like a fingerprint) composed of these factors. This chapter provides a general description of pharmacokinetic principles and their significance in clinical practice. (Expanded discussion for each area of pharmacokinetics is provided in appendix A.)

Absorption

Most drugs are initially, and predominantly, absorbed in the stomach or small intestine. The degree of absorption in the digestive tract can be affected by patient-dependent factors, such as whether the medication is taken with or without food. Further, as a drug proceeds to its ultimate destination, it may have numerous barriers to cross, depending on the absorption characteristics of the drug itself. For instance, in the central nervous system (CNS), the blood-brain barrier allows passage of only certain molecules into the brain. Penetration of medication into the CNS is restricted by a host of factors which protect the CNS from exposure to toxins, although this barrier is not absolute or impenetrable. (See appendix A for discussion of related factors of bioavailability and first-pass phenomena.)

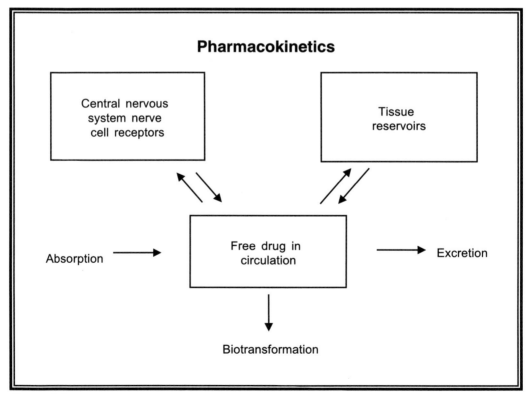

Figure 4-A

Case 6

Patricia A. is a 45-year-old female referred to the day treatment program at your hospital. She is an intelligent, energetic woman whose chief complaint is "difficulty remembering things." She is moderately anxious about this symptom, since she is expecting to return to work in two weeks after a six-month medical leave of absence. She was diagnosed with breast cancer seven months ago, for which she received chemotherapy and radiation treatment. Tests indicate that her cancer has not spread, and her physician reports an excellent prognosis.

Patricia is a member of a support group for cancer survivors which has helped her "tremendously." She is hoping someone in your program can help her "get a handle on this memory thing." Her job requires that she retain and recall detailed numerical data, and she does not want to return to work "less than 100 percent." You will be providing psychotherapy to her on a daily basis for the next ten days.

During your initial session with her, she tells you that she is sure that her memory loss is related to the effects of her chemotherapy and is therefore somewhat doubtful that you will be able to help her. You find that this might be a reasonable question to pursue before proceeding too far in therapy with her. Your program relies heavily on interdisciplinary treatment, so you request psychological testing from the psychologist and a medication review from the pharmacist. Psychological testing results show Patricia to be above average in intelligence with no evidence of organicity or personality disorder. The pharmacist reports that none of the chemotherapeutic agents that Patricia received crosses the blood-brain barrier appreciably or affects healthy brain tissue.

Typical memory loss secondary to cancer treatment is short term and is usually attributable to pretreatment antianxiety medications. Based on these reports, you feel confident in moving ahead with therapy and exploring Patricia's anxiety and memory loss from a nonorganic focus.

Distribution

Once a drug has been absorbed and reaches the bloodstream, it is then distributed to various organs or sites of action throughout the body. Certain medications have characteristic distribution patterns, which are extremely important in understanding response to treatment. A critical example in psychiatry is the extensive depositing of tricyclic antidepressants and antipsychotic medications in fat and muscle cells. In effect, these areas act as reservoirs or holding tanks. In some instances, concentrations of a drug in reservoir areas will exceed levels in the bloodstream. This explains why serum levels of antidepressants are not absolutely indicative of total body concentration. (See appendix A for a detailed description of distribution phases and protein binding.)

Case 7

Helen P. is an obese 27-year-old woman who has been taking the antidepressant desipramine. She was started on a low dose and gradually increased to a dose of 300 mg daily, which she has been taking for the past three months. Even though Helen has only in the last two months been able to notice an effect, she now reports a significant improvement in her depression and no side effects. Her physician has forwarded results of periodic desipramine blood levels to you, and all are within therapeutic range. However, Helen recently discovered that a coworker also takes this medication, in a dose of 150 mg daily, and is doing well. She reveals to you that without consulting her physician she has cut her dose in half over the last two weeks because she thinks her dosage was too high.

You firmly encourage Helen to discuss this matter with her doctor, and point out to her that a dose of 300 mg is still within the standard accepted dosage range and that blood level monitoring has shown this dose to be right for her. You further remind her of the risk and consequences if her depression should recur. Because you are aware that this tricyclic antidepressant is probably extensively stored in her fat tissue you are able to provide needed reassurance that her treatment is reasonable and being safely monitored.

Biotransformation

The body's reaction to drugs as foreign substances results in several processes of elimination, one being metabolism (biotransformation) and the other excretion. Metabolism occurs primarily in the liver, via specific action of enzymes that change the original chemical into compounds that are more easily excreted by the kidneys. Biotransformation is a complex process. Understanding metabolic activity is crucial in medication management, especially when medication treatment is not working adequately.

When medications are chemically altered by the process of biotransformation, the results are the production of numerous chemical by-products, called *metabolites*. Some metabolites are useful and desirable, in that they produce desired effects; for instance, the reduction of psychiatric symptoms. Unfortunately, some metabolites affect various bodily tissues and result in undesirable side effects. In addition, since most medications undergo significant metabolism, the risks of drug *toxicity* (poisoning due to excessively high levels of a drug) must be considered whenever metabolism is impaired. Antidepressants, antipsychotics, and anticonvulsants are all extensively metabolized by liver enzymes. Thus, impaired liver functioning can result in abnormal metabolism of these medications. Conversely, increased activity of liver enzymes can cause excessive metabolism, resulting in a decreased drug level and an inadequate response to treatment. (Appendix A contains additional information regarding metabolic enzymes and drug metabolites.)

Case 8

Susan is 45-year-old women whom you have been seeing in therapy, off and on, for several years. You have diagnosed her with dysthymia and currently she meets the criteria for major depression. In the past, you and her primary care physician have recommended antidepressant treatment, which she has declined. She is motivated to "manage her moods" without chemicals and maintains a regular exercise regimen and stays in close contact with friends when she feels sad. However, she reports recent worsening of insomnia and daytime fatigue and is finding it harder to keep herself "under control." Her doctor has suggested she may be perimenopausal, which can be associated with sleep disturbance and mood lability.

Due to her worsening symptoms, she reluctantly agreed to antidepressant treatment. Six weeks ago her doctor prescribed paroxetine (Paxil), 20 mg daily, with an upward titration from 10 mg daily for the first five days. Susan experienced extreme drowsiness, dry mouth, and constipation and stopped the medication after two weeks. Her physician then prescribed venlafaxine (Effexor), at a very low starting dose, but again, after several weeks, Susan continued to experience intolerable side effects of dizziness, blurred vision, and profuse sweating. She agreed to one more trial of an antidepressant, although she expressed her frustration with this aspect of treatment. She is currently taking sertraline (Zoloft), 75 mg daily, and after two weeks has tolerated the medication well. She is encouraged by the lack of side effects compared to the other antidepressants and is willing to continue taking it as long as necessary.

You are curious as to the pattern of side effect response that Susan experienced and confer with her doctor. Her physician speculates that Susan may be a slow metabolizer of medications metabolized by the CYP2D6* system, which is the case for paroxetine and venlafaxine. Slow metabolizers often experience severe side effects to low or average doses of medications. This assumption is supported by Susan's tolerability of sertraline which is metabolized by the CYP2C9* and CYP3A* systems.

Excretion

Excretion is the process by which drugs are eliminated from the body. Excretion occurs primarily via the kidneys, although other routes include the gastrointestinal tract, the respiratory system, and sweat, saliva, and breast milk. Adequate excretion is dependent on effective kidney function. Disease- or drug-induced damage to the kidneys can lead to kidney failure, resulting in a toxic accumulation of medications in the bloodstream.

An important characteristic of medications is the *half-life* ($t_{1/2}$), which is defined as the amount of time required for the serum concentration to be reduced by 50 percent (Benet, Mitchell, and Sherner 1990b). Half-life is used to determine dosage amounts and intervals for most medications.

Half-life measurements are used to estimate the time required for a drug to reach what is called *steady state*. Steady state occurs when concentrations of a medication in the bloodstream have reached a plateau, so that the amount administered is equal to the amount being eliminated. It is generally accepted that for most drugs steady state is attained after four half-lives; for example if the half-life is 24 hours, then steady state is usually reached in four days. It is important to remember that reaching steady state does not always correspond to a drug's onset of desired action. With antidepressants, for instance, steady state will be reached long before a therapeutic effect is noted. (See figure 3-B; also see appendix A for discussion of a related topic, the therapeutic index.)

---

* These are specific classes of liver enzymes (see appendix A).

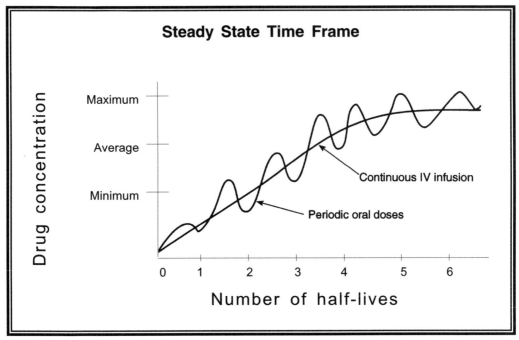

Figure 4-B

Case 9

Frank is a 24-year-old honor student, majoring in engineering, who you have been seeing for four months through the student counseling center. He initially presented with major depression, although he has never been suicidal. He has significant narcissistic and passive-aggressive traits. He began treatment with Prozac, 20 mg daily in the morning, two weeks ago. His agreement to take medications came after much discussion with you and the psychiatrist, including detailed information regarding dosage range, onset of action, and side effects.

During today's session, he angrily informs you that the medication is not working and challenges you to answer some questions he has formulated after reading the *Physicians' Desk Reference*. His opinion, based on mathematical calculations, is that the drug has had plenty of time to reach a therapeutic level. He concludes that "the whole idea is some sort of placebo experiment" and threatens to terminate treatment.

This behavior is characteristic of Frank, and you respond in a calm and nondefensive way. You acknowledge his need to thoroughly understand the medication and that it can be frustrating to wait for indicators that the drug is working. However, you remind him that the typical response time for most antidepressants is three to four weeks and is not absolutely related to serum level of the medication. You suggest other sources of information, written for patients, which may more specifically address his needs. You also offer encouragement that he has tolerated the medication without significant side effects.

Medication Effects

When medications are chemically reorganized into various metabolites, these resulting compounds produce a variety of effects—some desirable, some undesirable. All medications, including psychotropics, typically have five primary effects:

- *Pharmacological effect*—the desired therapeutic effect, such as antipsychotics reducing hallucinations.

- *Side effects*—typically considered to be undesirable effects, such as constipation, dry mouth, blurry vision, and so on. Occasionally side effects can be used to benefit the patient, for example, using a medication's sedating side effect to help an anxious patient fall asleep at night. Side effects, although generally undesirable, are by definition fairly common and predictable and may be somewhat preventable. Side effects are generally considered extensions of the pharmacological properties of a drug, and account for 70 to 80 percent of adverse drug events (Glazener 1992).

- *Idiosyncratic effects*—extremely rare, adverse effects, and are difficult to predict. They are often specific to an individual or to certain groups of patients who share common genetic or biologic features.

- *Allergic reactions*—some individuals have an immune response to medications, generally a skin rash or hypersensitivity. The body may respond to the medication as if it was a foreign substance or organism and produce allergic symptoms. A severe type of allergic reaction, called anaphylaxis, can include difficulty breathing, fever, and irregular heart beat. Anaphylactic reactions are potentially fatal, as is, for example, an allergy to penicillin.

- *Discontinuance syndrome*—response to stopping or interrupting medication treatment. Examples are narcotic withdrawal or "cholinergic rebound" when tricyclic antidepressants or antipsychotics are abruptly stopped.

Drug Interactions

Basic pharmacologic principles apply as much to drug *interactions* as to drug actions. Each kinetic property—absorption, distribution, metabolism (biotransformation), and excretion—is potentially affected by the presence of coadministered medications. Drug interactions involving metabolism are of particular clinical significance. The reader is referred to appendix A for an expanded discussion on this topic. Drug interactions follow a variable time-course pattern, from immediate to delayed. Consequently, it is important to remember that several weeks may elapse before the effects of an interactive combination are evident.

And the comorbidity of medical and psychiatric disorders requires at least some degree of multiple drug prescribing. For example, many patients suffering from serious physical disorders as well as depression will require medication treatment for both conditions. Examples include diabetes mellitus, cancer, and cardiovascular disease. Familiarity with drug interactions can be an important addition to diagnostic skills.

Although significant interactions for specific drugs will be addressed in subsequent chapters, case 10 illustrates the most frequently encountered of all drug interactions, enzyme inhibition (Hansten and Horn 1990). This interaction occurs when two drugs rely on the same enzyme system for metabolism. In this "competition," one drug usually wins over the other and is preferentially and completely metabolized. Conversely, metabolism of the other drug is inhibited, leading to an increased serum level. This increase can at times produce greater effectiveness than anticipated from a given dose, or it can produce serious adverse effects, such as toxicity.

Case 10

Eugene is a 60-year-old man who is being treated for a first episode of major depression. Eugene's wife died unexpectedly a year ago and he has had difficulty "coming to terms" with life alone. He reports decreased appetite, sleep disturbance, tearfulness, and anhedonia. He began taking 10 mg of fluoxetine daily one week ago, and is scheduled to increase his dose tomorrow to 20 mg daily. This is his first psychiatric treatment. Eugene has a history of hypertension, which has been well controlled for many years with metoprolol, a beta-blocker.

This week, during your session with Eugene he appeared fatigued and complained of shortness of breath and lightheadedness. His blood pressure, taken at home the morning you saw him, was 100 over 60. He asked you if the antidepressant could be causing these side effects. You recommended that Eugene be seen by his doctor that same day. You called and arranged for an appointment after your session was over. Eugene's physician called you later that day to report that Eugene's blood pressure and pulse were both dangerously low, which she suspected was due to a drug interaction between fluoxetine and metoprolol, causing an increased level of the latter. Eugene's doctor changed his antidepressant to citalopram (Celexa), which he tolerates without problems.

There is a likelihood that psychiatric patients (especially older people) will be receiving multiple medications. People with clinical syndromes that include associated physical symptoms, such as anxiety disorders and depression, are often initially treated by a nonpsychiatrist prescriber. The medications prescribed can include gastrointestinal agents, antihypertensives, analgesics, and sedative-hypnotics. Subsequent referral to a psychiatrist may result in the addition of a psychotropic medication. Thus the psychotherapist may ultimately inherit this patient with the attendant possibilities of drug interactions.

The presentation of this material does not suggest that psychotherapists are responsible for identifying and monitoring drug interactions. That is a job best left to physicians and pharmacists. However, in certain cases the effects of interactive drugs will be evident in therapy. For example, when a previously good medication response has abated, or when the intensity of side effects is inconsistent with dosage, ruling out drug interactions is helpful. Also, psychotherapists often have more complete information about a client's treatment than do individual physicians, each of whom may be independently prescribing potentially interactive medications. In these situations, it is the psychotherapist who often sounds the initial warning.

Medication Effects on a Cellular Level

For most psychiatric mediations to have an effect on symptoms, they must first gain entrance to the brain. (Notable exceptions are most beta-blockers, which have an effect primarily in the periphery, not in the central nervous system. See chapter

1.) The central nervous system is protected by dense membranes and tightly packed capillaries, collectively referred to as the *blood-brain barrier*. The blood-brain barrier controls chemical access to the brain, preventing the entry of a host of molecules that could be potentially toxic to the brain. Drugs that are *lipophilic* are generally better able to penetrate the blood-brain barrier, and most effective psychiatric medications are highly lipophilic. Once in the brain, the next step is for medications to have an effect on individual nerve cells.

As noted in the previous chapter, the functioning of nerve cells is maintained or altered by the effects of various molecules, which are able to bind to receptors located on the surface of neuronal cell bodies, dendrites, and nerve terminals. (Note: Some receptors are also found in the interior of nerve cell bodies.) Molecules that are able to bind to a receptor are referred to as *ligands*. Ligands include neurotransmitters, hormones, and certain exogenous agents such as drugs, or trace elements (e.g., lithium) and some chemicals found in foods and herbs.

For a ligand to bind to a receptor it must have a highly specific molecular shape, much in the same way that a key must precisely fit a lock in order to open it.

Cellular response to ligand binding: There are two fundamental ways to understand the cellular response. The first involves an *agonist* effect, where a ligand activates the receptor. The second involves an *antagonist* effect which occurs when a ligand occupies a receptor site but does not activate it. The process of *antagonism*, also known as *blocking*, prevents other molecules from activating the receptor. This has been likened to the lock and key metaphor again, in that some keys can be inserted into a lock, but if it is not the right key, it cannot open the lock. However, as long as it occupies the lock, other keys cannot be inserted; i.e., it blocks the lock.

The nervous system must be capable of making adaptive responses to changes in the external environment (e.g., stressors) and to shifts in the internal biologic milieu. Receptors represent a physiological mechanism by which stimulation can influence the action of nerve cells. Via agonism or antagonism of receptors, a host of molecules (including psychiatric medications) can have an impact on cellular functioning.

Specific Receptors, Receptor Actions; Drug Effects and Side Effects

The ideal psychiatric drug would be a highly selective molecule that would be targeted to bind to a specific receptor on specific nerve cells in the brain *and* have no effect on other receptors or neurons. It would also be administered in the most direct and convenient way possible for the patient. Such drugs do not exist, but are highly sought after by pharmaceutical companies. Three major problems stand in the way of development of such ideal drugs.

First, many molecules, owing to their unique molecular shape, inadvertently bind to more than one receptor. For example, a number of antipsychotics bind not only to postsynaptic dopamine receptors (which creates a dopamine blockade and presumably accounts for antipsychotic effects), but also lock onto acetylcholine muscurinic receptors (this can result in a number of side effects including memory impairment, blurry vision, and constipation, to mention but a few of the common anticholinergic side effects).

A second problem is that a particular drug molecule, for example, binds to some dopamine receptors in the limbic system, producing desired, antipsychotic effects. However, it simultaneously binds to other dopamine receptors but they are located in the basal ganglia, and there it produces significant extrapyramidal side effects (such as tremors). Such drug molecules cannot be delivered to just one part of the brain and be sequestered there, but rather, they are disseminated to numerous brain regions.

The third problem is that, among classes of receptors, numerous subtypes have been discovered and drug molecules typically do not just interact with one subtype. For example, currently fourteen different serotonin receptors have been identified. Drugs that, in a global sense, increase brain serotonin levels, have multiple effects since some serotonin receptors are inhibitory and some are excitatory.

The pharmacologist may want to target serotonin (abbreviated 5-HT) 5-HT1a receptors to have an antidepressant effect, but also can't help but activate all other 5-HT receptor subtypes, provoking numerous side effects. Thus, the development of highly selective molecules that potentially could target particular receptor subtypes, and leave others alone, is the dream and the challenge for many pharmaceutical company chemists. An important perspective for understanding medication effects and side effects requires a knowledge of the various types of receptors that are found on the surfaces of particular nerve cells in the brain; it also requires becoming familiar with the assortment of actions that drugs have on the receptors. Many hundreds of receptors have been identified, but a smaller and more manageable list of those most relevant to psychopharmacology are outlined below.

Specific Receptor Actions

Receptors[1]	Action	Drugs that can produce this action	Desired Effects	Adverse Effects
NE (in general)	Activate	Antidepressants	Antidepressant	Sympathomimetic (increase heart rate, blood pressure, sweating, tremors, jitteriness, and anxiety)
NE α-1	Activate	Antidepressants	Increase alertness	Increase blood pressure
NE α-2[2]	Activate	Clonidine	Decrease aggression Reduce hyperactivity	Decrease blood pressure; causes lightheadedness
NE α-2	Block	Yohimbine	Combats sexual dysfunction	Sympathomimetic
5-HT1A	Activate	SSRIs	Antidepressant, anti-anxiety, impulse control, reduce aggression	
5-HT 2[3]	Activate	SSRIs		Extrapyramidal effects, apathy, emotional blunting, sexual dysfunction
5-HT 2[3]	Block	Remeron	Atypical antipsychotics Antipsychotic (?) Antidepressant	Counters extrapyramidal
5-HT3	Activate	SSRI's		Nausea
5-HT3	Block	Remeron		Reduces nausea
DA	Block	Antipsychotics	Antipsychotic	Counters extrapyramidal effects, apathy, emotional blunting, increases prolactin secretion
DA	Activate	Cocaine, stimulants Wellbutrin	Antidepressant; Reduces hyperactivity	Psychosis; anxiety
H1	Block	Benadryl, tricyclics, some antipsychotics	Sedation (to promote sleep)	Sedation; weight gain; hypotension
ACH	Block	Tricyclics, some antisychotics, Paxil	Reduces acute extrapyramidal effects	Constipation, urinary retention, blurred vision, increase heart rate, memory impairment, confusion, dry mouth

(1) Receptor Abbreviations: NE (norepinephrine), 5-HT (serotonin), DA (dopamine), H-1 (histamine), Ach (acetylcholine/muscurinic).

(2) NE α-2 receptors are inhibitory and thus stimulating them, in essence, activates a braking mechanism and reduces arousal.

(3) 5-HT2 inhibitory receptors on the surface of dopamine neurons. Thus when *stimulated* (i.e., activates the brake), it reduces dopamine activity. When this happens in the basal ganglia it can cause extrapyramidal effects and amotivation. If 5-HT2 receptors are *blocked* on dopamine nerve cells in the frontal cortex, it can reduce apathy and amotivation (i.e., reduce the negative symptoms of schizophrenia).

Figure 4-C

Part Two

Clinical Syndromes: Etiology, Diagnosis, and Treatment Implications

In part two of this book we address in some detail the biological etiology and differential diagnosis of major clinical syndromes. In our approach to diagnosis, we incorporate some *DSM-IV* criteria. However, at times alternative classifications and criteria are employed. Our aim is to provide a useful and clinically relevant approach that will help the therapist in decision making, particularly with regard to referral issues and medication treatments.

This section of the book begins with a chapter on preliminary diagnostic considerations. Following this are chapters addressing the most common clinical syndromes. The specifics of medication treatment (dosing, effects, side effects) will follow in part three.

5

Preliminary Diagnostic Considerations

Before launching into a detailed discussion of major psychiatric disorders, it is important to explore some preliminary diagnostic issues. These issues should be considered in the initial workup of any client for whom medications are being considered.

The most common approach to diagnosis (that of the *DSM*), and the approach we present in this book, is based on the identification of specific target symptoms that make up a particular disorder or syndrome. Such an approach certainly has merit. Yet it is crucial to keep in mind that any particular behavior, symptom, or trait *may* have diverse etiologies. That is, identical symptomatic behaviors may spring from biochemical dysfunctions, social learning experiences, or characterological sources. The three most common sources of etiologic confusion will be discussed in this chapter: the interaction between Axis I and Axis II; substance abuse and psychiatric symptomatology; and finally physical illnesses that present with cognitive, emotional, and behavioral disturbances. Successful pharmacologic treatment often depends on a thorough understanding of these important issues.

Axis I and Axis II: Complex Interactions

DSM-IV employs a multiaxial diagnostic system. Axis I includes major psychiatric symptom disorders and syndromes, and Axis II is reserved for long-standing personality styles and disorders. This distinction between the more acute, episodic, symptomatic disorders (Axis I) and more trait-like, pervasive, and enduring personality problems (Axis II) is a useful and important advance over earlier diagnostic systems. Differentiating state and trait variables has helped researchers and clinicians alike to identify more clearly and reliably a host of psychiatric disorders. The distinction also has been useful in planning therapeutic interventions, in understanding treatment outcomes, and in making predictions about the course of disorders and their prognosis. Yet, in many respects, the boundaries between Axis I and Axis II are not entirely clear-cut. Understanding the complex interactions between Axis I and II is as important in pharmacological treatment as it is in psychotherapy. Axis I and II disorders influence one another in four common ways:

- Axis I disorder evokes or intensifies Axis II characteristics
- Axis II dynamics predispose to Axis I disorders
- Axis II characteristics reflect atypical or mild chronic Axis I disorders
- Axis II dynamics influence Axis I treatment response

Let's take a look at each of these interactions.

Axis I Disorder Evokes Axis II Characteristics

Axis I disorders oftentimes enhance or exaggerate preexisting personality traits. For example, sometimes an Axis I disorder unearths behavior that was not at all evident prior to the clinical episode. The clinician may conclude that a patient has a major depression *and* a personality disorder, only to discover that the personality disorder disappears with successful treatment of the Axis I disorder. This is frequently seen in individuals diagnosed as borderline personalities in which the impact of serious depression or panic disorder results in psychological regression. During the Axis I episode there are, in fact, features verging on borderline. However, in as many as a third of such patients, with resolution of the major symptom disorder, their level of functioning resumes its normal or (more often) neurotic preclinical level. Since borderline characteristics were not evident prior to the major episode of depression or panic, and the history was not one of "stable instability," to call such a patient borderline is technically inaccurate.

Case 11

Barbara M., 35, was admitted to an inpatient psychiatric unit after she developed suicidal ideas and incidents in which she repeatedly sliced the inside of her calf. Her admitting diagnosis was major depression and borderline personality disorder. The borderline diagnosis was based on the rather bizarre self-mutilation. The treating

---

Key Terms

Agonist. Drug or chemical that acts on a receptor to mimic the effects of a naturally occurring substance (such as a hormone or neurotransmitter), or of another chemical; for example, beta adrenergic agonist medications mimic epinephrine and produce relaxation of bronchial (lung) muscles to treat asthma.

Antagonist. Substance or drug capable of blocking (at the receptor) the activity of an agonist without exerting any effect itself. For example, antipsychotics are dopamine receptor antagonists.

Differential diagnosis. The process of considering diagnostic possibilities based on a comparison of signs and symptoms of two or more disorders or diseases.

Egodystonic. Symptoms subjectively experienced by the patient as being aversive, undesirable, or alien.

Egosyntonic. Signs or symptoms judged to be pathological by others but not experienced as distressing by the patient.

Etiology. The study of the causes of disorders and diseases.

Pathophysiology. The underlying physiological dysfunction or disease which contributes to the manifest symptoms of a disease.

continued

psychiatrist informed the patient's family that her acute depression could indeed be treated, but that the apparent personality disorder would likely be a serious, ongoing problem and the prognosis was more guarded.

Barbara's history, however, failed to reveal any previous signs of psychiatric problems. She was a very successful owner of a small print shop and had a history of solid interpersonal relationships. Her depressive disorder occurred after her best friend had been tragically killed in a boating accident. After five days of hospitalization, she was discharged. Five weeks later, after twice weekly psychotherapy and antidepressants, she was virtually symptom-free. There was no hint of the primitive personality disturbance evident when she was first hospitalized.

Target symptoms. In this book, the distinctive symptoms that are the focus (target) of medication treatment.

Toxicity. Serious medication-related adverse effects associated with actual or potential damage to tissues, organs, or the entire body system. Toxicity may be directly related to critically elevated blood levels of a drug and may be acute (as in tricyclic antidepressant overdose) or chronic (as in prolonged, moderately elevated lithium level). A drug may also produce "toxic effects" at therapeutic doses (such as phenothiazine's potential for inducing bone marrow damage, which in turn causes decreased production of white blood cells).

Another common example is when a very severe depression or anxiety disorder pulls the rug out from under a person. As a result, we may see the emergence of helplessness and overly dependent behavior. This *may* be an exaggeration of preexisting dependent traits, but it may also be the kind of regressive behavior seen across many personality styles when one is laid low by a serious, debilitating illness.

Axis II Dynamics Predispose to Axis I Disorders

Certain personality disorders may predispose an individual to increased risk of developing an Axis I disorder. We can see this emerge in at least two ways. First, people with personality disorders often, if not always, experience particular, unique areas of emotional vulnerability. For example, histrionic, dependent, avoidant, and many borderline patients have strong dependency longings and an exquisite sensitivity to separation stresses. As a group, these people are at higher risk for developing major depressions, serious anxiety reactions, or both in the wake of interpersonal losses. For these patients, relatively minor social rebuffs, rejections, or losses may precipitate significant depressive reactions. In a parallel manner, obsessive and paranoid personalities highly value being in control. Even minor life stresses that decrease one's sense of control or predictability can plunge these people into states of high anxiety, hypervigilance, and ruminative self-doubt.

A second way Axis II problems can increase risk is that repetitive maladaptive behavior patterns can result in recurring interpersonal stressors. For example, the clinging, overly dependent personality may, by his or her interpersonal style, repeatedly drive people away. Here the maladaptive behavior provokes numerous rejections, which in turn can lead to episodes of depression.

Thus, when medications are used to treat various Axis I disorders, it is well to keep in mind that, despite the success of drug treatment, ultimate therapeutic success and relapse prevention may depend heavily on the role Axis II factors play.

Axis II Characteristics Reflect Axis I Disorder

It is possible that what initially appear to be characteristic symptoms of personality disorder may reflect some form of mild, chronic, or atypical Axis I disorder. Let's consider several examples. For years clinicians described certain patients as suffering from masochistic or depressive personalities. These people were often seen as chronically pessimistic, bitter, irritable individuals, and the implication was that the low-grade depressive traits were manifestations of personality—that is, etched into the character of the individual. Although certainly this is the case for some people, in recent years a significant number of dysthymic patients have experienced very positive results when treated with antidepressants.

These so-called depressive characters likely have suffered from a form of chronic, low-grade biological depression. Similarly, recent reports of successful treatment of social anxiety in "avoidant personalities" using MAO inhibitors or SSRIs may indicate another group of patients whose character pathology seems to be rooted in a type of biochemical disturbance.

Undoubtedly, many people presenting with personality problems are best understood as exhibiting true disorders of character, and for these people medication treatment is not appropriate. However, it is very important not to conclude automatically that such behaviors are solely attributable to character pathology (see figure 5-A). Certain behavioral characteristics or traits seen in various personality disorders *may* be due to subtle neurochemical malfunction, which may respond to medication.

Just because a trait is long-standing, it is not appropriate to automatically assume that it is truly characterological. Figure 5-A can serve as a reminder to consider the *possibility* that certain characteristics may be due to chronic biochemical dysfunction. (See interesting discussions of this topic in Peter Kramer's best-selling book, *Listening to Prozac* 1993.)

Axis II Dynamics Influence Axis I Treatment Response

As mentioned in chapter 2, individuals' particular personality style and unique psychodynamics will often dramatically influence how they respond to pharmacotherapy. Robert Michaels (1992) has commented that in general clinical practice two-thirds of patients with Axis I disorders appear to respond quite well either to medication treatment or to brief, targeted psychological interventions, such as cognitive-behavioral or interpersonal therapy. However, a significant minority of patients with clear-cut Axis I disorders don't respond well to such treatments, primarily due to serious comorbid character pathology. In treating these people, at the very least the clinician must be alert to how personality factors influence treatment outcome; often medication treatment must be accompanied by more intensive psychotherapy that addresses the personality disorder.

Substance Abuse

Substance abuse can directly cause or contribute to a wide array of psychiatric symptoms: depression, anxiety disorders, psychosis, mania, and so on. Not only can the use of recreational drugs produce psychological symptoms, but frequently such substances markedly interfere with psychological or psychiatric treatment. A

Personality Traits That May Reflect Biochemical Disorders

Axis II Traits	Medication-Responsive Axis I Disorder	Psychotropic Medication Options
Chronic boredom; emptiness; irritability; hypochrodriasis; low energy; chronic fatigue; pessimism, negative thinking; feelings of shame, humiliation	Depression	Antidepressants
Easily hurt by criticism; helplessness, dependency; difficulty making decisions	Depression, anxiety disorders	Antidepressants
Social anxiety, avoidance	Social phobia, panic disorder	Antidepressants, beta blockers, benzodiazepines
Magical thinking; odd speech	Psychotic disorders	Antipsychotics
Excessive worry	Generalized anxiety disorders	Antidepressants, buspirone, benzodiazepines
Impulsiveness; stimulus seeking; affective instability	Attention deficit disorder, bipolar disorder	Stimulants, antidepressants, lithium
Separation stress; nonassertivenes	Anxiety disorders	Antidepressants, benzodiazepines
Perfectionism; preoccupation with rules, order, details, lists, or cleanliness; workaholic	Obsessive-compulsive disorder	Antidepressants (SSRIs)

Figure 5-A

common example of this occurs when moderate-to-heavy alcohol use adversely affects liver functioning, causing prescribed psychotropic medications to be inadequately metabolized. The result can be inadequate blood levels of the medication, as in the following case.

Case 12

Jerry H. was first seen for psychiatric consultation six months ago. He presented with a classic major depression, which had emerged during an especially difficult marital separation and divorce. Jerry had initially reported only occasional social drinking, "a few times a month." After five months of psychotherapy and aggressive antidepressant treatment he was still quite depressed. Three antidepressant medications had been tried in conjunction with cognitive-behavioral psychotherapy, with little improvement. It was eventually learned that Jerry actually had been consuming four to six beers every night. Three weeks after the alcohol use had been curtailed he began to show his first positive response to the antidepressant. The alcohol use (unknown to the therapist for five months) had been the main culprit in preventing antidepressants from ever reaching adequate blood levels.

Although a very wide range of prescription and nonprescription drugs can cause psychiatric symptoms, the three most commonly encountered in clinical practice are nicotine, alcohol, and caffeine. (In subsequent clinical chapters additional specific drugs will be listed as they contribute to particular psychiatric disorders.) It is always important to get a complete drug history on each person being evaluated.

In general, more than 1.5 ounces of alcohol (or the equivalent: one beer, or one glass of wine) per day, may directly contribute to psychiatric symptoms, may interfere with proper metabolism of psychotropic medications, or both. Obviously, excessive use often leads to two additional complications: addiction or dependence and the use of the drug as a means of acting out (emotional numbing), which can interfere with the process of self-exploration, abreaction, or "working through" in psychotherapy. Appropriate psychotherapy and pharmacotherapy can (and often do) fail because of ongoing and often unrecognized substance abuse.

In general, over 250 mg (especially amounts over 500 mg) of caffeine per day can cause or contribute to psychiatric symptoms, especially anxiety, irritability, sleep disturbance, and agitation. Figure 5-B provides a guideline for a caffeine history—which should be done on every person being evaluated.

Finally, moderate to heavy smoking can interfere with liver metabolism and ultimate blood levels of some psychotropic medications.

Physical Illness

A number of investigators have found that a rather substantial minority of people seeking psychiatric services are actually suffering from undiagnosed physical illness. The primary medical disorder either causes or contributes to the emergence of psychiatric symptoms. Let's sample a couple of studies: Hall et al. (1978) carefully evaluated 658 consecutive psychiatric outpatients. These researchers found that 9 percent had medical disorders that were the primary cause of psychiatric symptoms. Koran et al. (1989) found an even higher number of psychiatric patients with underlying medical disorders—17 percent.

Robert Taylor (1990) has aptly referred to such cases as "psychological masquerade." Here, unrecognized medical disorders either directly or indirectly affect the biochemistry of the brain and produce a host of emotional, cognitive, and behavioral symptoms.

Caffeine Content of Common Substances

Beverages			**Over-the-Counter Drugs**	
Coffee,	6 oz	150 mg	Appetite-control pills	100–200 mg
Decaf coffee	6 oz	5 mg	NoDoz	100 mg
Tea	6 oz	50 mg	Vivarin	200 mg
Hot cocoa	6 oz	15 mg	Anacin	32 mg
Soft drinks	12 oz	40–60 mg	Excedrin	65 mg
(colas, Mountain			Midol	132 mg
Dew, Mr. Pibb,			Vanquish	33 mg
Mello Yello,			Triaminicin	30 mg
Dr Pepper,			Dristan	16 mg
Big Red)			Extra Strength Excedrine	100 mg

Prescription Drugs		**Foods**	
Cafergot	100 mg	Chocolate candy bar	15–20 mg
Fiorinal	40 mg	Hot cocoa	15 mg
Darvon compound	32 mg		

Source: FDA National Center: Drugs and Biologics (as cited in Avis 1998).

Figure 5-B

It is crucial to identify those people suffering from psychological masquerade for two reasons: First, various medical illnesses need to be treated early. Failure to recognize and treat them may result in prolonged suffering, permanent impairment, progressive physical decline, and, at times, death. Second, one's best efforts at providing psychological treatment may be in vain if the underlying medical condition goes unrecognized. However, nonmedical therapists are not trained in medical diagnosis. So what steps can they take to identify those patients who have a physical illness?

The role of the nonmedical therapist is not to make definitive medical diagnoses, but rather to be alert to certain warning signs that may signal the presence of a physical illness or that at least increase one's index of suspicion. Obviously, when a medical illness is suspected, a referral to a physician or emergency medical facility is in order.

For practical purposes we can divide medical illnesses with psychiatric symptomatology into three categories:

- Illnesses and conditions that do not directly affect the CNS, but can lead to secondary (reactive) emotional responses. These conditions are generally recognized and reported by the patient. Examples are a person who develops a serious reactive depression after sustaining a spinal cord injury and paralysis and an individual who is diagnosed with glaucoma and may be facing blindness.

- Illnesses and conditions that affect the CNS and impair cognitive functioning. These conditions are of greatest importance—where the medical problem may go unnoticed and what predominates are psychiatric symptoms.

- Illnesses and conditions that affect neurochemistry, but do not affect cognitive functioning. The latter two conditions include some primary disorders of the nervous system (such as brain tumors and certain degenerative diseases) and a host of systemic illnesses that indirectly influence brain chemistry.

Illnesses and Conditions Affecting Cognitive Functioning

Disorders affecting cognitive functioning can be further subdivided into: acute and chronic or insidious categories. Acute disorders tend to have a more profound effect on brain functioning and have an impact on the following cognitive functions:

- Patients may appear to be drowsy and suffer from what is called "clouding of consciousness."

- Attention and concentration may be impaired.

- Speech may be slurred.

- Content of speech may reveal confused and disorganized thinking.

- Gait may be unsteady.

- The person can become disoriented.

- Recent memory (the ability for new learning and recall) is impaired.

- There may be agitation and/or labile emotions.

These areas of functioning can be evaluated by the use of a brief neuro-cognitive mental status exam (see appendix E). Acute disorders affecting the CNS have multiple etiologies (see figure 5-C). Many of these conditions can be potentially life threatening, thus immediate medical attention is indicated.

Acute Organic Brain Syndromes

- Anoxia
- CNS infections
- CVA (strokes), hemorrhages
- Head injuries
- Metabolic disorders such as hypoglycemia, adrenal disease, vitamin deficiencies, electrolyte imbalances
- Organ diseases such as hepatic encephalopathy
- Pernicious anemia
- Toxic reactions, such as drug interactions or overdoses

Figure 5-C

Causes of Chronic Organic Brain Syndromes

- AIDS or HIV dementia
- Alzheimer's disease
- Chronic sequelae of head injury
- Cognitive disorders associated with chronic substance abuse
- Pick's disease
- Wilson's disease

- Multi-infarct disorder
- Multiple sclerosis
- Neoplasms (CNS tumors)
- Parkinson's disease

- Huntington's chorea
- Hydrocephalus

Figure 5-D

Chronic, insidious brain syndromes usually do not present with a clouding of consciousness; patients appear fully awake. Also, disturbances in gait and slurred speech are *generally* not seen. (Exceptions do exist, however. For instance, in Parkinson's disease there is a gait disturbance.) The onset of symptoms is gradual. Hallmark symptoms usually include: impaired recent memory, poor ability to reproduce geometric designs, impaired concentration, and an erosion of higher level cognitive abilities (such as impaired reasoning and judgment). These disorders can also be evaluated using the brief neuro-cognitive mental status exam in appendix E, and by taking a complete history from the patient and an informed relative. If a chronic brain syndrome is suspected, a medical referral is indicated. Figure 5-D lists causes of common chronic brain syndromes.

Medical Illness Checklist

- Onset of psychiatric symptoms has "come out of the blue"—not precipitated by identifiable psychosocial stressors.

- The patient is over 55, thus at increased risk for a host of medical illnesses.

- The patient takes multiple medications—which may interact adversely.

- No personal or family history of similar psychiatric symptoms.

- Recent history of head injury.

- Hallucinations or illusions—especially visual, olfactory, tactile, or gustatory (such perceptual disturbances are indicative of neurologic disease).

- The patient looks physically ill or has abnormal vital signs (such as very low blood pressure, fever, weak pulse).

Source: Taylor 1990

Figure 5-E

Specific Physical Symptoms Checklist

Physical Symptoms	Psychiatric Symptoms	Possible Disorder
Abdominal pain, jaundice, constipation	Depression	Pancreatic cancer
Weight gain, cold intolerance, dry skin, hair loss, puffy face, fatigue	Depression, psychosis	Hypothyroidism
Weight loss, heat intolerance, sweating, tremors, wide-eyed state	Anxiety, agitated depression	Hyperthyroidism
Bad breath, urine odor, frequent urination	Depression	Diabetes mellitus
Weakness, dizziness, lightheadedness, sweating, tremors	Anxiety (acute onset)	Hypoglycemia
Muscular weakness, fatigue	Depression	Myasthenia gravis
Sensory disturbances, paresthesia, transient motor disturbances	Depression, euphoria, conversion symptoms	Multiple sclerosis
Weakness, fatigue, diffuse pain, incoordination	Depression, impaired memory	Pernicious anemia
Abdominal pain, weakness, confusion after ingestion of alcohol or barbituates	Anxiety	Porphyria
Increased skin pigmentation, weight loss, diarrhea, muscle cramps, low blood pressure	Depression	Hypoadrenalism (Addison's disease)
Muscle weakness, moon face, hirsutism, hypertension	Irritability, euphoria, depression	Hyperadrenalism (Cushing's disease)
Hypertension, headache	Anxiety	Pheochromocytoma (adrenal gland tumor)
Fever, malaise	Depression, agitation	Viral or bacterial infection
Fatigue, joint pain	Depression	Various rheumatoid disorders (e.g., fibromyalgia), chronic fatigue syndromes
Headaches, weakness changes in vision	Depression, mania, personality changes	Brain tumor
Any physical symptoms	Any psychiatric disorder	Drug effects or side effects

Note: This listing does not cover all possible medical disorders that may cause psychiatric symptoms; however, these do represent those most commonly encountered in clinical practice.

Figure 5-F

Illnesses and Conditions Affecting Neurochemistry

There are a number of medical disorders that have little or no effect on cognitive function but can adversely affect the biochemistry of the limbic system and other subcortical brain areas. Thus, although individuals suffering from these conditions may appear intact on the brief neuro-cognitive mental status exam, they may exhibit pronounced psychiatric symptoms as the systemic medical illness dysregulates the chemistry of the brain.

How might the nonmedical therapist detect the presence of such medical disorders? We will look at two approaches: to evaluate for global warning signs (see figure 5-E), and to ask about particular physical symptoms (see figure 5-F). In each case, the clinician should do a brief overview of various signs and physical symptoms. The goal again is not to make a medical diagnosis but rather to either raise or lower one's index of suspicion. If a medical condition is suspected, a referral for appropriate medical care is indicated.

Many of the symptoms listed in figure 5-F are fairly nonspecific and may be elicited from many patients, but some particular physical symptoms should raise your index of suspicion, such as when there are several physical complaints, not just a simple nonspecific complaint like fatigue. When in doubt, refer for evaluation. In fact, it is probably advisable that anyone with a significant psychiatric disorder have a medical evaluation.

Keep in mind that medications and other drugs are a very common cause of emotional symptoms—this includes prescription, nonprescription, and other recreational drugs and alcohol. Obtaining collateral history from family members may be helpful. Also conducting the "bag test"—having the person bring in *all* (this cannot be stressed too much) medications he or she is taking for the therapist to see and make a record of.

In summary, after assessing for the presence of Axis II characteristics and understanding how these may influence the primary symptom disorders, and after ruling in or out substance abuse and coexisting medical illnesses, the clinician is ready to formulate a clinical diagnosis. The following chapters address major diagnostic groups with a focus on clinical presentation, differential diagnosis, etiology, and treatment decision making. In each area we pay particular attention to which diagnostic characteristics indicate the need for psychotropic medication treatment.

6

Depressive Disorders

Depressive disorders (also often referred to as affective or mood disorders) represent an extremely broad, heterogeneous group of disorders. These clinical syndromes share some common symptoms (especially dysphoria), but in fact reflect a number of disorders that have diverse etiologies: characterological, acute reactive, and biologic. (Note that bipolar disorder, or manic-depressive illness, is covered separately, in chapter 7.) The symptoms, course, prognosis, and response to treatment vary considerably depending on the particular type of depressive disorder seen clinically; thus a solid understanding of the differential diagnosis is crucial for treatment-oriented decision making.

Differential Diagnosis

It is helpful to first view depressive disorders as falling broadly into three primary groups: reactive sadness, grief, and clinical depression.

Reactive sadness is characterized by relatively low-grade mood changes—sadness, disappointment, despair—that occur in response to minor losses and disappointments. The emotional responses are considered to be normal and appropriate. They are transient, and, most importantly, these mood disturbances do not typically interfere with functioning; that is, they have little impact on academic, occupational, or social or interpersonal functioning.

Grief, or uncomplicated bereavement, can be a much more prolonged and intensely painful experience. Grief is a normal and emotionally necessary response to major losses, such as death of a loved one or divorce. Most normal grief reactions result in significant degrees of emotional distress for a period of six to twelve months and continued, albeit less intense, grieving often lasts for an additional one to three years. Social and occupational functioning can be derailed for a while, although most people experiencing a grief reaction do continue to work and socialize.

There are two important features that distinguish grief from clinical depression. First, as noted in Freud's classic, "Mourning and Melancholia" (1917), with grief, self-esteem remains relatively intact, despite significant dysphoria. Second, as painful as it is, the grieving process is healthy and adaptive; it is an active process of mourning that eventually leads to emotional healing. In clinical depressions self-esteem almost always erodes, and true depression is a clearly pathological condition.

Certainly, what appears initially to be a grief reaction often disintegrates into a true clinical depression, so the boundary between these disorders is not always sharply defined. When the following symptoms emerge in the wake of a serious loss, this signals that normal grief has evolved into a clinical depression:

When Grief Becomes Clinical Depression

- Marked erosion of self-esteem

- Agitation*

- Early morning awakening*

- Serious weight loss*

- Suicidal ideation or attempts

- Anhedonia (loss of the ability to experience any pleasure)*

- Marked impairment of social, interpersonal, academic, or occupational functioning

* When this clinical picture emerges, psychotherapy, psychotropic medication treatment, or both, become necessary. These symptoms marked with an asterisk are targets for antidepressant medications.

The vast majority of individuals encountering uncomplicated bereavement do not need psychological or psychiatric treatment. However, it is estimated that 15 to 25 percent of individuals do in fact develop a clinical depression following a major loss.

Clinical depressions are characterized by their intensity, duration, impact on functioning, and a host of symptoms. Most true clinical depressions result in tremendous personal suffering, can last for months to years (left untreated), and normal daily functioning is severely affected.

We can further divide *clinical depressions* into the following categories:

Types of Clinical Depression

- *Major unipolar depressions:* reactive, biological, reactive-biological, atypical

- *Bipolar disorder:* manic and depressive episodes (see chapter 7)

- *"Minor" depressions:* dysthymia, chronic residuals of partially recovered major depressions

---

Major Unipolar Depressions

For practical purposes and to aid in treatment decision making, it is useful to conceptualize three primary types and one atypical version of major depression. All have in common marked impairment in functioning, a typically long duration, and one or all of the core symptoms listed below:

Core Symptoms Common to All Depressions

- Mood of sadness, despair, emptiness

- Anhedonia (loss of the ability to experience pleasure)

- Low self-esteem

- Apathy, low motivation, and social withdrawal

- Excessive emotional sensitivity

- Negative, pessimistic thinking

- Irritability

- Suicidal ideas

Note: Some degree of decreased capacity for pleasure (anhedonia) may be seen in all types of depression. In depressions that involve a biochemical disturbance, this loss of ability to experience pleasure can become so pronounced that the patient has almost no moments of joy or pleasure. Such people are said to have a "nonreactive mood," which means that they are unable to get out of their depressed mood even temporarily.

Reactive depressions

Classic reactive depressions (sometimes referred to as psychological depressions) can range in intensity from mild or moderate (for example, adjustment disorders with depressed mood) to severe (major depression). These disorders occur in response to identifiable psychosocial stressors. These stressors may be acute and intense (such as loss of a loved one), insidious (as in the case of a gradual deterioration in the quality of marital relationship), or in the distant past (for example, the emotions experienced by a survivor of child abuse who in adulthood begins to recall long-forgotten abusive events).

In its pure form, reactive depression can present with severe levels of symptomatology, yet basic physical functions (sleep, energy levels, and so on) are relatively unaffected. Note that many, if not most reactive depressions do take on biological features, as will be described below, but the pure reactive disorder noted here is seen without major physiological symptoms.

Biological depressions

Biologically based depressive disorders, in their purest form, are not seen as a reaction to stressors. In fact, they can emerge apparently spontaneously, "out of the blue"—in individuals encountering little in

Depression Facts

- Lifetime prevalence for depressive disorders is 19 percent.

- Suicide rate for patients with major depression is 9 percent.

- 18 million people per year suffer from major depression in the United States. Another 7.5 million experience chronic low-grade depression.

- The incidence of depression ratio of women to men is 2:1.

- Only one in three Americans who suffers a bout of major depression seeks treatment. Yet treatment is effective in up to 80 percent of depressed patients—even those suffering with very severe depressions.

Medical Disorders That Can Cause Depression

- Addison's disease
- AIDS
- Anemia
- Asthma
- Chronic fatigue syndrome
- Chronic infection
  (mononucleosis, tuberculosis)
- Chronic pain
- Congestive heart failure
- Cushing's disease
- Diabetes
- Hypothyroidism
- Infectious hepatitis
- Influenza
- Malignancies (cancer)
- Malnutrition
- Multiple sclerosis
- Parkinson's disease
- Pre-menstrual dysphoria
- Porphyria
- Rheumatoid arthritis
- Syphilis
- Systemic lupus erythematosus
- Ulcerative colitis
- Uremia

Figure 6-A

Drugs That Can Cause Depression

Type	Generic name	Brand name
Alcohol	Wine, beer, spirits	Various brands
Antianxiety drugs	Diazepam Chlordiazepoxide	Valium Librium
Antihypertensives (for high blood pressure)	Reserpine Propranolol hydrochloride Methyldopa Guanethidine sulfate Clonidine hydrochloride Hydralazine hydrochloride	Serpasil, Ser-Ap-Es Inderal Aldomet Ismelin sulfate Catapres Apresoline hydrochloride
Antiparkinsonian drugs	Levodopa carbidopa Levodopa Amantadine hydrochloride	Sinemet Dopar, Larodopa Symmetrel
Birth control pills	Progestin-estrogen combination	Various brands

Corticosteroids
and other
hormones
	Cortisone acetate
	Estrogen
	
	Progesterone and
	  derivatives
		Cortone
		Premarin, Ogen,
		  Estrace, Estraderm
		Provera, DepoProvera,
		  Norlutate, Norplant,
		  Progestasert

Figure 6-B

terms of life stress. The trigger for biological depressions can be traced to any of a number of conditions that alter neurotransmitter function in key areas of the limbic system. The conditions responsible for biological depressions fall into four categories:

- Medical illnesses that lead to systemic changes and ultimately to brain dysfunction (see figure 6-A).

- Female sex-hormone fluctuation, especially noted postpartum, during menopause, and premenstrually.

- Medications and recreational drugs (see Figure 6-B). (Note that alcohol and minor tranquilizers are often used or abused during times of emotional stress, and, almost invariably, eventually make depression worse.)

- Endogenous biological depressions. These disorders appear to emerge spontaneously in certain at-risk individuals, in the absence of stressful events. The prevailing theory (discussed below) is that such disorders likely reflect a genetically transmitted biologic vulnerability that leads to repeated dysfunction of selected neurons in the limbic system and resulting recurring depressive episodes.

In experimental settings, researchers have been able to identify some biological markers for these disorders, including reduced frontal cortex metabolic activity, abnormalities shown on sleep EEGs, and neurotransmitter metabolite irregularities in cerebral spinal fluid. However, for practical, economic, and safety reasons, such tests are not used in clinical settings. What have been and continue to be the most reliable markers of biological depression are the emergence of depression in the absence of identifiable psychosocial stressors *and* the presence of any of the following physiological symptoms:

Physiological Symptoms of Depression

- Appetite disturbance—decreased or increased, with accompanying weight loss or gain.

- Fatigue.

- Decreased sex drive.

- Restlessness, agitation, or psychomotor retardation.

- Diurnal variations in mood—usually feeling worse in the morning.

- Impaired concentration and forgetfulness.

- Pronounced anhedonia—total loss of the ability to experience pleasure.

- Sleep disturbance—early morning awakening, frequent awakenings throughout the night; occasionally hypersomnia (excessive sleeping). Note that initial insomnia (difficulty in falling asleep) may be seen with depression, but is not diagnostic of a major depressive disorder. Initial insomnia can be seen in anyone experiencing stress in general. Initial insomnia alone is more characteristic of anxiety disorders than of depression.

These symptoms are commonly referred to as *vegetative* or *neurovegetative* symptoms. Not only are these symptoms a marker of biological depression, they also serve as our major target symptoms—alerting the therapist that the patient should be referred for antidepressant medication treatment.

Typically, for the diagnosis to be more definitive, the patient must have one or more of these symptoms on a sustained basis: present most days for a period of at least two weeks. Sporadic or occasional vegetative symptoms may hint at a neurotransmitter abnormality, but do not suggest an entrenched clinical depression.

Reactive-biological depression

Sometimes referred to as endogenomorphic depressions, reactive-biological depressions represent a very large number of the depressions seen clinically. These disorders begin in much the same way as the more classic reactive depressions described above. However, with time, we see the emergence of various physiological symptoms. These disorders are not truly endogenous; however, at some point the effects of psychological stress appear to adversely influence brain functioning. What emerges is a sort of mixed depression—with both psychological-reactive and biologic symptoms.

Atypical depressions

Atypical depression, or hysteroid-dysphoria as it is sometimes called, is a subtype of major depression characterized by the following symptoms:

Symptoms of Atypical Depression

- Reactive dysphoria—sadness or despair comes and goes in response to psychological stressors

- Profound fatigue, low energy

- Hypersomnia (excessive sleeping)

- Increased appetite and weight gain

- Sensitivity to interpersonal rejection or separation

- Phobias and panic attacks

As we will see later, this type of depressive disorder has been shown to be effectively treated with a particular subtype of antidepressants called monoamine oxidase inhibitors (MAOIs). Recent findings suggest that atypical depressions may also respond to selective serotonin re-uptake inhibitors (SSRIs).

Efficacy of medication treatment

Major depressions can certainly occur once and never again. Yet, 66 percent of people experiencing a major depression encounter recurring episodes (on average, six per lifetime). Thus treatment and resolution of the current episode is crucial, but relapse prevention is also an important treatment goal. The eventual suicide rate for individuals with major depression is 19 percent. The economic burden to society is staggering: Direct and indirect costs are estimated to be $44 billion per year in the United States, not to mention the incalculable personal suffering of patients and their families. Good patient education especially focused on the early signs of recurrence can go far to avert future episodes.

There is a large body of research supporting the finding that, when physiological symptoms are present, antidepressant medications are quite effective. Presumably the presentation of the symptoms listed above (physiological and atypical) signals the presence of an underlying dysregulation of particular neurotransmitters, especially norepinephrine, serotonin, and/or dopamine. These symptoms continue to be our most reliable behavioral markers of an underlying biological dysfunction. Thus very few people suffering from pure reactive-psychological depressions benefit from antidepressant medication treatment. However, improvement rates for the more physiologically based disorders (biological, reactive-biological, and atypical depressions) when treated with antidepressants are as high as 80 percent[1]. Thus, the presence of the sustained physiological symptoms listed above can serve as primary target symptoms for antidepressant medication treatment.

It is very important to note that medical treatment of depression focuses primarily on restoring normal biological functioning (that is, improvement in physiological symptoms) and only secondarily affects mood, self-esteem, and so forth.

Psychotic Depressions

Major depression and bipolar illness (the subject of chapter 7) can, if extremely severe, manifest psychotic symptoms. Typically, the hallucinations and delusions seen in psychotic mood disorders are said to be "mood congruent," which means that the themes of these symptoms are congruent with the dominant mood. For example, a psychotically depressed patient might have delusions that she is the most disgusting or evil person in the world and should be executed. This delusional belief embodies the depressive themes of extremely low self-esteem and guilt. Compare this to schizophrenic symptoms, which most often are bizarre and unconnected to a dominant mood state, for example, the anxious man who believes a radio transmitter has been implanted in his thumb so that neighbors can hear broadcasts of his inner thoughts.

When symptoms of major depression and psychosis coexist, medication treatment is always warranted. (Often hospitalization, ECT, or both may also be necessary.) Psychotically depressed patients do not respond to psychotherapy alone, and they represent a *very* high suicide risk when actively psychotic. It has been firmly documented that treatment with antidepressants alone is not very effective (only 25 percent). Likewise, treatment with antipsychotics alone produce disappointing results (35 percent effective). However, combined antidepressant-antipsychotic treatment is significantly more effective (60 to 75 percent). Electroconvulsive treatment is really the gold standard in the treatment of psychotic mood disorders (90 percent effective). (See chapters 15 and 18, on treatment with antidepressants and antipsychotics, respectively.)

---

1. The high improvement rates are seen in those individual for whom the diagnosis is correct and for whom treatment is appropriately managed. Diagnostic and treatment errors abound, and in general clinical practice success rates usually fall far below 80 percent.

"Minor" Depressions

The depressive disorders described below are sometimes referred to as minor depressions because they do not reach the depths or intensity seen in major depression. However, the term *minor* may be a misnomer. Although these disorders are low-grade, they tend to be very long-term, often having their onset in late childhood or early adolescence, and potentially lasting a lifetime. The cumulative toll such disorders exact on the quality of life and productivity over a lifetime are not minor at all! These chronic, low-grade depressions fall into two categories: dysthymia and chronic residuals of partially recovered major depression.

Dysthymia is characterized by the following symptoms:

Dysthymic Symptoms

Core Psychological Symptoms

Low-grade sadness

Irritability

Negative thinking

Low self-esteem

Possible Biologic Symptoms

Low energy

Decreased capacity to experience pleasure

Note: These biologic symptoms may be considered as targets for medication treatment.

Unfortunately dysthymic individuals can also suffer not only from chronic, low-grade depression but also from periods of major depression. These more severe episodes are superimposed on the chronic depression, and often, upon recovery from the major episode, the patient returns to his or her preclinical norm: low-grade depression. Such disorders have been termed "double depression" (see figure 6-C).

Double Depression

Normal mood

Low grade depression

Major depression

Figure 6-C

These minor depressions have long been seen as characterological and difficult to treat. However, during the past decade a large number of studies conclude that 50 to 55 percent of dysthymic patients do respond, and respond well, to treatment with antidepressants. (For review articles see Stewart, Quitkin, and Klein 1992 and Akiskal and Weise 1992.) It is likely, based on these findings, that approximately one-half of dysthymic patients may, in fact, be suffering from a type of chronic low-grade biologic depression. The other half may be experiencing more of a true characterological depression. For example, in unpublished data, Nicholas Ward (1992) finds that a history of serious early child abuse (emotional, sexual, or physical) in the context of dysthymia does not portend well for a good response to antidepressants. This finding should *not* preclude the use of antidepressants in survivors of child abuse, but rather serves to highlight the possibility that this version of dysthymia may issue more from pervasively tragic life circumstances and characterological problems than from disordered neurotransmitters.

A final type of minor depression is seen in those 15 to 20 percent of individuals who experience only a partial remission of symptoms following a major depressive episode. These people may clinically *look* dysthymic but are not. Typically, they do not have a lifelong history of low-grade or characterological depression. Usually these patients need ongoing and often more aggressive treatment to truly resolve the persistent depressive symptoms.

Seasonal Affective Disorder

Organisms evolve in ways that promote adaptation to the environment. Examples of this, seen in numerous species (both plant and animal), are the biologic functions influenced by photic stimulation (i.e., exposure to sunlight). Many hormones and neurotransmitters exhibit diurnal variations and are powerfully influenced by environmental stimuli, especially photic stimulation. The first five million years of human evolution took place in equatorial regions that experience a highly stable ratio of sunlight to darkness year-round (basically twelve hours of daylight, twelve hours of darkness). It was around these environmental stimuli that some fundamental biologic processes evolved and remain to this day.

About 150,000 years ago humans began to migrate to other geographic regions where seasonal changes in patterns of light and dark were first encountered (the further away from the equator, the more pronounced changes are evident). As the human organism had to adapt to new environmental circumstances, this likely set the stage for difficulties. Apparently, many people manage this adaptation rather well, while others do not. Some of the more vulnerable people are hypothesized to suffer from seasonal affective disorder (SAD), a mood disorder that is ushered in by reduced exposure to bright light.

SAD is also seen in individuals who work at night (and sleep during the day)—some 20 percent of the work force—and in people who live in areas that experience significant cloud cover and/or pollution.

SAD can present with a full range of depressive symptoms with intensities varying from mild states of dysphoria to severe, major depression. Interestingly, the majority of people with SAD have symptoms that resemble *atypical depression*; i.e., appetite increase, weight gain, fatigue, and hypersomnia. It is theorized that the basic underlying neurotransmitter dysfunction primarily involves serotonin, thus suggesting that if antidepressants are used to treat SAD, the drugs of choice are SSRIs or MAO inhibitors. Additionally, *light therapy* has been found effective in treating SAD. This involves daily exposure to bright light (either by way of a commercially available light box which provides between 2500–10,000 lux of light, or by encouraging the patient to go outside for at least one hour per day).

For more detailed information regarding SAD, the reader is referred to the book *Winter Blues*, by N. E. Rosenthal, Guilford Press (1993).

Premenstrual Dysphoric Disorder (PMDD)

Approximately 5 percent of women experience severe mood changes premenstrually. This may involve irritability, anxiety, and/or depression. When depressive symptoms are evident, they sometimes reach a level of severity suggestive of major depression. This disorder is characterized by the tremendous regularity in the onset and remission of symptoms. Mood symptoms generally occur for only a few days beginning several days prior to menses. Generally, there are no psychosocial stressors (i.e., it is best seen as an endogenous disorder). The limbic system contains estrogen receptors and it is hypothesized that fluctuations seen in female hormones premenstrually may destabilize neurotransmitter functioning in key limbic areas. Clinical experience rather strongly supports the hypothesis that serotonin is the primary neurotransmitter underlying PMDD. The most effective pharmacological treatments currently available for PMDD are SSRIs.

Postpartum Depression

Subtle mood changes are seen in the majority of new mothers. The so-called "baby blues" occur in 50 to 80 percent of women following childbirth. However such changes are not pathological and do not exclusively involve sadness. These mood changes involve increased sensitivity to the whole range of emotions, including happiness. Such enhanced sensitivity may enable new mothers to be even more attuned to the nuances of their child's emotions.

Postpartum depression is another story. It occurs in 10 percent of women and can have devastating effects. Generally, the onset is two to six weeks after delivery, and if left untreated, it may last from one to two years. Postpartum depressions are often severe and not only cause suffering for the woman, but can significantly interfere with crucial mother-child bonding.

Those most prone to postpartum depressions are women who also have experienced premenstrual dysphoric disorder. In addition, it is not rare that the stresses, the normal changes, and the sleep deprivation following delivery can precipitate a first episode of bipolar illness in a woman genetically predisposed to this disorder. Severe manias, obsessive-compulsive disorder, and psychoses may also develop following the birth of a child.

Etiology

It is easy to be seduced by surface symptoms and make assumptions about etiology and treatment. If all sore throats were treated with antibiotics, only about 10 to 15 percent would respond because most sore throats are due to viral rather than bacterial infections. Likewise with psychiatric disorders: Common symptoms should not automatically lead to conclusions regarding common etiologies.

The causes of depression have been viewed from a number of developmental and psychological perspectives, including the following:

- Psychodynamic models focusing on retroflexed rage and inadequate psychological "metabolism" of aggression and the development of an overly punitive superego

- Attachment theories and the role that loss plays in precipitating depression or mourning, in humans and in animals (Bowlby 1986)

- Object relations theory, which implicates faulty separation-individuation experiences and a failure to develop self-soothing introjects (Mahler et al. 1975)

- The learned helplessness model, in which depression is seen to emerge when people (or animals) perceive that "No matter what I do, I have no ability to influence aversive experiences" (Seligman 1990)

- The cognitive model, in which certain life experiences contribute to the development of pervasive cognitive schemas or cognitive distortions—negative mental sets and expectations that automatically influence ongoing perceptions, conclusions, and predictions about the future (Beck 1976)

Clearly, these models all have merit in helping to tease out complex factors that can contribute to the development of depression. These psychological causes also very likely influence much of what goes on in the so-called biologic depressions. However, the focus of this section is limited to a discussion of current theories of biological causation—causes that either underlie or contribute to the development of the biologic-based depressions listed above.

The dominant theories of biologic causation draw from a diverse source of research, which will be highlighted only briefly here:

- Genetic studies (primarily derived from population, family, twin, and adoptive studies) suggest that certain depressive disorders may have a genetic loading, especially bipolar and unipolar depression.

- In both human and animal studies, exposure to two general classes of stress may result in the neurotransmitter abnormalities underlying depression. These include experiences of loss and exposure to highly stressful situations where no avoidance, escape, or coping is available (resulting in an eventual state of "learned helplessness").

- Certain medical illnesses can result in systemic biochemical and hormonal changes that affect the central nervous system (e.g., thyroid disease; viral infections, etc.; see figure 6-A).

- Numerous drugs have been shown to have a negative impact on 5-HT (serotonin), NE (norepinephrine), and DA (dopamine), in vulnerable individuals (see figure 6-B).

- Primary neurological disease may affect or destroy brain areas responsible for affect regulation (e.g., Parkinson's disease, Alzheimer's disease).

- Severe early neglect can result in persistent abnormalities in corticotropin releasing factor (CRF), which can result in exquisite vulnerability to depression (Nemeroff 1997).

- Decreased photic (bright light) stimulation can cause depression.

- Decreased physical exercise can cause or exacerbate depression.

- Very poor nutrition can result in a deficiency of certain amino acids that are essential for the production of neurotransmitters, resulting in depression.

Monoamine Hypothesis

The aforementioned data, coupled with numerous positive outcome studies of the effectiveness of antidepressants, has led to the development of the *monoamine* (or biogenic amine) *hypothesis* of depression. The theory holds that depressive symptoms are ushered in by a malfunction of norepinephrine (NE), serotonin (5-HT), and/or dopamine (DA) neurons, which play critical roles in the functioning of the limbic system and the adjacent hypothalamus. The basic neuronal malfunction is felt to be identical for NE, 5-HT, or DA neurons.

Recall the discussion in chapter 3 of normal chemical events at the level of the synapse. The monoamine hypothesis holds that several abnormalities may develop in NE, DA, or 5-HT neurons in the brain. The first is excessive reuptake (see figure 6-D). The effect of this abnormality is that significant amounts of neurotransmitter, that have already been released from the presynaptic cell, are rapidly reabsorbed. The result is decreased ability to stimulate postsynaptic receptors. The nerve cells, in a sense, are then unplugged. A second hypothesized malfunction involves decreased release of neurotransmitters into the synapse. This may be due to a reduction in the synthesis of the neurotransmitter, and an inability to adequately store neurotransmitters in vesicles, and/or abnormalities in the process of vesicle migration and the creation of transmembrane pores.

A third way NE, DA, and 5-HT cells can shut down is when the naturally occurring enzyme, monoamine oxidase (MAO), becomes too active, excessively degrading neurotransmitters. This results in major depression, but often a depression with its own unique symptomatic signature (see "Atypical depression," above).

A final type of cellular dysfunction may be traced to abnormalities in receptors. This might involve a shift in the absolute numbers of receptors (or the ratio of inhibitory-to-excitatory receptors) and/or altered levels of receptor sensitivity, both of which can change the excitability levels of nerve cells. Such changes appear to be due to alterations in gene expression, which are likely to be secondary to the effects of second messengers.

Which of the cellular changes appear first and how they interact is not fully understood. However, as those conditions come to affect thousands of NE, DA, or 5-HT cells throughout the limbic system and hypothalamus, biologic rhythms (such as sleep cycles) and drives including hunger and sex get off track; pleasure centers fail to respond (anhedonia); and emotional-control structures in the limbic system fail (resulting in lability or emotional dyscontrol). With time, the emergence of neurovegetative symptoms is seen. Without treatment, this abnormal condition can persist for many months (on average six to eighteen months), and then it may begin to reestablish normal functioning; that is, the condition is often self-limiting, again, for reasons that are not well understood.

Biologic Consequences

Numerous physiological consequences can occur with severe depression (above and beyond the symptoms listed earlier). These are mentioned here, briefly:

- Extraordinarily high, sustained levels of cortisol (hypercortisolemia), seen in about 50–60% of those with major depression, have been associated with cell death in the hippocampus (Sapolsky 1996) and damage to the interior walls of arteries. The latter likely contributes to the higher incidence of coronary heart disease seen in people with chronic depression.

- Hypercortisolemia in mothers during pregnancy may be harmful to the fetus (Sapolsky 1994).

- Abnormal brain metabolic states occur during depressive episodes, including

- Hypo-metabolism in the frontal lobes (especially: medial-orbital area, anterior cingulate, and the lateral, dorsal pre-frontal cortex).

- Hyper-metabolism in hypothalamus, amygdala, hippocampus, and infra-limbic cingulate (Mayberg 1997).

- Reductions in secretion of growth hormone that may contribute to osteoporosis and, in children, retarded growth and failure to thrive.

- Immune-suppression (likely due to multiple factors including chronic sleep deprivation and hypercortisolemia).

- Reduced synthesis of brain-derived neurotropic factor (BDNF), which is essential for neuronal maintenance and repair (Thoenen 1995).

This list is not all-inclusive. It is clear that beyond the tremendous emotional suffering, depressive disorders often take a significant toll on physical health.

Treatment

Treatment with antidepressant mediations is described in detail in chapter 15. However, discussion of some issues regarding treatment is warranted at this point.

Although atypical depression often presents with unique symptoms, depressions associated with DA, NE, or 5-HT dysfunction can look similar from a behavioral perspective. Until safe, cost-effective lab tests are available to practitioners, the psychiatrist is faced with an uncertainty regarding the underlying biochemical disorder. Is it NE, DA, or 5-HT-based? Antidepressants fall into four broad classes: those that target NE, DA, or 5-HT (the SSRIs), or MAO inhibitors (see figure 6-E). Chapter 15 which covers antidepressants will present some general guidelines for medication choices.

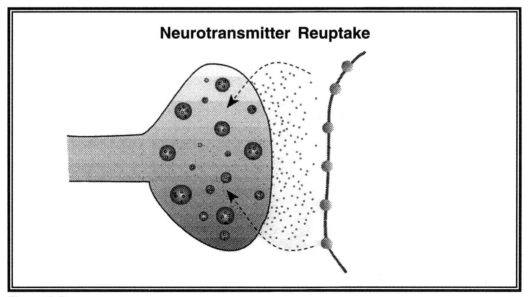

Neurotransmitter Reuptake

Figure 6-D

Selective Action of Antidepressant Medication

Generic Name	Brand Name	Serotonin Effects	Norepinephrine Effects	Monoamine Oxidase Effects	Dopamine Effects
imipramine	Tofranil	+++	++	0	0
desipramine	Norpramin	0	+++++	0	0
amitriptyline	Elavil	++++	+	0	0
nortriptyline	Aventyl, Pamelor	++	+++	0	0
protriptyline[a]	Vivactil	+	++++	0	0
trimipramine[a]	Surmontil	++	++	0	0
doxepin[a]	Sinequan, Adapin	++	+++	0	0
maprotiline	Ludiomil	0	+++++	0	0
amoxapine	Asendin	+	++++	0	0
venlafaxine	Effexor	+++	++	0	+
trazodone	Desyrel	+++++	0	0	0
fluoxetine	Prozac	+++++	0	0	0
paroxetine	Paxil	+++++	+	0	0
sertraline	Zoloft	+++++	0	0	0
bupropion[b]	Wellbutrin	0	++	0	++
nefazodone	Serzone	+++	+	0	0
fluvoxamine	Luvox	+++++	0	0	0
clomipramine	Anafranil	+++++	0	0	0
mirtazapine	Remeron	+++	+++	0	0
citalopram	Celexa	+++++	0	0	0
isocarboxazid	Marplan	+++	+++	+++++	+++
phenelzine	Nardil	+++	+++	+++++	+++
tranylcypromine	Parnate	+++	+++	+++++	+++

a Uncertain, but likely effects

b Atypical antidepressant; uncertain effects but likely to be a dopamine and norepinephrine agonist.

Figure 6-E

When the appropriate medication is found, generally after two to four weeks of treatment, the person begins to notice a reduction in symptoms (especially vegetative symptoms). Under ideal circumstances, the depression may be largely resolved within six to eight weeks (although it often takes longer). The clinical improvement is believed to correspond with a normalization of neuronal functioning. At such time, despite the improved clinical picture, medication discontinuation is not advised. Stopping medication at the point of symptomatic improvement has been associated with a very high acute relapse rate. Although the medication has returned the nerve cells to a more normal state, the cells are unstable and easily can regress if medication is not on board. Thus, continued treatment with the antidepressants is necessary for at least six months. Then, cautious discontinuation generally results in stable functioning (the acute relapse rate drops to below 10 percent). Recurrence can occur months to years in the future, however, owing to the episodic/recurrent nature of depression.

Many millions of depressed patients have been helped with antidepressant medication. Clearly, these drugs work; when they are properly prescribed. Also, other approaches have been shown both to reduce depression and alter neuro-biology, including the following:

- Electro-convulsive therapy (ECT)

- Bright light therapy

- Repetitive Trans-cranial Magnetic Stimulation (rTMS)

- Vagus nerve stimulation

- Exercise

- Psychotherapy

- Psycho-surgery (rarely used)

It is important to underscore the fact that a number of the personal, emotional, and existential issues that make up the experience of a major depression are not magically resolved by antidepressants. Even under ideal circumstances when medications work well, most patients must engage in a good deal of soul-searching, mourning, and working-through. The combined approaches of pharmacotherapy and psychotherapy offer the best chance of successful recovery from depression. This has been documented in studies investigating the combined use of antidepressants and three forms of psychotherapy especially designed for treating depression: cognitive-behavioral (Beck 1976), cognitive-behavioral analysis (McCullough 2000), and inter-personal psychotherapy (Klerman, Weissman, Rounsaville, and Chevron 1984).

QUICK REFERENCE
When to Refer for Medication Treatment

Event	Symptoms
Grief becomes clinical depression	Early morning awakening Serious weight loss Anhedonia Agitation
Major depression has vegetative symptoms	Sleep disturbance Appetite disturbance Fatigue Decreased sex drive Agitation or psychomotor retardation Anhedonia
Major depression has atypical symptoms	Pronounced fatigue Hypersomnia Increased appetite and weight gain Rejection sensitivity Panic symptoms Reactive dysphoria
Dysthymia presents with sustained symptoms	Low energy Anhedonia
Daily functioning is markedly impaired	
Presence of severe suicidal impulses or psychotic symptoms	
Major depression or dysthymia fails to respond to psychotherapy	

7

Bipolar Disorders

The bipolar disorders (historically referred to as manic-depressive illness) are mood disorders characterized by the essential diagnostic feature of mania or hypomania. In general, these disorders follow cyclic patterns of mood, behavior, and thought alterations, alternating between mania or hypomania and depression. These episodic changes are only core features of a variable, heterogeneous group of illnesses. *DSM-IV* classification distinguishes between bipolar I, bipolar II, cyclothymia, and bipolar disorder not otherwise specified. Further diagnostic distinctions are made depending on severity of symptoms and time-course patterns. Pharmacologic treatment of the bipolar disorders is rapidly evolving, with the bulk of useful data having been generated in the last decade.

Differential Diagnosis

Mania rarely occurs as a primary psychiatric condition by itself, so the presence of a manic episode usually leads to a diagnosis of bipolar disorder, even in the absence of a clear depressive history. The manic episode as defined by *DSM-IV* is "a distinct period of abnormally and persistently elevated, expansive, or irritable mood lasting at least one week (or any duration if hospitalization is necessary)." Additionally, manic episodes are defined as mild, moderate, or severe. If severe, psychotic features may be present, but this is not always the case. Associated with this mood disturbance are combinations of racing thoughts, pressured speech, grandiosity, increased activity, engaging in pleasurable activities, distractibility, and decreased need for sleep. If the above patterns are severe enough to impair occupational or social functioning, or to cause hospitalization, a diagnosis of mania is assigned.

A hypomanic episode, defined as lasting at least throughout a four-day period, is marked by an observable change in functioning and disturbance in mood that is uncharacteristic of the individual's usual nondepressed mood and level of functioning. Hypomania is distinguished from mania by the absence of the significant impairment, or hospitalization, described above.

The onset of mania can follow an abrupt or a gradual course. A useful stage-model categorization of acute mania has been described by Carlson and Goodwin (1973), as follows:

Stages of Acute Mania

Stage 1 (corresponds with hypomania):

- Increased psychomotor activity

- Emotional lability

- Euphoria or grandiosity

- Coherent but tangential thinking

Stage 2 (frank mania):

- Increased psychomotor activity

- Heightened emotional lability

- Hostility, anger

- Assaultive or explosive behavior

- Flight of ideas, cognitive disorganization

- Possible grandiose or paranoid delusions

Stage 3 (exhibited by some patients):

- Frenzied psychomotor activity

- Incoherent thought processes

- Ideas of reference, disorientation, delirium

- Florid psychosis (indistinguishable from other psychotic disorders, although usually mood congruent)

Case 13

George M. is a 32-year-old man you saw briefly a number of years ago for several intensive therapy sessions following the death of his mother. You know of no other psychiatric history. His family history is significant for his mother being hospitalized twice with "some sort of mental problem." George was in law school at the time and was not informed of the specifics of his mother's illness. His paternal uncle committed suicide when George was 14.

He is, by his report, in a stable marriage of ten years and has two children. He has just been made a partner in a small, successful law firm. He prides himself on being skilled in various areas, including athletics and music.

George called your office yesterday requesting an appointment to discuss recent feelings of "anxiety and stress." When George arrives at your office he is loud and demands to see you immediately because his "time is so valuable." The receptionist is able to escort him to your office fairly quickly, but not before he has attempted to pass out his business cards to other patients in the waiting room. He appears slightly disheveled, is unshaven, and states that he is "afraid to go to his office today," although will not elaborate further.

During the interview he is unable to remain seated for very long and paces in front of the window. He states the reason for the appointment is for you to "help him straighten a few things out." He specifies that he has been working until 2:00 A.M. every day for the last week because of an upcoming case. He describes this as the "biggest case in recent history" for which he "will become famous." His speech is pressured, and his thought processes are tangential. When you comment that he smells of alcohol, he admits that he regularly needs "a couple of drinks" a day to bring himself "down." You recognize that George's symptoms may indicate a manic episode, and with some difficulty you persuade him to see one of your psychiatrist colleagues for further evaluation.

Bipolar Disorder Facts

- Lifetime prevalence:
  Type I: 0.8 percent
  Type II: 0.5 percent.

- Suicide rate: 20%.

- Incidence of psychotic features: 47 to 75 percent.

- Ratio of men to women:
  Type I: 1:1
  Type II: women>men.

- 60 to 65 percent of patients have positive family history.

- Over-representation in higher socioeconomic and educational groups.

- First episode is usually:
  mania in males
  depression in females.

- Range of age of onset:
  20–40 years.

- Average episodes in a lifetime: 7 to 9.

- Average recovery time for depressed state: 9 weeks.

- Average recovery time for manic state: 5 weeks.

- Average recovery time for mixed state: 14 weeks.

Mania may develop as a consequence of a general medical condition (see figure 7-A) or as a result of pharmacologic treatment (see figure 7-B).

Medical Conditions Associated with Mania

- Central nervous system trauma, for example, post-stroke

- Metabolic disorders such as hyperthyroidism

- Infectious diseases such as encephalitis

- Seizure disorders

- Central nervous system tumor

Figure 7-A

Bipolar I Disorder

One or more manic or hypomanic episodes with one or more major depressive episodes generally constitute the diagnosis of bipolar I disorder. Depression in bipolar disorder meets diagnostic criteria for major depression, with the exceptions of shorter duration and increased frequency. Depending on the current presentation, bipolar disorder is subclassified as one of the following (*DSM-IV*):

Bipolar I Subclasses

- Single manic episode—only one manic episode, no previous major depressive episodes.

- Most recent episode hypomanic—current (or most recent) episode hypomanic with at least one previous manic episode.

- Most recent episode manic—current (or most recent) episode manic with either at least one previous major depressive episode or at least one previous manic or hypomanic episode.

- Most recent episode mixed—current (or most recent) episode of at least one week's duration and criteria for both major depressive episode and manic episode are met on a daily basis. Also at least one previous episode of major depression or one previous episode of mania or hypomania.

- Most recent episode depressed—current (or most recent) episode is major depressive and at least one previous manic episode.

- Most recent episode unspecified—current (or most recent) episode meets criteria for major depression, mania, or hypomania (except for duration), with significant distress or functional impairment. Also at least one previous manic episode.

Between episodes, most bipolar patients are relatively asymptomatic, although many will continue to experience functional impairment after symptom resolution. With increasing age episodes become more frequent and prolonged. As more recent outcome studies are published, evidence mounts that for many patients the course of their disease will be particularly difficult, resulting in significant psychosocial morbidy. Unfavorable outcomes may be especially common in rapid cycling, secondary mania, and mixed mania (Keller, Lavori, Coryell, Endicott, and Mueller 1993; American Psychiatric Association 1994; Solomon, Keitner, Willer, Shea, and Keller 1995; Goldberg, Harrow, and Grossman 1995; Evans, Byerly, and Greer 1995; Calabrese, Fatemia, Kujawa, and Woyshville 1996; Keck, and McElroy 1996).

Beginning with Kraepelin's (1921) systematic classification of dysphoric mania, considerable attention has been paid to mixed states of bipolar disorder. Kraepelin's model was based on variable symptom patterns expressed in three areas: mood, thought, and motor activity. Once considered to be uncommon, current estimates suggest that the prevalence rate for dysphoric, or mixed mania, is approximately 30 percent (McElroy et al. 1992). Debate continues regarding the status of mixed mania as a distinct affective state versus a form, or stage, of typical mania. However, there is convincing evidence to support the opinion that mixed episodes can be more severe, chronic, and difficult to treat than pure manic or depressive episodes (Clothier, Swann and Freeman 1992; McElroy et al. 1992; Dilsaver, Swann, Shoaib, Bowers, and Halle 1993; Bowden et al. 1994; Swann 1995; Sachs 1996).

Recent attention has focused on developing more precise diagnostic indicators and treatment regimens for bipolar depression, mixed mania, and rapid cycling. It is speculated that continued research may lead to the identification of separate and distinct bipolar I processes. (2000; Goldberg 2000). For the treating therapist, it is important to point out that there is ongoing controversy regarding the role of antidepressants in bipolar depression. The potential for antidepressants to induce mania is well documented. Concerns about this effect has led, by extension, to the suggestion that antidepressant treatment may play a role in the development of rapid cycling. Correspondingly, the literature and expert guidelines are not in concordance regarding the use of antidepressants in bipolar I depression, especially for sequential courses of therapy. Likewise, there is disagreement regarding recommendations for the length of antidepressant treatment. Chapter 16 addresses medication treatment issues in more detail.

Bipolar II Disorder

Bipolar II disorder is defined as one or more depressive episodes and at least one episode of hypomania. It has been postulated that bipolar II is difficult to differentiate from major depression, for several reasons. First, many patients subjectively do not recognize periods of elevated mood as dysfunctional—or may even deny the existence of such periods because of the predominate depressive element. Second, the patient may primarily manifest irritability rather than classic mood and behavior symptoms of hypomania. Finally, there is considerable variation between individual clinicians' ability to reliably assess for hypomania.

Drugs That Can Induce Mania

- Stimulants (amphetamines)
- Antidepressants (especially tricyclic antidepressants)
- SAM-e
- Antihypertensives
- Corticosteroids (prednisone) in higher doses
- Anticholinergics (benztropine, trihexyphenidyl)
- Thyroid hormones (levothyroxine)

Figure 7-B

Case 14

Cheryl R. is a 28-year-old married woman with two children under three years of age. She has been referred by her family doctor, who has been treating her depression for nine months with fluoxetine 20 mg daily. Her physician states that medication adjustment is not indicated and thinks "talking therapy" will be beneficial. Her psychiatric history is negative for hospitalizations, and she has never been in therapy. She describes a "lifetime of sadness" with periodic episodes of suicidal ideation during late adolescence.

Cheryl reports moderate improvement in her depression since starting the medication and wants to continue taking it. However, she says that some of her initial symptoms of irritability, tearfulness, and tiredness have never really improved. She reports continued initial insomnia and describes lying awake worrying about things.

Her major concern is that she is not the "best mother" she can be. On particularly "bad days" she places the children in front of the television and retreats to her room. She wishes she had more "good days," which occur about every three months and last about a week. During these periods she begins sewing and crafts projects for the house, socializes with neighbors, exercises, and "feels on top of the world."

She appears slightly nervous and describes her mood as "pretty bad." She describes her marriage as "average" and her children as the "center of her life." She is moderately impatient with the interview questions relative to history taking, since she wants to "get on with things."

You are encouraged by Cheryl's motivation for treatment. However, you internally question whether she may fit the profile for bipolar II. In the process of the diagnostic interview, you elicit enough information indicative of hypomanic periods that predated the initiation of fluoxetine to warrant further consultation with her original prescriber or a psychiatrist.

Cyclothymia

The features of cyclothymia include periods of alternating depression and elation, of at least two years' duration, that do not meet criteria for either major depression or mania (see figure 7-C). During this two-year period, symptoms are never absent for more than two months. Social and occupational impairment may occur during the depressive phase, but typically not during the hypomanic period. However, for many individuals the pervasive, irregular pattern of mood lability eventually affects personal and work relationships. Because "mood swings" are a frequent complaint of individuals with certain personality disorders, it is important to identify the presence of the associated behavioral criteria for hypomania or depression before establishing a diagnosis of cyclothymia.

This is a chronic disorder, with approximately one-third of individuals later developing a major affective disorder (Akiskal et al., cited by Hirschfeld and Goodwin 1988). Cyclothymia is so strikingly consistent with bipolar disorder with regard to symptoms, family history, course, and treatment response, that some clinicians argue for its categorization as a variant of bipolar disorder.

Cyclothymia Criteria

- History of numerous hypomanic and depressive episodes

- The intensity of episodes does not warrant a diagnosis of major depression or full-blown mania

- Not due to any established organic factors or substance abuse

---

Figure 7-C

While the "classic" manic is readily diagnosed, differentiating between diagnostic subtypes may be more difficult, especially when a seasonal pattern exists. Further disorders to rule out in the differential diagnosis include attention deficit hyperactivity disorder, schizophrenia, and schizoaffective disorder.

Bipolar Disorder Not Otherwise Specified

Disorders with bipolar features which do not meet any specific bipolar disorder criteria fall into this category. *DSM-IV* provides examples of recurring hypomania without major depression symptomatology, mania superimposed on certain delusional or psychotic disorders, or situations in which bipolar disorder cannot be determined as primary or secondary to medical conditions or substances.

Course Specifiers

Course specifiers for bipolar I or bipolar II disorder are as follows:

- With rapid cycling

- With seasonal pattern—demonstrated temporal relationship between onset of symptoms and time of the year

- With postpartum onset—must be within four weeks postpartum

Rapid cycling bipolar disorder warrants special attention, due to the diagnostic and treatment challenges it presents. Rapid cycling is defined as at least four episodes of either mania, hypomania, or major depression in the previous twelve months. The characteristics of rapid cycling are these:

Rapid Cycling Bipolar Disorder

- Estimated incidence: 10 to 20 percent of bipolar patients

- Poor lithium response

- More common in women, especially postpartum and postmenopausal

- Subclassified as early onset (initial rapid cycling) and late onset (change from "regular" to rapid cycles)

Suggested Model for Expanded Spectrum of Bipolar Disorders

In addition to the theoretical questions raised relative to dysphoric mania, other symptom patterns have been discussed as possible variants of bipolar disorder. Akiskal (1996) and Akiskal and Bowden (2000) has presented an extensive case in support of defining bipolar disorders across a broader spectrum. Key points in his theory address softer expressions of bipolar I and bipolar II disorders, temperamental dysregulation, and the overlap between cycling affective states and personality disorders. Akiskal acknowledges that his ideas are controversial and await formal research examination. His arguments are included in this book, not as a criticism of established *DSM-IV* criteria, but as a means of acknowledging that these ideas may be evident in clinical practice. Therapists may be faced with situations in which physician colleagues ascribe to this wider spectrum nosology, and elect to utilize mood stabilizing agents, or combinations, in the absence of the classic target symptoms of bipolar disorder. There are obvious challenges presented to the therapist in these scenarios, especially regarding assessment, treatment planning, therapeutic approach, and patient education.

Etiology

Even though manic-depressive illness was first described by Kraeplin in 1898, causational and treatment questions persist. The introduction of lithium as an effective treatment in the 1970s sparked renewed research interest. Since that time numerous theories have been investigated, most of which focused more on neurobiology and genetic transmission than on environmental influences, although the latter is not without importance. The complexity and expense of studying this disorder places limits on achieving consistent and replicable data. Throughout the 1970s, 1980s, and into the mid-1990s the theories focused on a variety of neurologic processes: neurotransmitters, synaptic activity, cell membrane function, and second messenger systems.

- **Dysregulation Theory.** J. Rosenthal et al.'s (1986) dysregulation theory includes (but by definition is not specific to) bipolar disorder. In this model, mood is regulated by several homeostatic mechanisms. The failure of a component part leads to the expression of mood outside of set limits, which are identified as the "symptoms" of mania and depression. R. Post, S. Weiss, and O. Chuang (1992) offer a similar explanation: that overactivity in either of the mediating "circuits" of mania or depression leads to the appearance of associated behavioral manifestations.

- **Chaotic Attractor Theory.** The chaotic attractor theory of J. P. Crutchfield et al. (1986) is intriguing and may help explain the unpredictable course of bipolar disorder. This model is predicated on a biochemical defect leading to dysregulation of neurotransmitter synthesis. The type of dysregulation is consistent, but the symptom presentation (either mania or depression) depends on the physiological or environmental conditions at the moment. Building on chaos theory, Gottschalk, Bauer, and Whybrow (1995) obtained results confirming a low-dimensional chaotic process in bipolar disorder.

- **Kindling Theory.** J. C. Ballenger and R. M. Post's (1980) kindling model of mood disorder is not completely adequate, but it has provided some valuable contributions to the reconceptualization of several psychiatric disorders. This hypothesis states that some psychiatric symptoms are the result of cumulative subclinical biochemical changes in the limbic system. This progressive buildup causes neurons to become more excitable until, eventually, clinically observable symptoms appear. The kindling model has been offered as an explanation for the progression and changes in bipolar disorder over time, especially the increasing frequency and severity of episodes that often occurs with aging.

In the late 1990s, research expanded to include a greater focus on molecular and cellular processes, signaling networks, and neuroplasticity. In the models summarized below, the evolution of this research is apparent. Due to the complex nature of this research we have outlined and clarified the major theoretical models, especially those that present new and thought-provoking ideas. Manji (2001) and Manji and Lennox (2000) have recently published very complete review articles that are referenced below, along with many secondary references.

- **Catecholamine Theory.** Although conclusions vary regarding the results obtained, in general, there is evidence suggesting that the catecholamine hypothesis of mood disorders extends to bipolar disorder, but probably not in a primary causative capacity (Goodwin and Jamison 1990; Schatzberg and Schildkraut 1995; Manji and Porter 1997, as cited in Manji 2001). Noradrenergic abnormalities predominate and are measured by concentrations of norepinephrine, and its major metabolite, MHPG. Overall, urinary MHPG levels are lower in bipolar depressed patients, and are higher during manic episodes. Urinary MHPG levels are lower in bipolar depression than in unipolar depression. In mania, CSF concentrations of NE and MHPG are elevated. There is less clear evidence for the role of other catecholamines in bipolar disorder. Serotonergic abnormalities have not been substantiated. However, areas that are being researched include reduced serotonin levels and alterations in the serotonin transporter. Preliminary research regarding the dopaminergic system implicates a decreased CSF concentration of HVA, the major dopamine metabolite (Willner 1995).

  Although there are studies that have investigated the role of the cholinergic system in bipolar disorder, at this time there is no strong clinical evidence that implicates cholinergic abnormalities.

- **The HPA Axis Theory.** The HPA axis has been studied widely in mood disorders (see chapter 3). The strongest association between overactivation of the HPA axis and bipolar disorder appears to be in mixed states and in bipolar depression, with less convincing evidence in classic mania (Goodwin and Jamison 1990; Garlow, Musselman, and Nemeroff 1999).

- **Protein Signaling Network Theory.** At least two signaling pathways are thought to be implicated in bipolar disorder, the G protein pathway, discussed in chapter 3, and the protein kinase C (PKC) pathway. There is more evidence to support the proposed role of G proteins than of PKC, but research involving the latter is expanding. These systems have been likened to "cellular cogwheels" (Manji 2001) in that they function to integrate complex biochemical input and output and to regulate feedback mechanisms. In addition, these systems may play a role in maintaining cellular memory and plasticity (Bhalla and Iyengar 1999; Weng, Bhalla, and Iyengar 1999).

- **Calcium Signaling Theory.** Abnormalities in calcium signaling has long been postulated to play a role in bipolar disorder, extrapolated from evidence of higher than normal intracellular calcium levels in bipolar patients. However, the exact nature of what gives rise to these increases and how that might affect bipolarity has yet to be elucidated. The lack of convincing evidence that calcium channel blocking drugs are effective in treating bipolar disorder further complicates conclusive interpretations.

- **Neuro-anatomical Theories: Cellular Resiliency.** As in schizophrenia research, efforts have been made to explore neuro-anatomical abnormalities in mood disorders from a causational approach, as well as from a disease-consequence approach. To date, neuro-imaging and postmortem studies have shown enough positive results that research in this area is likely to expand greatly (Soares and Mann 1997; Manji, Moore, Rajkowska, and Chen 2000). Key initial findings point to a decrease in CNS volume and cell numbers, neurons and/or glia, in mood disorders. Some results apply to major depression and some to bipolar disorder. An unexpected finding of these studies is the identification of a cytoprotective protein in the frontal cortex. This finding has sparked interest in defining the mechanism by which lithium and other mood stabilizers increase levels of this protein (see chapter 16 for further discussion). The existence of neuroprotective proteins holds great promise for furthering the understanding of mood disorders and for developing effective treatments.

- **Genetic and Familial Theories.** Familial, twin, and adoption studies support the theory that bipolar disorder is heritable. Bertelsen's early Danish twin studies have been supported in the intervening years, and it is generally accepted that the concordance rate for monozygotic twins is 50 to 60 percent for bipolar disorder (Tsuang and Faraone 1990). Even though the risk factor association in first degree relatives is four to six times higher than in the general population, the exact mode of transmission has yet to be identified. Genetic linkage studies are complex and difficult to replicate. However, multiple chromosomes have been identified in various studies conducted over the last decade. Chromosome 22 has been implicated in both bipolar disorder and schizophrenia, raising questions as to how distinct the two conditions really are (Nurnberger and Foroud 2000; Potash and DePaulo 2000; Kelsoe et al. 2001).

In summary, these various theories, although focusing on different aspects of neurobiology, tend to support a strong biological base for bipolar disorder. Probably the most convincing evidence in favor of a biologic etiology remain the relatively good response to pharmacotherapy and the extremely poor response to purely psychological interventions. Unlike the biological theories discussed in chapters 6 and 8–11 of this book, at this time the precise neurochemical dysfunctions in bipolar disorder have not been clearly established. Our intent is to provide you, as the therapist, with the fundamental knowledge necessary to address your patients' questions about their disorder and the medications prescribed.

Treatment

The evidence is so strongly compelling that bipolar is largely a biologic-based disorder that pharmacologic intervention is the mainstay of treatment. The details of treatment with various pharmacologic agents are discussed in chapter 15.

Although medications are the primary treatment modality for bipolar disorder, it is important to consider the impact of medications in conjunction with other forms of treatment. For instance, milieu therapy, when inpatient care is necessary, will be most effective after initial medication response has reestablished some degree of cooperation and insight. Psychotherapy, especially cognitive, behavioral, and psychoeducational approaches, is effective with the medication-stabilized patient. Group therapy, which can include families, will often revolve around acceptance of the disease as well as of the need for long-term medication treatment, and include a consideration of the side effects and the implications of noncompliance. In instances of medication resistance or contraindications, ECT should be considered.

QUICK REFERENCE
When to Refer for Medication Treatment

Event	Symptoms
Mood indicates mania or hypomania	Expansiveness, overconfidence, euphoria, irritability, labile mood
Mood indicates depression	Criteria for major depression is met (see chapter 5)
Mood indicates mixed state	Coexistence of above
Thought process and judgment become impaired	Lack of insight, flight of ideas, grandiosity, tangentiality, paranoia, delusions, hallucinations
Behavior becomes inappropriate	Pressured speech, psychomotor hyperactivity, decreased need for sleep, hypersexual or promiscuous, increased spending, gambling
Grief becomes clinical depression	Early morning awakening, serious weight loss, anhedonia, agitation
Major depression has vegetative symptoms	Sleep disturbance, appetite disturbance, fatigue, decreased sex drive, agitation or psychomotor retardation, anhedonia
Major depression has atypical symptoms	Pronounced fatigue, hypersomnia, increased appetite and weight gain, rejection sensitivity, panic symptoms, reactive dysphoria
Dysthymia presents with sustained symptoms	Low energy, anhedonia
Daily functioning is markedly impaired	
Presence of severe suicidal impulses or psychotic symptoms	
Major depression or dysthymia fails to respond to psychotherapy	

8

Anxiety Disorders

Anxiety disorders encompass a broad, heterogeneous group of psychiatric problems. Like depression, anxiety disorders have multiple etiologies. Some appear to be clearly related to biochemical abnormalities, while others are psychogenic in origin. And treatments vary considerably depending on the diagnosis and presumed underlying pathophysiology. Anxiety disorders have often been erroneously seen as mild or benign disorders. However, recent clinical and epidemiological studies indicate that anxiety disorders are quite common—more common even than depression—and exact a heavy toll on individuals and society alike. The current view sees anxiety disorders as often serious, chronic mental illnesses. Especially in severe cases, such as panic disorder, suicide rates are high; alcohol abuse rates reach 30 percent or more; medical services are inappropriately overutilized; and the cardiac-death rate is higher than average.

Differential Diagnosis

Before outlining the main features of each anxiety disorder, it is necessary to define two terms: *panic attacks* and *anxiety symptoms*. Panic attacks are very brief but extremely intense surges of anxiety. The major differences between a panic attack and more generalized anxiety symptoms are differences in the onset, duration, and intensity (see figure 8-A). Panic attacks often "come out of the blue"; that is, they are not necessarily provoked by stress. They come on suddenly, are *extremely* intense, and last anywhere from one to thirty minutes and then subside. The patient feels as if he or she will actually die or go crazy, as we are not talking about uneasiness but full-blown panic.

The person may continue to feel nervous or upset for several hours, but the attack itself lasts only a matter of minutes. If a patient says, "I've had a continuous panic attack for the past three days," he or she may be having intense anxiety symptoms, but not a true panic attack. In anxiety disorders without panic attacks, the anxiety symptoms can be very unpleasant, but are much less intense; they also can be prolonged or generalized—that is, present most of the day and lasting from days to years. The distinction between anxiety and panic is very important when it comes to making an accurate diagnosis and choosing appropriate treatments. The symptoms of anxiety are as follows:

Symptoms of Anxiety

- Trembling, feeling shaky, restlessness, muscle tension
- Shortness of breath, smothering sensation
- Tachycardia (rapid heartbeat)
- Sweating and cold hands and feet
- Lightheadedness and dizziness
- Paresthesias (tingling of the skin)
- Diarrhea, frequent urination, or both
- Feelings of unreality (derealization)
- Initial insomnia (difficulty falling asleep)
- Impaired attention and concentration
- Nervousness, edginess, or tension

Although *DSM-IV* includes twelve types of anxiety disorders, the list of disorders in this chapter is somewhat more brief. Patients suffering from post-traumatic stress disorder (PTSD) and a related disorder, acute stress disorder, often do present with a host of anxiety symptoms; however, anxiety is but one aspect of PTSD. This syndrome also often includes symptoms of depression, transient psychosis, and dissociation. Thus, we have chosen not to address it here, but in a separate chapter (see chapter 11). Additionally, although obsessive-compulsive disorder (OCD) is considered to be an anxiety disorder, its pathophysiology and treatment varies enough from the anxiety disorders to warrant a separate chapter (see chapter 9).

Anxiety Symptoms Versus Panic Attacks

	Anxiety	Panic
Onset	Can be gradual	Very sudden
Duration	Prolonged	1 to 30 minutes
Intensity	Mild to moderate	Severe
Precipitated by stressors	Generally	Often not

Figure 8-A

Ten anxiety syndromes can be distinguished, as follows:

- Generalized anxiety disorder (GAD)

- Anxiety associated with psychological stress (adjustment disorder with anxiety)

- Specific phobias

- Social phobias/social anxiety disorder

- Agoraphobia without panic

- Anxiety symptoms due to a general medical condition

- Substance-induced anxiety disorder

- Anxiety symptoms secondary to a primary mental disorder

- "Neurotic" anxiety

- Panic disorder

Anxiety Facts

- Lifetime prevalence rates for anxiety disorders: 25 percent.

- Thirty-seven million people per year suffer from anxiety disorders in the United States.

- Panic disorder patients are eighteen times more likely to make suicide attempts than normal controls.

- Incidence of anxiety disorders, women to men: 2:1.

- It is estimated that only 30 percent of patients with panic disorder receive treatment. Yet treatment is effective in 70 to 90 percent of those so afflicted.

Generalized anxiety disorder

Generalized anxiety disorder is characterized by chronic, low-level anxiety (without panic attacks). Patients with this disorder may have no specific current stressors. Life in general is stressful for them. Such people are often high strung and are chronic worriers.

Anxiety associated with acute psychological stressors

In such disorders, anxiety symptoms are not evident prior to the onslaught of stressors; preclinically the person functioned well. Symptoms emerge in the wake of acute life stress.

Specific phobias

These phobias involve fears of specific objects, such as dogs, or places, such as heights. Anxiety is seen only in the phobic situation.

Social phobias/social anxiety disorder

Social phobias involve serious anxiety symptoms experienced only when the person is in social or interpersonal settings, such as speaking before a group, participating in a social gathering, or asking someone for a date.

Agoraphobia without panic

This disorder is characterized by intense fears of being in situations or places from which escape might be difficult or embarrassing. As in other phobias, the anxiety is accompanied by a strong tendency to avoid being in such feared places. Agoraphobia commonly develops in the course of panic disorder, but in agoraphobia without panic, there is no history of full-blown *spontaneous* panic attacks (see "Panic disorder," below). Experiences of anxiety are always associated either with entry into a feared place or situation such as entering a crowded store or with anticipation of such an event.

Anxiety symptoms due to general medical conditions, substance use or abuse, or another primary psychiatric disorder

In these disorders, the anxiety symptoms are secondary to another etiology.

Neurotic anxiety

Neurotic anxiety arises when an individual is beset by significant emotional issues or conflicts but maintains tight defenses against awareness of these inner issues. In other words, the conflicts are unconscious, and what one sees overtly are anxiety symptoms—often "generalized" and *sometimes* in the form of occasional panic attacks. Another version of neurotic anxiety is seen in individuals who are plagued by more conscious conflicts. Often such conflicts take the form of approach-avoidance, such as the person very much wanting to do something but worrying about offending others or violating certain internalized rules or "shoulds." The person feels inwardly torn and will often experience feelings of generalized anxiety.

Panic disorder

Panic disorder is characterized by recurring, intense panic attacks. Many times these attacks appear to be spontaneous, not provoked by identifiable stressors. As the disorder progresses, most patients begin to develop considerable anticipatory anxiety (a rather continuous, mild-to-moderate generalized anxiety as they come to worry when the next attack will occur)—and phobias (agoraphobia is especially common). With time, alcohol abuse and depression commonly develop.

Since the etiology and treatment of these anxiety syndromes vary significantly, each is discussed separately below, with greater detail provided for the disorders that are felt to be more strongly biologically based.

Etiology

For decades, the psychoanalytic theory of neurosis rested on Freud's fundamental notions of the psychogenic origin of anxiety (Freud's second, or revised, theory of anxiety, 1923). Most neurotic disorders were felt to arise from the unconscious perception of danger: realistic anxiety (danger from the environment), moral anxiety (danger from the superego), and id anxiety (danger from the id). Such unconscious judgments involving potential danger provoked "signal anxiety" and ignited defensive operations. When defenses failed, patients experienced manifest anxiety symptoms.

Other dominant psychological views of anxiety have been proposed by cognitive theorists such as Beck. The cognitive model suggests that anxiety is generated when people overevaluate the danger in certain situations or underestimate their coping ability. The perception of danger and loss of control can provoke fight-or-flight responses even in nondangerous circumstances. With anxious people, their perceptions of reality are skewed such that there are many misperceptions and "false alarms."

These psychological theories are not at all incompatible with biologic ones, though they were developed before the physiology of anxiety was well understood.

Biologic Theories

Let's now explore theories of biologic etiology. "Hard-wired" into the nervous system of humans and many animals is a complex network of nerve pathways, brain structures, and glands that are responsible for eliciting the fight-or-flight response. This response triggers a multilevel neurochemical and hormonal reaction designed to mobilize the body and mind during times of potential danger. Nonessential physiological processes shut down (such as digestion, reproduction), and energy is channeled into a host of bodily functions preparing the organism for rapid action. The nervous system also shifts into a state of hyperarousal and vigilance. All of these changes, which occur rapidly and automatically, have evolved to assure survival when a person or animal confronts actual danger situations. Thus, fundamentally, the biologic mechanisms and processes underlying the fight-or-flight response are necessary and adaptive.

The basic components of the fight-or-flight mechanism are depicted schematically in figures 8-B and 8-C. As stressful events are perceived at the level of the cortex and also processed in a crude way on the subcortical level (the amygdala), lower brain areas become activated. In a sense, the limbic system is put on alert. Should ongoing perception result in a conclusion that there is imminent danger, a burst of excitation emanates from a cluster of nerve cell bodies in the brain stem called the locus coeruleus (LC). The LC has sometimes been called the adrenal gland of the brain. The LC nerve cells, which project to the limbic system, are mediated by the neurotransmitter norepinephrine.

The limbic system and adjacent hypothalamus shift into high gear, and by way of the pituitary gland (and other downstream endocrine glands) and the sympathetic nervous system, a multitude of stress hormones are released into the system. The brain and body alike are ready for action.

It is also important to discuss yet another feature of the nervous system that plays a role in anxiety. On the surface of about 60 percent of nerve cells in the brain

Figure 8-B

Figure 8-C

(including cells in the LC) are tiny gateways referred to as chloride ion channels (see figure 8-D). Chloride ions, which carry a slight negative charge, are in abundance in the fluid surrounding nerve cells. The ion channel can be activated (opened) when stimulated by the naturally occurring neurochemical gamma-aminobutyric acid, GABA for short (see figure 8-D, 2).

As the gate opens, the chloride ions are drawn in. When the nerve cell is infused with negative ions, its electrical characteristics are altered, resulting in decreased excitability; that is, the cell relaxes. This operates as a sort of biological braking mechanism, serving to dampen "limbic alert" and calm overall brain excitation. Benzodiazepine molecules (the substances found in antianxiety medications) also bind to the chloride ion channels, further enhancing the in-flow of negative ions and thus producing a widespread calming in many areas of the brain (see figure 8-D, 3).

This model provides an understanding of the mechanism of action of antianxiety medications. It also has led to a theory that may explain some anxiety disorders. Since there is a receptor on the chloride ion channel that responds to benzodiazepine molecules, there is speculation that an endogenous benzodiazepine-like chemical may exist in the CNS. To date, however, such a chemical has yet to be identified (although some researchers believe that adenosine may be the chemical). However, should this theory hold true, it may provide an explanation for why some individuals are temperamentally more "high-strung" and less able to stay calm during stressful times, and why others experience chronic, generalized anxiety. Such individuals *may* suffer from a deficiency of this yet-to-be-identified endogenous neurochemical.

Excitability in the locus coeruleus (LC) is also mediated by serotonin (in this area of the brain, serotonin receptors are inhibitory). Thus any number of factors that lead to a global decrease in serotonin may affect the LC (i.e., it can become disinhibited and thus more sensitive to activation).

Acquired fears appear to be mediated primarily by the amygdala. After exposure to very frightening events, in a sense, the amygdala encodes certain elements of the memory. Such memories have been shown to be quite indelible and highly resistant to extinction. Once etched into the memory circuits of the amygdala, this brain structure develops a sort of persistent hypersensitivity to activation by similar stimuli. One result is that re-exposure to a similar anxiety-provoking event can result in significant or extreme reactivity. Also, generalization often occurs such that non-dangerous stimuli that somewhat resemble the original stressful event may readily provoke intense anxiety reactions. For example, the traumatized combat veteran who now experiences strong surges of anxiety when hearing the backfire from an automobile. There is speculation that serotonin also plays a role in inhibiting cellular reactivity in the amygdala (and serotonergic antidepressants are now considered to be first-line treatments for many anxiety disorders).

Neurobiologic structure and functioning underlying normal separation anxiety in young mammals also plays a role in intense anxiety states in adult life; especially so with panic disorder. Often in the six to twelve months prior to the emergence of panic disorder, people with the disorder experienced a significant interpersonal loss.

Figure 8-D

This raises the speculation that such experiences may resensitize those neural circuits that once played a role in normal separation anxiety.

Finally, research on the impact of early child abuse and neglect suggests that such experiences may permanently alter the HPA axis and thus set the stage for chronic vulnerability to anxiety (Nemeroff 1997).

Please note: Biologic theories regarding obsessive-compulsive and post-traumatic stress disorder are dealt with in separate chapters (9 and 11, respectively), which deal specifically with these disorders.

With these biological models in mind, let's begin to look at specific anxiety disorders, many of which represent some type of malfunction in this otherwise-adaptive physiological system.

Generalized anxiety disorder and anxiety associated with acute stress

In GAD the individual is almost continuously predicting, anticipating, or imagining "dangerous" (unpleasant) events. The limbic system is kept in a perpetual state of alert—on guard for a multitude of "what-ifs." Since daily life rarely presents GAD patients with severely traumatic or life-threatening events, the level of activation does not reach the intensity of threshold of full-blown fight-or-flight. The result is a low-grade, but chronic, state of anxiety.

GAD is primarily felt to be a psychogenic disorder. However, there is some speculation that at least some GAD patients may suffer from a biologically mediated disorder. One hypothesis is that mentioned above: a deficiency of neurochemicals. Another model has emerged more recently. Treatment with serotonin agonists such as buspirone and 5-HT antidepressants (SSRIs) has been shown to reduce "what-ifing" (worry) in GAD patients. However, the mechanism of action and underlying pathophysiology are not well understood.

In stress-induced anxiety disorders, actual psychological stressors have evoked another version of ongoing limbic alert. And in the wake of severe stress, such patients often can have *occasional* full-blown panic attacks. These disorders emerge in response to life-threatening stressors (natural disasters, combat, assaults, automobile accidents) and in response to a host of emotional stressors (loss of a job, serious illness in a relative, marital separation). In many cases, the anxiety symptoms can be seen as normal responses; that is, they are not pathological. However, the symptoms can be severe enough to warrant treatment.

With GAD and stress-related anxiety, in all likelihood the basic neurobiology is not grossly abnormal. Rather, real or imagined stresses are provoking psychological reactions—which, of course, ultimately are biologically mediated.

Specific phobias

Phobias such as the fear of snakes, closed-in spaces, heights, and so on, are generally considered to be associated either with age-appropriate fears (fears that subside with maturation) or conditioned responses. There is little evidence that these disorders are due to biological dysfunction, and medication treatment is generally not warranted.

Social phobias

Social phobias are certainly influenced by developmental and other life experiences (such as the quality of early attachments, the development of appropriate social skills, and adequate experience interacting with others). At the same time, there is rather compelling evidence suggesting that social phobics (and their more pervasively impaired cousins—avoidant personalities) may have a biologically based disorder.

Animal studies have shown that when baby animals are separated from their parents, they typically enter a state of high arousal and agitation—frequently producing some form of vocal distress signal. This is obviously the case with human infants as well. Separation stresses appear to elicit extremely high levels of neuronal activity in the locus coeruleus. One hypothesis holds that this brain area, in addition to its role in evoking fight-or-flight responses, may be a key brain structure designed to trigger arousal and distress behavior in infants separated from caregivers. Presumably, with psychological development and neurologic maturation, the threshold of LC activity gradually raises. Behaviorally, we see an increased capacity to tolerate separation as children and young animals mature.

What does this have to do with social phobias? One view is that the underlying fear in many social phobias is that the person will be embarrassed, humiliated, and ultimately rejected, which is equivalent to separation. This fear of rejection is also seen in avoidant personalities, so-called hysteroid-dysphorics (see chapter 5), and many people suffering from borderline personality disorders. Animals treated with heterocyclic antidepressants and MAO inhibitors (drugs shown to reduce excitation in the LC) exhibit markedly decreased distress in the face of separation stresses. And during the past decade, clinical trials with antidepressants and MAO inhibitors have shown improvement in broad groups of patients with social phobias and rejection sensitivity. The theory contends that such patients may be chronically experiencing very low thresholds of arousal at the level of the locus coeruleus—accounting for their exquisite sensitivity to humiliation, separation, and rejection.

Agoraphobia without panic

The anxiety experienced with this disorder only occurs when the patient must go into feared situations (such as a store) or in the moments before entering the phobic situation (anticipating anxiety). Although such experiences of anxiety ultimately do involve an activation of the limbic system, the primary disorder is felt to be largely psychogenic, a conditioned fear response. Medications are sometimes used to treat agoraphobia without panic; however, this disorder is not felt to be biologically based.

Anxiety symptoms due to general medical conditions

Certain systemic medical illnesses and primary neurologic disorders can dysregulate CNS neurotransmitters and cause or contribute to anxiety symptoms (see figure 8-E). Note that most anxiety symptoms associated with these medical conditions present in the form of generalized anxiety, generally not panic attacks.

Substance-induced anxiety disorders

A common cause of anxiety symptoms can be traced to drug use or abuse (see figure 8-F).

Anxiety symptoms secondary to primary psychiatric disorders

Certainly, anxiety symptoms are seen in a very wide range of psychiatric disorders, including schizophrenia, mania, PTSD, agitated depressions, and severe personality disorders. It is important to keep in mind that anxiety symptoms do not necessarily signal a diagnosis of anxiety *disorder*. Almost without exception, however,

Medical Disorders Associated with Anxiety

- Adrenal tumor
- Alcoholism
- Angina pectoris
- Cardiac arrhythmia
- CNS degenerative disease
- Cushing's disease
- Coronary insufficiency
- Delirium[a]
- Hypoglycemia

- Hyperthyroidism
- Ménière's disease (early stages)
- Mitral valve prolapse[b]
- Parathyroid disease
- Partial-complex seizures
- Postconcussion syndrome
- Premenstrual syndrome
- Pulmonary embolism

a Delirium can occur as a result of many toxic and metabolic conditions and often produces anxiety and agitation.

b The mitral valve prolapse probably does not cause anxiety, but it has been found that MVP and anxiety disorders often coexist. This may be due to some common underlying genetic factor.

Figure 8-E

Drugs That Can Cause Anxiety

- Amphetamines
- Appetite suppressants
- Asthma medications
- Caffeine

- CNS depressants (withdrawal from)
- Cocaine
- Nasal decongestants
- Steroids

Figure 8-F

when anxiety is associated with a more primary mental disorder, psychotropic medication treatment is aimed at the primary disorder. (Refer to appropriate chapters for descriptions of etiology and treatment.)

Neurotic anxiety

Although the term *neurosis* has fallen out of favor in some professional circles, the concept still has merit. As conceived of here, neurotic anxiety is a condition in which manifest symptoms of anxiety are evident but the underlying problem can ultimately be traced to unconscious conflicts, or unrecognized inner emotional issues. A common example of this is illustrated in case 15.

Case 15

Rob S. is 42 and recently lost his wife to breast cancer. Emotionally, he grits his teeth and blocks his inner grief. But the overcontainment of his inner feelings of loss has resulted in a tense, brittle adaptation. Rob feels little sadness, but his heart races, he experiences tension headaches, and he has initial insomnia. The problem does not lie in disordered neurons, but in overdefensiveness; and the solution is not to be found in a pill, but rather in the process of working through and mourning (possibly in the context of psychotherapy). To assume a biological etiology and attempt to medicate away anxiety symptoms with this man would only create more distance between his conscious awareness and his inner painful emotional concerns.

As mentioned earlier, some neurotic conflicts that generate anxiety may also be experienced on a conscious level. But again, these are best seen as psychogenic rather than as biologically rooted problems.

Panic disorder

The biological factors that set the stage for the emergence of panic disorder may arise spontaneously (be truly endogenous) or can be set in motion by major life stressors as noted earlier. Biochemical factors likely operate to alter cellular functions in the LC, lowering the excitation threshold for those neurons.

Panic disorder begins with the eruption of full-blown panic attacks—many of which (as mentioned earlier) occur "out of the blue" in low- or no-stress situations. Some individuals with panic disorder suffer from relatively infrequent attacks (a few per month); in more severe cases, attacks can occur several times a day and oftentimes even during sleep. The *noradrenergic hypothesis* holds that the intense, recurring attacks are caused by hypersensitive neurons in the LC or a dysfunction in the natural braking mechanism in the LC nerve cells or both (see figure 8-G).

The nerve axon in figure 8-G impinges back on itself and releases its neurotransmitter norepinephrine (also called noradrenaline, hence the term "noradrenergic hypothesis"). The neurotransmitter typically stimulates inhibitory receptors on the cell body, acting to reduce excitability. However, in panic disorder, the inhibitory-α-2 receptors ("brakes") are felt to be dysfunctional (in a state of sub-sensitivity). Once stimulated, the LC cell continues to fire alerting signals to the limbic system, uninhibited by the normal braking mechanism. Antipanic medications (especially antidepressants) are hypothesized to have their effect by normalizing the operation of LC inhibitory receptors (see chapters 15 and 17). Other molecules also have been found to exert inhibitory effects on LC neurons including: serotonin, GABA, and opiates. This helps to explain how SSRIs are often useful in treating panic disorder, and how certain minor tranquilizers may reduce panic symptoms (e.g., alprazolam, lorazepam, and clonazepam along with GABA activate chloride ion channels). Although opiates are not approved or indicated for use in treating anxiety disorders, many narcotic addicts may be self-medicating with opiates to reduce anxiety symptoms.

Treatment

Generalized anxiety disorder

For many patients, psychological approaches are the treatment of choice. These techniques include stress management, cognitive-behavioral treatment[1], relaxation training, meditation, and psychotherapy. Also, for GAD patients in good health who do not experience coexisting panic attacks, a program of regular, aerobic-level exercise can be very beneficial. Note that individuals with panic disorder may experience an *exacerbation* of panic attacks when involved in strenuous exercise.

---

1. For a review of cognitive-behavioral treatments for anxiety disorders, the reader is referred to *Depression and Anxiety Management*, an audiotape by John Preston, New Harbinger Publications, 1993.

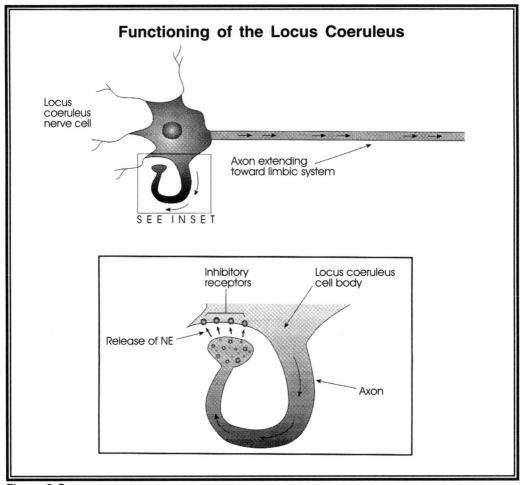

Figure 8-G

When medication is indicated, the clinician has three choices:

- Benzodiazepines (the class of drugs often termed minor tranquilizers or anti-anxiety medications) can be used in severe cases of GAD. However, the use of benzodiazepines to treat GAD has been the subject of considerable controversy. Great concern has arisen regarding potential benzodiazepine abuse and dependence. Certainly, people who chronically use benzodiazepines do develop a physiological dependence on these medications. Nonetheless, concern in the media and medical profession alike may have been overstated. The vast majority of chronically anxious patients do not abuse nor become addicted to these medications and rarely require progressive increases in doses. The individuals who do, in fact, present a significant risk of abuse are people with a personal or family history of alcohol or other substance abuse. With such individuals, benzodiazepines are not appropriate. (Guidelines and cautions regarding treatment appear in chapters 13 and 17.)

- The atypical antianxiety medication buspirone has been used with some success with GAD patients. This medication offers the benefits of reduced rumination and worry, but without the problems of sedation and potential drug dependence seen with benzodiazepines. Buspirone is not addictive and thus provides a treatment option for GAD patients with substance abuse risk.

- Both cyclic and serotonergic antidepressants (SSRIs) are being used increasingly to treat chronically anxious patients. (See chapter 15 for information regarding treatment with SSRI antidepressants.)

Anxiety associated with acute stress

Again, for most individuals, psychological approaches are best suited for treating acute stress reactions. However, antianxiety medications can be an important adjunct to treatment, especially when the patient is experiencing considerable amounts of agitation or insomnia. The classic form of anxiety-related insomnia is initial insomnia (difficulty falling asleep). Middle insomnia or early morning awakening should alert the clinician to a diagnosis of depression. Medications used to treat daytime anxiety include the whole range of benzodiazepines, and for sleep the so-called sedative-hypnotics (see chapter 17). Typically, drug treatment for acute stress is short-term (one to four weeks), in combination with crisis intervention and other psychological treatments.

Specific and social phobias

Specific phobias generally are not treated with psychotropic medications. Social phobias often respond well to cognitive-behavioral treatment. When medications are used, the clinician has two main alternatives: For occasional use—for example to reduce anxiety associated with theatrical performances or public speaking—the beta blocker propranolol has been shown to be quite effective. This drug does little to alter the cognitive aspects of anxiety (worry), but effectively reduces many physiological symptoms such as rapid heart rate. Anxious patients treated with propranolol take the medication only prior to the stressful event, ingesting 20–80 mg about one hour before.

More pervasive forms of social anxiety (and avoidant personality disorder) may be treated with MAO inhibitors or SSRIs (see chapter 15), in addition to psychotherapy and social-skills training.

Agoraphobia without panic

The treatment of choice for this disorder includes psychotherapy, relaxation training, and behavioral treatment (graded exposure to feared situations). Such approaches have a solid track record of effectiveness, and medication treatment as a sole therapy generally is not effective. However, often patients are treated with psychotropic medications in the early phase of graded exposure therapy. Minor tranquilizers (benzodiazepines) and beta blockers (such as propranolol) can be used to somewhat reduce the level of anxiety as the patient begins gradually to reenter anxiety-provoking situations. As the patient starts to experience success and a sense of mastery, the medications can be gradually phased out.

Anxiety symptoms due to general medical conditions, substance abuse, or primary psychiatric disorder

These symptoms usually are not directly treated with psychotropic medications. Rather the primary medical disorder is treated, or the patient is referred for treatment of a chemical dependency problem (see chapter 13). When psychotropics are employed, they generally are used for short periods of time. Medications of choice are the benzodiazepines (although they should be used with extreme caution in patients with a substance abuse disorder).

As noted earlier, when a primary psychiatric disorder is diagnosed, generally medication treatment targets the primary illness, such as antipsychotics for schizophrenia or antidepressants for agitated depression.

Neurotic anxiety

In neurotic anxiety, medication treatment is generally contraindicated, since the reduction of overt anxiety symptoms can serve to further block awareness of core emotional conflicts. The exceptions are these:

- If the patient has inadequate ego strength to tolerate a more "uncovering" psychological approach.

- If the patient is not psychologically minded or has a low level of cognitive functioning.

- If the clinician must work with a highly symptomatic client in very *brief therapy*.

- If manifest anxiety symptoms are severe. In such cases, short-term treatment with benzodiazepines may help reduce suffering, restore functioning in daily life, and help the patient stabilize. This can then be followed by medication reduction and psychotherapy.

Panic disorder

Panic disorder is the anxiety disorder for which medication treatment plays its most important role. This often-devastating illness is quite responsive to combined medication and psychological treatment. It is helpful to focus on four somewhat discrete aspects of this disorder, each of which requires targeted treatments:

- Panic attacks

- Anticipatory anxiety

- Phobias

- Associated features—alcohol abuse, depression

Panic attacks must be either eliminated or greatly reduced in the initial phase of treatment. Some behavioral and cognitive techniques have been developed to reduce panic attacks, although antipanic medications take effect more rapidly and have a solid track record as safe and highly effective drugs. Antipanic medications fall into three groups:

- High-potency benzodiazepines, such as alprazolam, clonazepam, and lorazepam

- Antidepressants (tricyclics and SSRIs)[2]

- MAO inhibitors

See chapters 15 and 17 for more on these types of medications.

The first goal of treatment is to stop or reduce attacks. However, even when this is successful, anticipatory anxiety and phobias can, and often do, continue unabated. Thus, the second step is to reduce anticipatory anxiety and phobic avoidance using behavioral techniques, especially graded exposure and desensitization (see Preston 1993). These techniques are highly effective, but only after there is good containment of panic symptoms.

Often, especially in more chronic cases, major depression, alcohol abuse or dependency, or both develop along with primary panic symptoms. In that event, appropriate antidepressant medication treatment and/or involvement in Alcoholics Anonymous or a chemical-dependency treatment program becomes necessary.

Finally, when primary anxiety or panic symptoms are resolved, many panic disorder patients often choose to pursue more traditional psychotherapy. As mentioned earlier, a number of panic patients have encountered major losses and must begin the journey of working through these major life changes. In our experience, however, insight-oriented treatment typically must await the resolution of primary panic symptoms.

Unfortunately a large percentage of patients relapse when medications are discontinued—as many as 70 percent have a return of panic symptoms if medications are withdrawn a year after treatment is initiated. Panic disorder, thus, appears to be an often chronic condition. To date, there are no very long-term follow-up studies tracking the course of this disorder. However, for practical purposes, the clinician should anticipate medication treatment lasting at least one year. Then a trial discontinuation or medication reduction can be implemented to determine if continued treatment is necessary.

---

2. To date, all antidepressants have been shown to reduce panic symptoms, with one exception: bupropion. This antidepressant can at times exacerbate panic attacks, and thus should be used with caution.

QUICK REFERENCE
When to Refer for Medication Treatment

The following anxiety disorders generally are *not* treated with psychotropic medications; a referral should be made only if the patient's symptoms are severe or fail to respond to psychological treatments:

- Generalized anxiety disorder
- Specific phobias
- Social phobias
- Agoraphobia without panic

If anxiety symptoms occur in the context of:

- A general medical condition
- Substance use or abuse
- Another primary psychiatric disorder

Then treat the primary disorder.

Psychotherapy is the treatment of choice for:

- Anxiety associated with acute stress
- Neurotic anxiety

Treat the following symptoms with medications only if symptoms are severe and fail to respond to psychological treatment:

- Initial insomnia
- Daytime agitation or restlessness
- Impaired concentration

Treatment with medication should be short term (1–4 weeks).

A combination of medication and psychological therapy is the treatment of choice for panic disorder, as demonstrated by the following:

Event	Symptom
Recurring panic attacks	Sudden onset Intense anxiety Short duration (1–30 minutes) Some attacks are spontaneous
Patient has had four or more attacks in past month	
Patient has developed significant anticipatory anxiety, phobias, avoidance	
Patient has developed secondary symptoms	Clinical depression Alcohol abuse

9

Obsessive-Compulsive Disorder

Obsessive-compulsive disorder (OCD) until recently was considered to be a very rare disorder. However, newer epidemiological studies show OCD to be just as common as panic disorder, and two to three times as common as schizophrenia or bipolar disorder.

OCD is a chronic psychiatric condition, often first emerging in childhood, and potentially lasting a lifetime. It results in considerable emotional suffering. Yet until recent times, few of those afflicted sought treatment. This is probably due to the common tendency for OCD patients to experience humiliation and shame over symptoms that they generally consider to be "crazy" or "irrational" and thus not to seek out professional help.

Differential Diagnosis

The major features of this disorder are recurring obsessions (persistent intrusive, troublesome thoughts or impulses that are recognized by the patient as senseless) and compulsions (repetitive behaviors or rituals enacted in response to an obsession, such as repeatedly checking to see if doors are locked, excessive hand washing, and counting). In order to meet the criteria for obsessive-compulsive disorder, the obsessions and compulsions must create significant distress and be time-consuming enough or otherwise interfere with normal routines, work, activities, or relationships (*DSM-IV*).

Two-thirds of OCD patients are plagued by obsessions regarding dirtiness, contamination, and germs, with corresponding compulsions such as cleaning and hand washing. Another 20 percent primarily are worried about safety issues and engage in repetitive checking rituals (checking to see if doors are locked, if the stove is turned off, retracing their route when driving to make sure they have not accidentally hit a pedestrian). The remaining patients are concerned with a sense of incompleteness, or lack of order or symmetry, and engage in rituals designed to make their environment

> ### Obsessive-Compulsive Disorder Facts
>
> - Lifetime prevalence: 2.5 percent.
>
> - Ratio of men to women: 1:1.
>
> - Age of onset: Although many cases of OCD begin in adolescence or early adulthood, about half begin in childhood. The incidence of OCD in children is 1 to 1.5 percent.
>
> - Course: Although some milder cases of OCD can be transient, most moderate-to-severe cases last for many years if untreated.

"just right." At the heart of most obsessions and compulsions are two key elements: excessive self-doubt and intense worry regarding the safety of oneself and others. In addition to OCD symptoms, which are a tremendous source of suffering in their own right, two-thirds of OCD patients also experience episodes of major depression.

Many people will experience occasional obsessions and compulsions, especially when under stress or when they sense some loss of control over the environment or inner emotions. These more minor, transient obsessions and compulsions do not constitute OCD, which in contrast is a chronic and often incapacitating disorder.

Some similarities exist between OCD and obsessive-compulsive personality disorder (OCP); however, there are notable differences. For treatment purposes, it is important to distinguish between OCD and OCP. With OCD the person feels "under attack" by the obsessions and compulsive rituals; the symptoms are quite painful and ego-dystonic. In contrast, OCP traits (perfectionism, stinginess, emotional rigidity, over-devotion to work) are experienced as a part of oneself, or ego-syntonic.

Some patients are described as suffering from impulse-control disorders (ICD): gambling, overeating, and so on. Although OCD patients subjectively feel "seized" by an impulse to carry out rituals, notable differences exist between OCD and true ICDs. Those experiencing impulse-control problems find the actions, such as overeating, to be pleasurable. In contrast, OCD patients never enjoy carrying out rituals (beyond *some* reduction in anxiety). Also, impulse-control patients rarely are riddled with self-doubt or worries about harming others—again in sharp contrast to OCD. Finally, the medication treatments successful in OCD (described below) have not been shown to be helpful in various forms of impulse-control disorder.

Anorectics often exhibit a host of obsessions and compulsions (regarding eating—sizes and portions, times for meals, body weight)—yet two notable differences exist between anorectics and OCD patients. Obsessive-compulsive disorder patients almost always admit that the worries and rituals are irrational, whereas most anorectics don't appreciate the irrationality of their acts. Also, medications found to be effective for OCD generally are not effective in the treatment of anorexia nervosa.

Etiology

Traditional psychoanalytic theories posited psychogenic theories for what was once called obsessive-compulsive neurosis. These primarily involved early developmental experiences with perfectionistic, overly strict, and rigid parents who imposed unrealistic standards and stifled the child's emerging autonomy. These theories likely do apply to the development of OCP, but not necessarily OCD. In recent years a number of findings from clinical practice and neurobiology have convincingly argued a biological basis for OCD. Let's take a look at some of this evidence.

The disorder emerges early, often in late childhood, and maintains remarkable symptomatic stability throughout life. The incidence in the general population is 2.5 percent, yet it is 7 percent in first-degree relatives, suggesting a possible genetic loading for the disorder. Also, diseases such as certain types of encephalitis, that selectively damage areas of the basal ganglia (subcortical brain structures) have been shown to result in OCD-symptoms.

Probably most convincing are the findings from pharmacological and neuroimaging studies. A very large number of clinical studies have shown that OCD patients can be helped by treatment with SSRI antidepressants. And this holds true even in OCD patients without coexisting depression. In addition, antidepressants that do not affect serotonin are not effective in alleviating OCD symptoms. The SSRI antidepressants selectively increase serotonin activity in the brain and probably more specifically in the basal ganglia, cingulate gyrus, and prefrontal cortex.

Finally, several studies of brain metabolic functioning reveal that in highly symptomatic OCD patients there is a significant increase in metabolic activity (thus increased activation) in the prefrontal cortex and basal ganglia. Furthermore, this abnormal metabolic activity becomes normalized when patients are treated with SSRI antidepressants (Baxter et al. 1992; Rapoport 1991).

Two theories have emerged from these data. The first is that the frontal lobes normally act to inhibit or override the emergence of primitive instinctual urges. However, in OCD this inhibition fails, and we see the eruption of innate urges, or behavioral routines that resemble nest building, grooming, and the checking of territorial boundaries—instinctual behaviors associated with more primitive species. In this model, ordering, straightening, cleaning, hand washing, checking door locks, and so forth may reflect human versions of a breakthrough of these more primitive urges.

A second theory holds that there are naturally existing neural pathways that typically serve adaptive purposes, especially when people are exposed to potentially dangerous situations. The frontal cortex serves as the launching site for worry. When exposed to dangerous stimuli, the frontal lobes guide and direct sustained perceptual focus and attention. In essence, arousal is passed through a feedback circuit (see figure 9-A). In normal individuals this serves to maintain alertness and vigilance until it is determined that there is no danger; then the inner reverberating loop shuts down. Presumably, this neural loop fails to inhibit itself in OCD. The brain continues to sense danger (or to "worry" about danger) despite cognitive evidence to the contrary. The patient gets caught in an ongoing repetition of worry and engages in behavioral attempts to reduce the worry (the rituals). The caudate is richly innervated by 5-HT neurons. When these nerve cells are activated by 5-HT antidepressants, the inhibitory serotonegic cells reduce the excessive metabolic activity, shut down the maladaptive loop, and OCD symptoms diminish.

Treatment

Standard psychotherapy is notoriously ineffective with OCD. To date, two approaches to treatment are, however, proving to be helpful in reducing symptoms in this truly devastating mental illness.

The first are behavioral techniques: exposure and response prevention. Exposure amounts to systematic, gradual exposure to anxiety-provoking stimuli; for example, for a patient afraid of contamination by germs, the exposure trial might

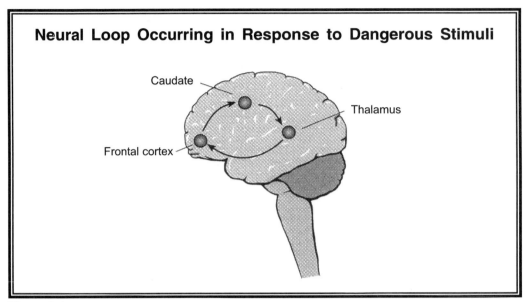

Figure 9-A

involve having the patient clean a toilet without using gloves. Response prevention amounts to helping the patient avoid rituals, such as avoiding hand washing. The rituals, if carried out, usually reduce anxiety. With response prevention, the initial experience is that the patient will encounter considerable anxiety as he or she avoids the ritualistic behavior. Yet, with repeated exposures or response prevention, gradually the anxiety diminishes. This is an emotionally difficult treatment to embark upon, but is one shown to be successful in 65 to 75 percent of patients—given an adequate number of trials, typically twenty to twenty-five sessions.

Medication treatment has become more successful with the advent of selective 5-HT antidepressants. These medications, as noted earlier, are given to OCD patients even if they are not clinically depressed. In addition to their antidepressant effects,

5-HT Antidepressants Useful in Treating OCD			
Generic Name	**Brand Name**	**Typical Depression Dose (mg/day)**	**Typical OCD Dose (mg/day)**
Clomipramine	Anafranil	150–200	200–300
Fluoxetine	Prozac	20–40	20–80
Fluvoxamine	Luvox	100–400	100–500
Sertraline	Zoloft	50–150	50–200
Paroxetine	Paxil	20–30	20–50
Citalopram	Celexa	10–40	20–60

Figure 9-B

these drugs reduce OCD symptoms directly. Treatment with medications for OCD *generally* requires doses higher than those used to treat clinical depression (see figure 9-B). Aside from higher doses, treatment guidelines are the same as for treating depression (see chapter 15).

Psychotropic medications are felt to be effective in 50 to 65 percent of OCD cases. Unfortunately, if patients stop medications, there is a 95 percent relapse rate; thus chronic treatment is necessary. In all likelihood, combined behavioral and pharmacologic treatment offers the best promise for successful outcome.

QUICK REFERENCE
When to Refer for Medication Treatment

Event	Symptoms
Persistent symptoms that are ego-dystonic, create significant distress, and/or interfere with normal routines	Obsessions—intrusive, troublesome thoughts or impulses
	Compulsions—repetitive rituals enacted to reduce anxiety generated by obsessions
	Comorbid clinical depression

10

Psychotic Disorders

This chapter deals with the group of disorders referred to as "psychotic disorders." The term *psychotic* is defined in *DSM-IV* as "gross impairment in reality testing and the creation of a new reality." Although a number of symptoms can be seen in the context of psychotic disorders, impaired reality testing is the central defining feature. Impaired reality testing may be seen behaviorally in the form of bizarre behavior. However, it is most clearly observed in patients' verbal output and content of speech; psychotic patients reveal false beliefs (delusions) and seriously impaired perceptions (hallucinations). You will note that the definition involves not only impairment of reality testing, which alone would only be confusion, but also the "creation of a new reality," such as delusions (I am being followed by the FBI) or hallucinations (I hear a voice telling me I am bad).

Psychosis, per se, is not a diagnosis but a symptom. There are a number of types of psychotic disorders, which have traditionally been classified into two broad groups: functional psychoses and organic psychoses. The term *functional* refers to those psychoses with a presumed psychological etiology and *organic* refers to those with a presumed biological etiology. Schizophrenia was traditionally classified as a functional psychosis; however, more recent research findings strongly suggest that schizophrenia has a biological basis; that is, it is an endogenous mental disorder. The distinction, however, is still important, but now different terminology is used. The functional disorders are referred to as primary psychiatric disorders and the organic disorders are referred to as "due to a general medical condition."

Differential Diagnosis

Psychotic Disorders Due to a General Medical Condition

The term psychotic disorder due to a general medical condition is used for those medical conditions that have psychotic symptoms. In the *DSM-IV*, these conditions are divided into the following:

Psychotic Disorder Facts

- 1 percent of the population has schizophrenia.

- 1 to 4 percent of psychiatric admissions have delusional disorder.

- 10 to 15 percent of medical-surgical patients in a general hospital have delirium.

- 15 percent of patients diagnosed with dementia have a treatable condition.

- Delirium is most common in the very young and the elderly.

- Psychotic disorders due to a general medical condition, with delusions or hallucinations

- Psychotic disorders due to a substance-induced disorder

Substance-related disorders that can be associated with psychotic symptoms can be produced by all classes of substances, i.e., alcohol, hallucinogens, opioids, phencyclidine, sedative-hypnotics, and stimulants. Sometimes psychotic symptoms are more often associated with intoxication and, sometimes, more with withdrawal. Many medical conditions can produce psychotic symptoms, but the most common can be grouped into the following categories:

Medical Conditions That Can Cause Psychosis

- Metabolic

    Organ failure, such as renal failure

    Hypoxia

    Hypoglycemia

    Vitamin deficiency

    Endocrinopathy, such as hyperthyroidism

    Fluid or electrolyte imbalance

    Porphyria

- Drug or alcohol intoxication or withdrawal

- Infections

- Epilepsy

- Head injury

- Vascular diseases, such as lupus

- Intracranial tumor

- Cerebral degenerative diseases

    Dementia, such as Alzheimer's disease

    Multiple sclerosis

    Huntington's chorea

    Parkinson's disease

Primary Psychoses

The primary psychoses can be divided into the following diagnoses:

- Brief reactive psychosis

- Delusional disorder

- Schizophrenia

- Schizophreniform disorder

- Schizoaffective disorder

- Induced psychotic disorder

- Psychotic disorder not otherwise specified (atypical)

- Major depression with psychotic features

- Bipolar disorder, manic

Brief reactive psychosis refers to a condition in which a person has psychotic symptoms lasting from a few hours to a month. There usually is some identifiable stressor that has precipitated the psychosis, and the person demonstrates significant emotional turmoil. The symptoms may be identical to those seen in schizophrenia, but they remit in a fairly brief period of time (less than one month).

Delusional disorder refers to a disorder with persistent nonbizarre delusions without bizarre behavior or prominent hallucinations. Thus, if someone has the delusion they are under surveillance by the FBI, they may meet the criteria. But if delusions are bizarre—for example, if a patient thinks she is under surveillance by Martians—she does not meet the criteria. The disorder is classified by type of delusion: erotomanic, grandiose, jealous, persecutory, or somatic.

Schizophrenia refers to a disorder of longer than six months' duration with prominent psychotic symptoms. This disorder is discussed in detail below. *Schizophreniform disorder* has the same criteria as schizophrenia, but is of less than six months' duration.

Schizoaffective disorder refers to a condition in which the person has not only schizophrenia but also significant episodes of mood disorder, either manic or depressive.

In *induced psychotic disorder*, the person develops psychosis as a result of an intense relationship and identification with someone who is already psychotic, for example, in folie à deux. Here the person typically has poorly defined self–other boundaries and will begin to mimic psychotic symptoms seen in the other individual. (Psychotic symptoms seen in severe affective disorders and mania and depressive psychoses are covered in chapters 6 and 7.)

Now let's discuss schizophrenia in more detail, using it as the prototype of primary psychosis.

Schizophrenia

Schizophrenia as a syndrome has been recognized for thousands of years. As long ago as the Hippocratic school, a syndrome called dementia (with behaviors and symptoms akin to schizophrenia) was recognized as distinct from mania and melancholia. Kraepelin (1898) described a syndrome he called dementia praecox. This referred to a psychotic disorder with progressive debilitation leading to severe impairment of social and intellectual functioning. In his view, this syndrome was invariably progressive, with a very poor prognosis, although more recent research questions the progressive nature of all schizophrenic disorders.

The clinical picture of schizophrenia varies depending on the particular phase of the disorder. *DSM-IV* divides the course of schizophrenia into three phases: prodromal, active, and residual. During the prodromal phase, patients show a deterioration in their level of functioning, without being actively psychotic. In this phase, the patient may show mostly "negative" symptoms (discussed below), such as isolativeness, blunted or flat affect, and lack of initiative. There may also be a disruption of sleep patterns. Often there is a deterioration of performance (at work or school), and sometimes in personal hygiene. There may be an abrupt change in behavior or lifestyle, e.g., a change of career. In the active phase, the person is floridly psychotic, with disorganized thinking, delusions, and hallucinations. In the following residual phase, the patient continues to be impaired, but without severe psychotic symptoms. Social isolation and peculiar affect and thinking may persist, to a degree.

For a diagnosis of schizophrenia, these three phases must last more than six months and must not be due to a mood disorder. Three types of schizophrenia are delineated: catatonic (prominent movement disorder), disorganized (severe thought disorganization), and paranoid (prominent paranoid delusions with mild disorganization of thinking). Undifferentiated and residual types are categories for those who do not fit the above three types but have a mix of features.

Case 16

George A. was a 19-year-old college student who was brought to the student health clinic by his roommate. It was difficult to get a clear history from George because he kept changing the subject and making odd and disconnected statements. His roommate reported George had been progressively more isolative the past four months. The past month he had been staying up late at night and had become somewhat secretive. He wrote notes to himself in a special notebook and made odd comments about God and Christ and about something "coming soon." His personal hygiene had deteriorated, and he sometimes went several days without bathing or changing clothes.

George reported that he felt that he was on a special mission to prepare for the second coming of Christ and that he sometimes heard God or the devil speaking to him. He thought it was necessary that he die or suffer in order to atone for his sins and the sins of the world. He admitted that he was doing poorly in school, but explained that doing God's work was more important. His roommate, who had known him in high school, described him as quiet, shy, and somewhat of a loner. He had never dated.

George was treated with antipsychotic medication, and the delusions and hallucinations resolved. But he continued to have difficulty in college and eventually dropped out of school and returned home to stay with his family.

This case illustrates the prodromal, active, and residual phases. George A. is described as having a somewhat schizoid premorbid personality, as is classically described (although some studies have shown that this is present in only about 50 percent of those diagnosed with schizophrenia). This case also illustrates what are called positive and negative symptoms. For practical purposes, it is helpful to group schizophrenic symptoms into four categories, as outlined below. (Note that characterological features are not psychotic symptoms per se, but do often accompany the more core positive or negative symptoms.)

The distinction between positive and negative symptoms appears to be significant because of both their differential responses to medication and their differing clinical course and probable differing etiology. Recently, a third symptom cluster has been identified, the disorganized cluster (Arndt et al. 1991; Liddle et al. 1989). This symptom cluster, like negative symptoms, correlates with cognitive impairment and frontal lobe dysfunction, but has different behavioral manifestations.

There are now several theoretical models of the neurophysiological basis for these different types of symptoms, and the course they follow in schizophrenia. They are discussed below.

Schneiderian First-Rank Symptoms

- *Thought broadcasting*—belief that one's thoughts are escaping aloud into the external world.
- *Experiences of alienation*—belief that one's thoughts, feelings, and actions are not one's own.
- *Experiences of influence*—belief that one's thoughts, feelings, and actions are being controlled by some external agent.
- *Complete auditory hallucinations*—hallucinations of voices coming from outside one's head.
- *Delusional perceptions*—a real, normal perception to which one attaches a private meaning.

Schizophrenia Symptoms

- Positive symptoms:
  Hallucinations
  Delusions
  Agitation
  Floridly bizarre behavior
  First-rank symptoms (see sidebar on this page)

- Negative symptoms:
  Anhedonia
  Apathy
  Blunted affect
  Poverty of thought
  Feelings of emptiness
  Amotivational states

- Disorganization
  Behavioral disorganization
  Distractibility
  Thought disorder

- "Characterological" symptoms:
  Social isolation or alienation
  Marked feelings of inadequacy
  Poorly developed social skills

Etiology

Over the centuries, there have been a multitude of theories about the etiology of schizophrenia. These have ranged from religious, social, and psychological theories to more recent biological theories.

Early evidence of biological factors came from genetic studies. Twin studies showed that the rate of concordance was much higher for monozygotic (identical) than for dizygotic (fraternal) twins. Adoptive studies done by Kety et al. (1971) have shown that schizophrenia is much more prevalent in the biological relatives than in the adoptive families of those adopted at birth who are later diagnosed schizophrenic. Since that study, many others have shown biological differences between schizophrenic subjects and controls:

- CT and MRI scans have demonstrated enlargement of the lateral ventricles and widened cortical sulci. This finding suggests that either there is brain atrophy or (more likely) that in some types of schizophrenia there has been abnormal brain development (Weinberger 1996). These abnormalities may increase over time.

- MRI scans have shown the presence of smaller anterior hippocampi (Weinberger et al. 1992) in schizophrenic subjects, which correlates with cognitive impairment (Nester et al. 1993).

- PET scan studies have shown decreased metabolic activity in the prefrontal cortex, which correlates with the severity of negative symptoms.

- Studies have found a positive correlation between levels of HVA (a dopamine metabolite) in plasma and clinical severity. Also, many studies have found an increase in the number of D2 receptors in the striatum and nucleus acumbens of schizophrenics (Bochus et al. 1996; Lieberman et al. 1996; Gur et al. 1998; Knoll et al. 1998).

The Dopamine Model

The dopamine model was the predominant theory of biological causation for the past two decades. This theory hypothesized that schizophrenia is caused by abnormal dopaminergic activity in the brain. Dopamine neurons are located in a number of different brain regions. In the basal ganglia, these nerve cells help to regulate motor functioning. In areas of the limbic and reticular systems, dopamine neurons appear to play an important role in emotional control and the screening of stimuli.

The dopamine model holds that the basic physiological pathology involves primarily overactive or hyper-reactive dopamine neurons. The excessive dopamine activity can lead to behavioral agitation, a failure to adequately screen stimuli, and disorganization of perception and thought. This theory is supported by two observations: The first is that the potency of antipsychotic drugs has correlated closely with their ability to bind to and block the postsynaptic dopamine (D2) receptors in the mesolimbic system (see figure 10-A).

The second observation is that drugs that increase dopamine activity (such as amphetamines) can product a paranoid psychosis similar to paranoid schizophrenia and, if given to schizophrenic patients, amphetamines may exacerbate psychotic symptoms.

Action of Antipsychotic Drugs on Dopamine Receptors

Figure 10-A

Although the dopamine model has merit, the basic theory has been modified to help explain some clinical data (Davis et al. 1991). One of the strongest stimuli has been the finding that clozapine, although effective in the treatment of schizophrenia, is only a weak D2 blocker. On the other hand, it is a fairly potent 5-HT2A and 5-HT2C antagonist. The 5-HT blocking ability appears to correlate with its effectiveness against negative symptoms. This has also been the case with newer atypical antipsychotics like risperidone and olanzapine (discussed in detail in chapter 18). Also, it has been shown that clozapine *does* significantly decrease dopaminergic activity in the mesolimbic area (despite the lack of D2 blockade) but not in the nigrostriatal tracts (thus the lack of extrapyramidal effects). What emerges is the following picture: In schizophrenia, there is hyperdopaminergic activity in the mesolimbic tracts that is associated with positive symptoms. In addition, there is decreased activity in the prefrontal cortex associated with negative symptoms. The exact relationship between these phenomena is not fully understood at this time. It has been suggested (Bochus et al. 1996) that hypofunction of the glutamate neurons, which interconnect the four main areas shown to be abnormal in schizophrenia (prefrontal cortex, mesolimbic, striatum/nucleus acumbens, and medial temporal lobe), may be the underlying pathophysiology. The different neurochemical basis dictates alternative treatment approaches: the use of atypical antipsychotics (discussed in detail in chapter 18).

The Phencyclidine Model

Another theory, proposed over thirty years ago (Luby et al. 1962), is the phencyclidine (PCP) model of schizophrenia. This is based on the discovery of a PCP receptor: the N-methyl-D-aspartate (NMDA) receptor, in the brain. Advantages of the PCP model are that, unlike amphetamines, PCP induces negativism and apathy in addition to disorganized thinking. It has been proposed (Javitt and Zukin 1991) that a primary NMDA dysregulation may lead to frontal cortex *hypo*dopaminergic activity and mesolimbic *hyper*dopaminergic activity. These questions remain to be clarified by future research.

The Neurodevelopmental/Neurodegenerative Model

The neurodevelopmental model proposes that in schizophrenia there is a defect, possibly genetically determined or from an event (e.g., a viral infection) during intrauterine or early infantile development, which leads to abnormal development later in life, especially during the synaptic "pruning" during adolescence (Hoffman and McGlashan 1997). This model suggests that the pathophysiological processes of schizophrenia develop over time until they produce overt symptomatology. Treatment would then be directed, not just at the final psychotic symptoms, but toward correcting the abnormal development.

Some evidence suggests that schizophrenia is a neurodegenerative disorder leading to poorer functioning and progressively diminished cognitive functioning after each psychotic episode (Lieberman 1999) and (Tsuang, Stone, and Faraone 2000). A number of studies using MRI imaging to measure brain and ventricular volume have shown progressive enlargement of the lateral ventricles, and corresponding loss of brain tissue. Furthermore, these changes correlate with deterioration in condition, and precede the first psychotic episode. Other studies have shown elevation of both dopamine and glutamate. Taken together, this evidence suggests that *in some cases* schizophrenia is a progressive neurodegenerative disorder with progressive loss of neurons and cognitive function. Newer evidence (Harvey and Keefe 2001) suggests that the atypical antipsychotics may greatly reduce, or possibly eliminate, this deterioration. The evidence suggests that early intervention and treatment may lead to marked improvement in the overall course of the illness. On the other hand, older studies (Bleuler 1968) have suggested that almost half of schizophrenic patients substantially improved or recovered.

Whatever the precise neurophysiological pathogenesis of schizophrenia may turn out to be, several things are clear:

- There is not just one type of schizophrenia. Different people with schizophrenia may have very differing courses, e.g., good prognosis vs. poor prognosis schizophrenia. These have differing neuro-anatomical findings and, presumably, differing pathogeneses.

- The etiology of schizophrenia is complex. A simple theory like the dopamine model cannot fully explain the disorder. A full understanding will take into account factors at the intracellular, synaptic, and neural network levels.

- The genetic factors are complex. They are certainly polygenic, and seem to overlap with other disorders.

Treatment

We can consider the positive and negative symptoms listed earlier as target symptoms for antipsychotic medication treatment. Antipsychotic medications are now considered an important, if not essential, component in the treatment of schizophrenia. The focus of treatment is not only the resolution of psychotic symptoms but also relapse prevention. Unfortunately, schizophrenia is a disorder in which relapse is extremely common. It is estimated that following a psychotic episode and subsequent recovery, 70 percent of patients will relapse within a year if treated with either placebo or no medication at all. With continued antipsychotic treatment the relapse rate can drop to 30 to 40 percent. Studies have shown that low-dose and intermittent treatment are associated with poorer outcome, as measured by number of hospitalizations (Carpenter et al. 1990; Kane 1990).

In addition, there is now evidence to support the notion that being psychotic is damaging to the brain (Loebel et al. 1992). It is as if the more the dopamine circuits are used, the more the psychotic pathways become etched into the brain. A. Loebel and associates studied the relationship between duration of illness and clinical outcome in a group of untreated, first-episode schizophrenic patients. The study showed that patients who had been psychotic longer prior to treatment tended to have a poorer treatment response. This is consistent with the observation that prolonged hallucinogen or stimulant abuse is associated with incomplete clearing of mental status. It also suggests some type of kindling phenomena or toxic effect of psychosis and supports the need for prompt treatment with antipsychotic medications.

Besides antipsychotic medications, both typical and atypical, other medications may be useful in the treatment of schizophrenia. These include lithium, carbamazepine, benzodiazepines, reserpine, propranolol, antidepressants, and antiparkinsonian drugs. Most of these are used to treat associated features of schizophrenia and are used in addition to, not instead of, antipsychotic medication. Lithium may be helpful to reduce psychotic and affective symptoms. It was once thought that lithium would benefit only those patients who were actually bipolar or schizoaffective, but even some patients without apparent affective symptoms can benefit from lithium. Benzodiazepines (minor tranquilizers) may be helpful relieving some of the negative symptoms, in addition to anxiety and agitation. Antiparkinsonian medications are usually effective for the extrapyramidal side effects of antipsychotic medications. Antidepressants may be helpful when there are significant comorbid depressive symptoms. Propranolol (a beta blocker) is often helpful for akathisia (a common side effect of antipsychotic medications) and can sometimes reduce agitation.

The goal of medication treatment is to reduce symptoms so that the person can function better and benefit more from other forms of treatment, such as individual, group, or family therapy and social or vocational rehabilitation. An important part of such therapy involves educating the patient about prodromal symptoms and effects and side effects of medications. It is also important to address patients' beliefs that taking medications means they are sick (and conversely, that not taking medications means they aren't). Especially with paranoid patients, the belief that medications are a means of being controlled by others must be worked through.

Sometimes people with schizophrenia feel better not taking antipsychotic medications because they are able to entertain more grandiose notions about themselves and thereby lift their mood. Even more commonly, premature discontinuation occurs because patients are plagued by very unpleasant medication side effects. Appropriate education of patients regarding side effects and medical intervention (many side effects can be controlled with other medications) can improve the quality of life and greatly enhance compliance. It may be helpful to present medications as a tool for the person to use to help them control their illness, as a diabetic uses insulin.

Any of the psychotic disorders, regardless of etiology, may respond to antipsychotic medications. Where there is an underlying medical illness causing the psychosis, it is crucial to treat the underlying disorder. However, even in that case, antipsychotic medication may help reduce symptomatology. In the case of drug-induced and brief reactive psychosis, it may be appropriate not to use antipsychotic medications initially and instead to await the resolution of the psychotic symptoms using only supportive treatments. In the cases of the other psychoses, it is usually best to treat with antipsychotic medications for at least six months.

QUICK REFERENCE
When to Refer for Medication Treatment

Event	Symptoms
Psychosis due to a general medical conditions	Delusions Hallucinations
Depression with psychotic features	Delusions Hallucinations Catatonic features
Schizophrenia	Positive symptoms
Other psychotic disorders	Delusions Hallucinations
Drug-induced state (including intoxication)	Severe paranoid delusions Hallucinations
Severe personality disorder	Disorganized thinking Prominent paranoia Poor impulse control
Manic episode	Prominent delusions Severe agitation

11

Post-Traumatic Stress Disorder

Natural disasters, catastrophic illnesses, incest, rape, and assault are but a few common life experiences that can unleash a wave of intense emotional stress. Acute stress reactions or "traumatic neuroses" were first addressed in the clinical literature during World War I, as thousands of soldiers returned from the front suffering from severe anxiety, insomnia, and nightmares attributed to "shell shock." The understanding of acute stress reactions was furthered by the pioneering work of Eric Lindeman.

In 1942, during an after-football celebration at the Coconut Grove nightclub in Boston, a disastrous fire claimed the lives of 499 people and stunned the community. Lindeman and his colleagues quickly rushed in and provided free counseling services for a large group of people, including survivors of the fire and relatives of the victims. At the same time they provided crisis intervention, the mental health team was able to carefully study this group of people. Lindeman discovered tremendous regularity in the symptoms that people reported: vacillation between overwhelming painful emotions and periods of numbness, a strong need or impulse to repeat the tragic events in their minds over and over again, nightmares, and a host of psychosomatic symptoms.

In 1976, psychiatrist Mardi Horowitz published a book entitled *Stress Response Syndromes*. In this landmark publication, Dr. Horowitz carved out a very useful model for understanding what appears to be a common pattern of human emotional response to significant stress and shed new light on the various aspects of PTSD symptomatology. Horowitz developed this model based on his review of numerous field studies (including Lindeman's), a good deal of clinical work treating mentally healthy people who had experienced major stresses, and even some experimental studies. Horowitz concluded that across a broad spectrum of stressful events (deaths of loved ones, physical assault, natural disaster, even viewing upsetting movies), most people exhibit a typical pattern of response. The various phases of the stress response syndrome helped to explain the differing and often dramatically shifting symptoms seen in PTSD.

Let's take a look at the stress response syndrome (see figure 11-A). The full stress response syndrome is seen most clearly in situations where the stressful event is sudden and intense. Although a host of events may trigger this reaction. Each of the boxes in the figure represents a state of mind or emotion. The stress response reaction begins with awareness of some painful event.

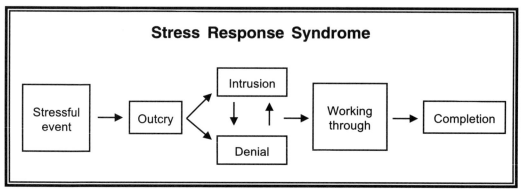

Figure 11-A

The first phase is Outcry. In a sense, a state of outcry is simultaneously an eruption of intense, unpleasant emotion (sadness, fear, and so on) *and* denial ("I can't believe it . . . it can't be true"). The person is in a state of shock and may be engulfed by very strong emotions. This phase of the reaction can last for a few minutes, a few hours, or a few days. Rather quickly, the person moves into phase two, which may be either a state of intrusion or a state of denial.

Intrusion occurs when a person experiences waves of intense emotion and a strong impulse to think about, imagine, remember, or mentally relive the stressful event. These experiences are deemed "intrusive" because generally the strong feelings and repetitive thoughts are not brought on willfully. During a state of intrusion, emotions feel very raw, and people feel extremely vulnerable, easily overwhelmed, and close to tears. They startle easily, don't sleep well, and often have nightmares. When intrusive experiences are especially intense, the individual may transiently lose reality testing and manifest psychotic-like symptoms, such as auditory or visual hallucinations.

Phase two includes a stage of Denial. Denial may occur directly following Outcry or may come on the heels of a period of intrusion. As noted earlier, denial is a state of emotional numbness; people often feel nothing. Other symptoms during the stages of denial include dissociative experiences (feelings of detachment, estrangement, impaired concentration, forgetfulness), avoidance of situations that may be associated with the trauma, and marked general social withdrawal.

Although *DSM-IV* includes post-traumatic stress disorder as an anxiety disorder, in some respects this may be a misnomer. Clearly, anxiety symptoms predominate in PTSD, but it is very common for PTSD patients to exhibit major depression, transient psychosis, and substance abuse as well. The symptoms of PTSD can be organized into six categories, as follows:

Symptoms of PTSD

- Persistent reexperiencing of the trauma

    Distressing, intrusive recollections of the event (images, affects, cognitions)

    Recurring nightmares regarding the trauma

    "Flashbacks" or déjà vu (sensations as if the traumatic episode were happening in the present)

- Increased arousal
    Sleep disturbances
    Startle response
    Irritability
    Hypervigilance

- Transient psychotic symptoms
    Derealization
    Illusions
    Hallucinations (visual or auditory)

- Avoidance
    Avoiding discussion of the traumatic events
    Avoiding activities or people and places that could provoke recollections of the trauma
    General social withdrawal

- Numbing
    Blunted affective responses
    Feelings of emptiness
    Feelings of estrangement or detachment
    Clouding of consciousness

- Associated features
    Major depression
    Panic attacks
    Substance abuse (often seen as an attempt to "self-medicate," to reduce anxiety or intrusive experiences)

Differential Diagnosis

PTSD is subdivided into the following clinical presentations: acute (duration of symptoms is less than three months) and chronic (duration of symptoms is more than three months). Also two versions of PTSD are seen clinically: acute onset (the traumatic event has just recently occurred) and delayed onset (the onset of severe symptoms occurs at least six months after the traumatic event). Beyond these

PTSD Facts

Lifetime prevalence rate may be as high as 14% (Zisook 1999). Each year a large number of people are exposed to overwhelmingly stressful events. Such encounters may be reflected by the following data. Each year it is estimated that:

- 1.5 to 2 million children are judged to be at risk for physical abuse by parents.

- 2.4 million children are *reported* to child protective services—49 percent for neglect, 27 percent for physical abuse, 16 percent for sexual abuse, and 8 percent for emotional abuse (Daro 1989).

- There are 1.9 million *reported* cases of violent crime—25,000 murders, 107,000 rapes. 24 percent of American households per year are victimized by crime.

- There are 36,000 infant deaths, 77,000 accidental deaths, 27,000 suicides, and many other sudden traumatic deaths.

- Countless thousands of people are exposed to natural disasters and traumatic medical crises, witness deaths or gruesome accidents, or are victims of some form of terrorism.

Most of those suffering from PTSD experience serious symptoms for many months or years, unless they are treated.

distinctions, other variables are extremely important to consider both in terms of diagnosis and treatment.

Lenore Terr (1991) aptly notes that *generally* single-blow traumas have a less devastating effect on psychologic functioning than recurring traumas. In the latter case are situations such as repeated child abuse and molestation, systematic terrorizing, and recurring spousal abuse. The age at which trauma occurs also plays a crucial role in our understanding of psychological sequelae. Very early, severe, recurring child abuse often not only results in primary symptoms of PTSD but may also interfere significantly with fundamental personality development. The outcome may be coexisting PTSD and borderline or other severe personality disorder.

Since PTSD can have a variety of symptomatic presentations (owing to the above-mentioned variables and whether the person is in the intrusion or denial stage of the stress response syndrome), it is wise first to formulate the overall diagnosis and then delineate particular target symptoms (see symptom list, above). In all forms of PTSD, ultimately the psychiatric symptoms can be traced to the patient's exposure to extremely overwhelming psychosocial stressors. And in almost all cases, a common element is the person's experience of extraordinary helplessness or powerlessness in the face of such stressors.

Etiology

Volumes have been written about the psychological origins and consequences of severe trauma, and it is beyond the scope of this book to attempt a review. Suffice it to say that the majority of PTSD symptoms can be understood as arising largely from psychogenic sources. However, some authors have proposed interesting theories regarding biological factors in PTSD, which we will review here. The primary work in this area has been done by Bessel A. van der Kolk (1987) and Charles Nemeroff (1997). In this chapter we will look at five models in which biology potentially can be altered by psychological stress.

Attachment and the repetition compulsion

PTSD due to early, severe child abuse or neglect may leave not only emotional scars; neurobiology may be altered. Severe stress during childhood and infancy in both humans and animals can result in an increased need for attachment and protection. Studies with birds, dogs, and monkeys show that infants will strongly seek out attachments even with abusive parents, especially under stress. "Thus attachment remains strong, even when the imprinted object no longer provides effective protection and nurturance" (van der Kolk 1987). This behavioral pattern seen so strongly in other species, may provide some understanding of the common human tendency for abused individuals to cling to and gravitate toward abusive parents and spouses. Since it is seen across diverse species, this may reflect an underlying neurobiologically mediated reaction pattern.

The repetitive involvement in apparently aversive or abusive relationships (sometimes called the repetition compulsion) may be related to hypersensitivity of the separation-stress center in the brain (see the discussion in chapter 8), which has been shown to respond favorably to treatment with antidepressants, especially MAO inhibitors and SSRIs.

Attachment and impaired affect modulation

When the traumatic experience has occurred early in life, another consequence, conversely, may be inadequate attachment and bonding. This may be especially true if the nature of the trauma was profound neglect. One common consequence of inadequate or insecure attachment is poor affective regulation. Studies with monkeys have revealed that isolated, neglected infants often develop persistent aggressive and self-destructive behaviors (such as biting) and, in general, impaired abilities for emotional regulation. Clearly many PTSD patients also show chronic problems with emotional control and at times manifest symptoms of self-mutilation (Harlow and Harlow 1971; Sackett 1965). This may account for both chronic emotional arousal and an increased vulnerability to later traumatic life events (van der Kolk 1987).

Following early trauma, permanent alterations in the nervous system have also been documented, including persistent elevations in the neuropeptide CRF and atrophy of the hippocampus (Post and Weiss 1997; Sapolsky 1996; Nemeroff 1997). Also, see chapter 12.

Hyperarousal

When animals are exposed to inescapable shock, they exhibit consistent behavioral reactions—initially hypervigilance or arousal and ultimately a profound state of withdrawal and "depression." In addition, such animals eventually show a significant depletion of norepinephrine, likely accompanied by changes in NE receptor sensitivity in parts of the brain. Alterations of receptor sensitivity may leave the animals in a state of chronic hyperarousal. In essence, their nervous systems may be permanently altered such that traumatized animals and people alike are relatively unable to dampen or inhibit excessive emotional arousal. Antidepressants that affect norepinephrine appear to alter receptor sensitivity, both in humans and animals. Serotonergic antidepressants may also indirectly inhibit hypersensitive NE cells (Nagy et al. 1993), and thus can play a role in treating hyperarousal in PTSD patients.

Intrusive symptoms

L. M. Nagy et al. (1993) report that PTSD patients treated with high doses of fluoxetine (a serotonergic antidepressant) showed a significant reduction in flashbacks and other intrusive symptoms. Interestingly, as intrusive experiences decreased so did symptoms of avoidance and numbing. (Again, the reductions were at levels that were statistically significant.) Furthermore, van der Kolk (1987) has hypothesized that flashback experiences may be traced (neurobiologically) to "stress-induced reaction of LC—hippocampus/amygdala pathways." As we saw in chapter 8, the locus coeruleus is mediated by norepinephrine, and selective serotonin antidepressants also clearly have an inhibitory effect on LC activation.

Kindling

Finally, it has been hypothesized that severely traumatic experiences may result in a sort of kindling effect, in which repeated episodes of trauma literally change brain functioning and even brain morphology. Severe trauma may *progressively* increase the likelihood that subsequent stresses are responded to with even more intense affective symptoms (see chapter 2). Animal models have suggested a kindling effect following emotional trauma (for instance, Kraemer et al. 1984), although at present this theory remains mostly speculative. There are clinical and anecdotal reports that some PTSD patients benefit from treatment with lithium carbonate, clonazepam, and carbamazepine, all of which have been shown to inhibit kindling effects.

Summary

Animal models strongly support the notion that severely traumatic experiences alter brain functioning and may more or less permanently change an organism's biologic capacity for response to stressful stimuli. It is likely that this occurs for human beings as well, although definitive conclusions await more sophisticated human studies. Thus, although PTSD can be seen as *induced by* environmental-psychologic

---

PTSD Symptoms That Respond to Medication

Target Symptoms	Class of Medication
Intrusive experiences "flashbacks"[a] and avoidance and numbing[b]	SSRI antidepressants; buspirone augmentation of SSRI
Hyperarousal[c]	Antidepressants, benzodiazepines such as clonazepam, anticonvulsants
Transient psychosis, marked derealization[d]	Low dose antipsychotics
Depression[a]	Antidepressants
Panic attacks	Antidepressants, MAO inhibitors, high-potency benzodiazepines

a Nagy et al. (1993); Davidson et al. (1991); Hidalgo and Davidson (2000); Connor et al. (1999); Hidalgo et al. (1999); Stein et al. (2000); van der Kolk et al. (1994); Brady et al. (2000); Davidson et al. (1990); Hammer et al. (1997); Wells et al. (1991)

b As intrusive symptoms are reduced and affective control improves, often numbing and avoidance diminish.

c van der Kolk (1987); Forster et al. (1995); Berigan and Holzgang (1995); Fesler (1991)

d Kapfhammer and Hippius (1998); Hori (1998); Joseph (1997); Krashin and Oates (1999)

Figure 11-B

stressors, the *impact* is on both psyche and soma. The resulting disorder is best understood as a psychological and neurobiological problem.

Treatment

The treatment of choice for PTSD is psychotherapy (most effective is exposure based cognitive therapy). It is essential that these patients gradually come to face the painful memories of traumatic experiences—come to terms with the realities of their lives. The process of "working through" is often quite prolonged and fraught with periodic emotional upheaval. Typically PTSD patients must navigate through repeated periods of intrusion and denial on their way toward psychological resolution and symptomatic improvement. During this treatment, it is crucial that affective reexperiencing of painful events be "dosed" (gradual, paced exposure) so as to not overwhelm or retraumatize the patient. Medications can be used in treating certain aspects of PTSD, but are not the primary treatment. In all cases, psychotropic medications should target particular, serious symptoms *as they arise*. Figure 11-B summarizes common target symptoms and provides treatment implications drawn from the limited studies and clinical experience available.

Central to appropriate pharmacological treatment of PTSD is the restoration of some sense of control over turbulent emotions. When medications are appropriately used, in the context of a solid and safe patient-therapist relationship, the improved emotional control can serve as a sort of antidote for what is otherwise a feeling of powerlessness. Ultimately, the ability to face painful realities with a degree of mastery is at the heart of recovery from PTSD.

At times, excessively high doses of benzodiazepines or antipsychotics have been used (often inappropriately) in desperate attempts to snuff out eruptions of painful affect. This approach can backfire, as it results in a chemically induced state of "dissociation." The patient may then be unable to access inner emotions or memories, and the process of working through comes to a halt. Also, overly aggressive medication treatment can be experienced by the patient as an assault in its own right—another case of being controlled by a powerful other. In cases of extremely severe intrusive symptoms or psychosis, aggressive pharmacotherapy may be necessary, but it should be seen only as a short-term solution that continues only until the patient has regained a measure of stability. At that time the dosage of benzodiazepines or antipsychotics should be reduced.

When the PTSD patient develops a full-blown clinical depression or a severe, entrenched panic disorder, antidepressants can be quite helpful. When PTSD patients are treated with antidepressants, the course of treatment almost invariably must be lengthy (as in treating all panic disorders and major depression)—at least nine to twelve months (see chapters 6 and 15).

QUICK REFERENCE
When to Refer for Medication Treatment

Psychotherapy is the treatment of choice for most cases of PTSD. Psychotropic medications can be used when the patient presents with any of the following:

- Persistent ego weakness and an inability to tolerate exploratory psychotherapy or exposure-based treatment.

- Low level of cognitive functioning.

- When the following target symptoms become too intense and overwhelming or markedly interfere with functioning in daily life, *short-term* medication treatment is indicated:

  Intrusive experiences, flashbacks

  Transient psychosis

  Marked derealization

  Avoidance and numbing

- When these target symptoms become too intense and overwhelming or markedly interfere with functioning in daily life, *longer-term* medication treatment is indicated:

  Major depression

  Panic disorder

  Persistent psychotic symptoms

12

Borderline Personality Disorders

The concept of borderline disorders has slowly emerged from Hoch's early description of pseudoneurotic schizophrenia and Grinker's landmark study in 1968. Nosological and theoretical controversy has surrounded this very common diagnostic group. It has often been referred to as a "wastebasket" diagnosis—a depository for those clients who are severely impaired, hard to diagnose, or especially difficult to treat. All therapists encounter people with severe levels of character pathology. These folks are said to exhibit a very "loud" form of psychopathology; they suffer a lot and cause great suffering in others. According to Allan Frances (1989) borderline patients often seek out psychotherapy and psychotropic medication treatment—and often overdose on both!

Differential Diagnosis

Borderline disorders have been viewed both from a behavioral-symptomatic perspective (such as that of *DSM-IV*) and a theoretical perspective (for example, borderline personality organization à la Kernberg and others). As Grinker and many subsequent researchers and clinicians agree, borderline patients are not all alike; they present in many different sizes and shapes. You can see borderline characteristics in the context of a number of different personality styles: schizoid-detached, obsessional, paranoid, narcissistic, and histrionic. However, all varieties share a few common characteristics as outlined in the box on the next page.

Beyond these commonalties are a considerable variety of symptomatic presentations. The particular behaviors observed are colored by the patient's style (obsessional, histrionic, and so on), the nature of their current social support network, and the presence or absence of comorbid Axis I disorders (see Preston 1997).

The critical defining feature that can help the clinician be more certain of a borderline diagnosis is the history. As noted in chapter 5, many individuals may transiently experience borderline characteristics while in the throes of a major Axis I disorder (for example, a depression), only to recompensate when the Axis I problem resolves. A more definitive diagnosis of borderline disorder emerges when there is a well-documented history of ego impairment dating back to adolescence or early adulthood—"stable instability."

Borderline Personality Disorders Facts

- The incidence of severe personality disorders in the general population is difficult to determine. However, in some community mental health clinics, up to 25 percent of clients present with an Axis II borderline personality disorder.

- Among borderline patients, the lifetime mortality rate by suicide may be as high as 10 percent.

- Recent longitudinal studies suggest that two-thirds of borderline patients experience a significant reduction in emotional instability and impulsivity after age 45. Thus appropriate crisis management and supportive medication treatment can play an important role in sustaining functioning and survival until patients reach their fourth decade.

Core Symptoms of Borderline Personality Disorders

- Generalized ego impairment
- Chronic emotional instability
- Chaotic interpersonal relations
- Feelings of emptiness
- Impaired sense of self
- Low frustration tolerance
- Impulsivity
- Primitive defenses, such as splitting, acting out
- Irritability and anger-control problems

DSM-IV focuses largely on one version of borderline disorder (a type of histrionic-dependent borderline). Speaking more broadly in this book, we will refer to borderline disorders as including a host of personality "styles" that share the common core features listed above. In addition, it is helpful to delineate three subgroups of borderlines. These subgroups have been derived both by research methods (cluster and factor analysis) and by a method that psychopharmacologist Donald Klein calls "pharmacological behavioral dissection." This latter approach looks at how different groups of patients respond to psychotropic medications; based on their response patterns, subtypes can be identified.

Hysteroid-dysphoric

These borderline clients present with a significant degree of emotional lability and are exquisitely sensitive to interpersonal rejection, loss, and abandonment. As a consequence, they often cannot tolerate being alone and may engage in desperate attempts to maintain attachments, including clinging behavior and manipulative suicidal threats or gestures. These patients are at great risk for recurring depression.

Schizotypal

These borderline patients chronically display odd thinking—ideas of reference, magical thinking, vagueness, very idiosyncratic beliefs—and periodically experience marked episodes of depersonalization or derealization and transient psychoses. Such people likely represent a truer sort of borderline schizophrenia.

Angry-impulsive

These people are characterized by their pervasively hostile-aggressive way of interacting with others. They have very low frustration tolerance and can be quite volatile. As a result, their interpersonal relations are replete either with ongoing intense friction or multiple rejections.

In addition to these subtypes, it is important to keep in mind that many, if not most, borderline personalities have comorbid Axis I disorders—especially common are major depression and substance abuse. These coexisting disorders always complicate the picture and must be dealt with in any approach to treatment. In particular, longitudinal studies following the course and outcome of borderline personality disorders over the life span suggest very clearly that those patients who continue to do poorly are those who continue to abuse alcohol and other substances. Thus treatment of chemical dependency problems *must* be addressed.

Etiology

Most writings addressing the etiology of borderline disorders focus on psychological factors—especially traumatic events and serious developmental failures in the early family of origin (Mahler, Kernberg, Kohut, Masterson, and so on). Biological theories are, at this time, only speculative. They include the following:

- In-born or constitutional factors in the CNS may leave certain children with defects in their ability to psychologically "metabolize" early interpersonal experiences adequately. Thus, even if raised in a "good enough" home, some kids simply may not acquire adequate emotional nurturance and sustainment from otherwise good parents.

- In-born or constitutional factors may lead to the development of a difficult temperamental style, such as an irritable, restless infant. Some children cry excessively, seem extremely sensitive to mild stressors, or are unable to be soothed. There certainly are times when such children evoke ongoing negative reactions in otherwise good parents (frustration, withdrawal of affection, and so on). Thus the child is both biologically at risk (less capable of handling stress, more sensitive) and prone toward behaving in ways that may provoke less-than-optimal parental interactions or bonding. The secondary parental-child friction likely contributes to ongoing problems with psychological growth.

- Early, severely traumatic experiences (especially neglect) *may* alter brain development, resulting in chronic neurotransmitter abnormalities (see chapter 11), and structural changes in the nervous system.

In the theories above, the particular biological-based abnormalities or dysfunctions may become manifest in various symptom clusters, as noted earlier: hysteroid-dysphoria, schizotypal, and angry-impulsive. It may be hypothesized that these subtypes of borderline disorders have neurochemical abnormalities, as outlined in figure 12-A. It must be emphasized, however, that at present such theories are quite speculative and not yet verified by well-controlled studies. Many studies attempting to identify biological markers in borderline disorders have shown inconclusive results. These results are largely due to designs in which diagnostic subtypes are collapsed into an overly heterogeneous group of patients in which there is no control for comorbid Axis I disorders.

Hypothesized Neurochemical Dysfunctions of Borderline Disorder Subtypes		
Subtype	**Neurotransmitter**	**Location**
Hysteroid-dysphoria	NE	Locus coeruleus
Schizotypal	DA	Mesolimbic, frontal cortex, and reticular formation
Angry-impulsive	5-HT	Amygdala

Figure 12-A

Treatment

No medication treatment can directly treat personality disorders, per se. Rather, psychotropic medications are used to ameliorate certain target symptoms. From results of the limited studies available, the medications of choice appear to be those listed in the Quick Reference (page 143). The reduction in target symptoms can contribute significantly to improved coping ability and reduced levels of emotional despair. It is clear that no magic pill can cure deep characterological wounds, but targeted medication treatment of borderline patients can be an important adjunct to psychotherapy and crisis management.

Cautions

Three cautions are important to note:

- Treatment with antianxiety medications (benzodiazepines) is risky with borderline patients. These patients are certainly at risk for tranquilizer abuse. In addition, clinical experience, as well as research, shows that benzodiazepines can contribute to emotional dyscontrol and increased suicidality with borderline patients (Cowdry and Gardner 1988; Hori 1998).

- Since many borderline patients are at risk for transient psychosis, the antidepressant bupropion (a dopamine agonist) should be used with caution. This drug, which is an effective antidepressant, may precipitate psychosis in prepsychotic individuals.

- Because this group as a whole engages in frequent suicidal acting out, it is advisable to treat borderline patients with medications that have been found to have a low degree of toxicity when taken in overdose. These include antipsychotics and the following antidepressants: fluoxetine, paroxetine, sertraline, citalopram, bupropion (note above caution), trazodone, and nefazodone. Most other antidepressants are quite toxic when taken in overdose.

QUICK REFERENCE
Medications for Treating Borderline Subtypes

Borderline Subtype	Class of Medication
Hysteroid-dysphoria[a]	MAO inhibitors, carbamazepine (anticonvulsant)
Schizotypal[b]	Low doses of antipsychotics
Angry-impulsive[c]	SSRI antidepressants; lithium
Comorbid major depression	Antidepressants
Comorbid panic disorder	Antidepressants

a Cowdry and Gardner (1988); Gardner and Cowdry (1986); Liebowitz and Klein (1981)

b Soloff et al. (1986); Francis and Soloff (1988); Goldberg et al. (1986); Gitlin (1993); Schulz et al. (1999); Coccaro (1998); Hori (1998)

c Norden (1989); Cornelius et al. (1991); Salzman et al. (1995); Markovitz et al. (1991); Hori (1998); Stein et al. (2000); Moleman et al. (1999); Coccaro (1998)

d General reviews: Kapfhammer and Hippius (1998); Hori (1998); Joseph (1997); Krashin and Oates (1999); Turner (1999); Turnbull (1998)

13

Substance-Related Disorders

Substance abuse and related disorders represent a major problem area facing the clinician. Despite the "war on drugs" they continue to be a widespread problem: At least 5 percent of Americans are alcoholic, and stimulant abuse is a serious problem among teenagers and young adults. Any solution to these problems will undoubtedly involve social and political factors in addition to clinical programs. This chapter focuses on the differing types of clinical syndromes related to each commonly abused substance and medications that may be useful as an adjunct to treatment.

Often the clinician will be confronted with a client who has substance-use problems in addition to a psychiatric disorder (comorbidity or dual diagnosis) or whose psychiatric disorder may be a direct result of substance use. In either case, treatment of the substance disorder will be crucial to the treatment of the psychiatric disorder. In the past, substance use was often seen as a form of self-medication—the person was using the drug to "treat" an emotional disorder, and psychotherapy was attempted in an effort to cure the person of the need for the substance—usually to no avail. In recent years, the evidence has shown that achieving abstinence is frequently a precondition for effectively dealing with psychological issues. In fact, the emotional problems may be significantly diminished by the person's achieving abstinence. For example, most (but not all) alcohol-related depression resolves within one to two weeks of abstinence. The interaction between substance-related disorders and other psychiatric disorders (like that between Axis I and Axis II disorders) is a complex one. We try here to clarify some of the more well-defined relationships.

Differential Diagnosis

Substance-related disorders are divided in *DSM-IV* into dependence, abuse, intoxication, and withdrawal. In addition, each substance may have related disorders phenomenologically similar to other disorders: delirium, dementia, amnestic, psychotic, mood, anxiety, sex, and sleep disorders.

Substance-Abuse Facts

- Alcoholism affects 5 to 10 percent of the adult population.

- Alcoholism plays a major role in the following causes of death: accidents, homicide, suicide, and alcoholic cirrhosis.

- One million Americans are reported to be addicted to cocaine, and over five million use cocaine regularly.

- Billions of dollars are spent annually on the treatment and prosecution of drug users.

- 30 to 50 percent of those in mental health treatment have a significant substance-abuse disorder.

Substance dependence is defined in *DSM-IV* as a pattern of substance use leading to significant impairment or distress, demonstrated by at least three of the following:

- Tolerance—diminished effect from the same amount of the substance, often leading to use of increased amounts to achieve the same effect

- Withdrawal—onset of withdrawal syndrome if the substance is discontinued, often leading to continued use to avoid withdrawal symptoms

- Substance is taken more than intended

- Persistent use despite efforts to cut down

- Great deal of effort is expended to obtain or continue use of the substance, or recover from its effects

- Other important activities are reduced in order to continue substance use

- Continued substance use despite knowledge that it is harmful

The *DSM-IV* defines *substance abuse* as a pattern of substance use leading to significant impairment or distress, demonstrated by at least one of the following:

- Impairment of home, work, or school performance as a result of substance use

- Hazardous behavior resulting from substance use

- Legal problems resulting from substance use

- Continued substance use despite significant resultant problems

Intoxication refers to an acutely altered mental state due to ingestion of (or exposure to) a substance that is not caused by a medical condition or other mental disorder.

Withdrawal refers to an altered state produced by cessation or reduction of use of a substance which causes significant impairment in functioning in important areas and is not caused by a medical condition or other mental disorder. The disorder may be "persisting"—may continue even though substance use has stopped and the withdrawal syndrome has been resolved.

Figures 13-A and 13-B list substances and the clinical syndromes they can produce. Not all substances can cause every syndrome. For example, phencyclidine (PCP) can produce a very severe psychosis during intoxication but has no withdrawal syndrome; whereas sedative-hypnotics (such as benzodiazepines) can produce all of the substance diagnoses, as can alcohol. In the remainder of this chapter we review several of the major classes of substances associated with clinical disorders.

Major Substance Diagnoses

Substance	Dependence	Abuse	Intoxication	Withdrawal	Persisting
Alcohol	X	X	X	X	X
Hallucinogens	X	X	X		X
Opioids	X	X	X	X	
Phencyclidine	X	X	X		
Sedative-hypnotics	X	X	X	X	X
Stimulants	X	X	X	X	

Figure 13-A

Substance-Induced Disorders That Mimic Other Disorders

Substance	Delirium	Dementia	Amnestic	Psychotic	Mood	Anxiety
Alcohol	X	X	X	X	X	X
Hallucinogens	X			X	X	X
Opioids	X			X	X	
Phencyclidine	X			X	X	X
Sedative-hypnotics	X	X	X	X	X	X
Stimulants	X			X	X	X

Figure 13-B

Alcohol

Alcohol (ethanol) is a water-soluble substance that is rapidly absorbed and readily crosses the blood-brain barrier. It is a CNS depressant and is metabolized by the liver. It is also a gastric irritant and is toxic to liver cells and neurons. Alcohol is probably the most-studied substance of abuse (and the most abused substance). It is associated with dependence, abuse, withdrawal, intoxication, delirium, dementia, amnesia, delusions, hallucinations, mood disorder, anxiety disorder, sexual dysfunction, and sleep disorder.

There is much evidence demonstrating that alcoholism is familial, but the exact biological mechanism remains unclear. Several studies have tried to find a biological marker for alcoholism. Studies have shown a differential sensitivity to alcohol in alcoholics versus nonalcoholics (Pollock 1992). M. A. Schuckit, E. Gold, and C. Risch (1987) have shown that sons of alcoholics had significantly lower prolactin levels in response to ethanol challenge. Smith et al. (1992) showed that alcoholics were more likely to show *Taq* 1 A1 restriction fragment length polymorphism of the D2 dopamine receptor gene (and dopamine controls prolactin release). The significance of these findings, however, remains speculative, and the search continues for the biological basis of alcoholism.

Psychiatric symptoms are very common in alcohol intoxication and withdrawal, but studies by Schuckit show that most of these symptoms improve greatly within one to four weeks of abstinence and are likely to abate over several months (Brown and Schuckit 1988; Schuckit, Irwin, and Brown 1990). The three diagnoses associated with increased risk of alcoholism are schizophrenia, mania, and antisocial personality disorder. As a depressant, alcohol tends to produce depressive symptoms during intoxication and anxiety symptoms during withdrawal and abstinence. These syndromes often mimic major depression or an anxiety disorder, but they will usually resolve within two weeks of abstinence and do not require prolonged treatment.

Medications can play an important role in the treatment of alcohol-related disorders. Figure 12-C lists medications that can be used in the treatment of alcohol-related disorders. Most of those medications are covered in part three of this book. The exception is disulfiram (Antabuse), a medication used to assist in the maintenance of abstinence. Disulfiram causes an accumulation of acetaldehyde if a person drinks alcohol while taking it, which leads to an unpleasant and potentially dangerous reaction involving flushing, throbbing headache, nausea, and vomiting. Only certain people are appropriate for disulfiram treatment. Some are able to remain abstinent without it; some will drink in spite of it. In between are those who will be able to reinforce their desire for abstinence by taking disulfiram 250 to 500 mg once daily. Naltrexone, an opiate antagonist, has also shown some promise in helping maintain abstinence by reducing craving for alcohol (Bender 1993).

Alcohol-Related Disorders and Medications for Treating Them

Disorder	Medication
Intoxication	Thiamine, folate, multivitamins
Withdrawal	Benzodiazepines
Abstinence maintenance	Antabuse, naltrexone,[a] lithium,[a] SSRIs[a]
Delirium	Benzodiazepines
Dementia	—
Amnesia	Thiamine
Delusional disorder	Benzodiazepines, antipsychotics
Hallucinosis	Benzodiazepines, antipsychotics
Mood disorder	Antidepressants
Anxiety disorder	Benzodiazepines, buspirone

a Likely, but not proven

Figure 12-C

Stimulants

Amphetamines ("crank," "speed," "bennies" "ecstacy [XTC]") and cocaine ("crack," "freebase") have become common substances of abuse. They are CNS stimulants that act on the dopaminergic system. Research suggests that a dopamine-medicated endogenous reward system in the limbic system is activated by amphetamines and cocaine. Amphetamines produce increased release of dopamine and norepinephrine along with their attendant peptides, and decreased reuptake. This leads to increased dopaminergic and noradrenergic activity and symptoms of euphoria, paranoia, and hyperexcitability. The half-life of dextroamphetamine is about ten hours. Cocaine produces similar pharmacologic effects but has a shorter duration of action and in some forms, especially crack cocaine, produces more intense effects, thus making it more addictive.

To understand the pharmacologic treatment of stimulant dependency it is helpful to look at the different phases of use on a neuronal level (see figure 13-D). During acute intoxication there is increased release of catecholamines (dopamine and norepinephrine) and enkephalins, along with decreased reuptake, leading to increased catecholamine activity. In the acute withdrawal state there is a reduction of available neurotransmitters (due to depletion and reduced reuptake). This leaves a state of reduced catecholamine activity and feelings of craving, depression, and restlessness. With chronic use, there is development of tolerance, further reduced availability of neurotransmitter, and an increased number of receptors (supersensitivity) leading to lower occupancy and feelings of craving, depression, and anhedonia.

Pharmacological treatment of stimulant use is different for each phase of use. During acute intoxication, medications can be used to block the effects of dopamine and norepinephrine. During withdrawal, medications are used to reduce craving (and hopefully subsequent use). The medications used to treat amphetamine use (see figure 13-E) generally potentiate the effects of norepinephrine, dopamine, or both. Most of those medications are discussed in part three of this book. Bromocriptine is a D2 dopamine agonist. Amantadine increases dopamine activity. L-dopa is a dopamine precursor that leads to increased dopamine synthesis. All these medications

Figure 13-D

Medications Used to Treat Phases of Stimulant Use

State	Medications
Intoxication	Beta blockers
	Clonidine
	Benzodiazepines
	Antipsychotics
Withdrawal	Desipramine
	Other antidepressants
	Bromocriptine
	Amantadine
	Lithium
	L-dopa
	Carbamazepine

Figure 13-E

increase dopamine activity, thereby reducing the feelings of craving produced by dopamine depletion. It should be noted, however, that dopaminergic medications can produce psychotic symptoms, so the dose must be monitored closely. The effectiveness of these medications continues to be under investigation. They are not a panacea, but are often helpful in reducing symptoms of withdrawal and craving.

Opiates

Heroin was first synthesized from morphine over a century ago. Since then, it has become one of the most abused substances. Research into why it produces such powerful effects has led to the discovery of specific opiate receptors and endogenous opioids (enkephalins and endorphins). These peptides appear to be neurotransmitters involved with the sensation of pain and pleasure. A number of opiates and synthetic opioids are available and can lead to dependency, including morphine, heroin, propoxyphene (Darvon), methadone, meperidine (Demerol), pentazocine (Talwin), hydromorphone (Dilaudid), oxycodone (Percodan Oxycontiu), and hydrocodone (Vicodin, Damason-P), and codeine.

Different medications are used to treat different phases of opiate use (see figure 13-F). Acute opiate (opioid) intoxication leads to sedation, pupillary constriction, and respiratory depression and can be fatal. There are specific opiate antagonists that block the opiate receptors and rapidly reverse these effects: naloxone and naltrexone. Opiate withdrawal is characterized by anxiety, agitation, sweating, gastrointestinal upset, tremulousness, and running nose. It is treated by using an opiate such as propoxyphene (Darvon), methadone, or clonidine, or a combination of these drugs.

There are two strategies for treating dependence or abuse. One is to use methadone, a long-acting synthetic opiate that is well tolerated and reduces craving for other opiates such as heroin. Methadone is used for maintenance treatment because, with its long half-life, it produces less of a "high" and is less prone to abuse. It is

Medications Used to Treat Phases of Opiate Use	
State	**Medication**
Acute intoxication	Naloxone (injectable) Naltrexone (oral)
Acute withdrawal	Opiates, especially methadone and propoxyphene Clonidine Benzodiazepines
Maintaining abstinence	Methadone Naloxone, naltrexone, or Bupreuorphine LAAM

Figure 13-F

now available only in certain federally approved treatment sites. The other is to have the client take an opiate antagonist (naloxone or naltrexone) so that the effect of the opiate will be blocked if it is used.

Hallucinogens

Various substances can produce transient psychotic states, often accompanied by visual, auditory, or olfactory hallucinations. These include LSD (lysergic acid diethylamide), mescaline, psilocybin, and PCP. These drugs are not associated with dependence or withdrawal, but they can produce a florid psychosis during acute intoxication. This effect can usually be allowed to run its course (usually twelve to twenty-four hours), but sometimes medications (such as antianxiety or antipsychotic) need to be used to decrease agitation and stabilize blood pressure.

Sometimes patients will report a reexperiencing or "flashback" of hallucinations they had during a previous ingestion of hallucinogen. These reactions likewise usually do not require treatment with medication but, when severe, may benefit from antianxiety or antipsychotic medication. Severe overdoses of PCP can lead to convulsions and may require emergency medical treatment.

Other Drugs

Other substances of abuse—including caffeine, cannabis, inhalants, and nicotine—are not covered here since they are less important clinically. Caffeine intoxication can lead to anxiety or confusion. Inhalants can cause an organic psychosis and are very neurotoxic—leading to permanent neurological deficit. Nicotine dependence can be treated with a nicotine gum or patch or buproprion (Zyban) (in conjunction with cognitive-behavioral treatment). Sedative abuse and dependence is discussed in chapter 17, on antianxiety medications.

QUICK REFERENCE
Treatment of Substance-Related Disorders

	Symptoms	Treatment
Alcohol		
Intoxication	Confusion, slurred speech, ataxia, delirium	Supportive; thiamine, vitamins
Withdrawal	Anxiety, agitation, possible hallucinations, possible convulsions	Benzodiazepines
Stimulants		
Intoxication	Anxiety, agitation	Supportive; benzodiazepines, beta blockers, clonidine
	Paranoid psychosis	Antipsychotics
Withdrawal	Anergia, irritabililty	Supportive; amantadine, bromocriptine
	Depressed mood	Cyclic antidepressants
Opiates		
Intoxication	Sedation, respiratory depression	Naloxone, naltrexone
Withdrawal	Anxiety, agitation, sweating, tremors	Clonidine, benzodiazepines, opiates (methadone or propoxyphene)
Hallucinogens		
Intoxication	Agitation, prominent hallucinations	Benzodiazepines, antipsychotics
Withdrawal	No withdrawal syndrome	

14

Other Miscellaneous Disorders

There are several types of disorders that, although they are encountered less often in clinical practice, we have chosen to discuss in this chapter. Compared to disorders discussed in earlier chapters, their biological basis is less well understood at this time, and the role of medications may be less clear. These disorders are: Tourette's syndrome, eating disorders (anorexia and bulimia nervosa), attention deficit disorder (ADD), self-mutilation, sleep disorders, obesity, aggression, and chronic pain.

Tourette's Syndrome

Tourette's (or Gilles de la Tourette) syndrome is characterized by motor and vocal tics—sudden involuntary movements or vocalizations. It is most known for coprolalia (sudden yelling of obscenities), but this is only seen in 25 to 30 percent of cases. Motor tics typically involve the head and neck. Vocal tics may be guttural sounds, repeated coughing, or words. Tourette's is now generally considered a neurological disorder, although symptoms may be exacerbated by anxiety or tension. It appears to involve dysfunction of dopaminergic pathways and is treated with dopamine D2 blockers—haloperidol or pimozide, in low to moderate doses. Persons with Tourette's have a higher incidence of obsessive-compulsive disorder (OCD), attention deficit disorder (ADD), and other learning disorders (Stern et al. 2000). This is probably because Tourette's can involve multiple areas of the brain, some of which are also associated with OCD and ADD. Theories regarding the etiology of Tourette's include genetic (Robertson and Stern 1997) and autoimmune mechanisms related to strep infection (Bowes 2001).

Eating Disorders

Eating disorders are divided into two main types in DSM-IV: anorexia nervosa and bulimia nervosa. Anorexia nervosa involves significant weight loss and maintenance of a very low body weight, by restriction of intake, purging, or both, often in combination with excessive exercising.

The *DSM-IV* diagnostic criteria are:

- Body weight less than 85 percent of that expected

- Fear of gaining weight

- Distorted perception of one's weight (thinking one is fat when actually very thin)

- Missing at least three consecutive menstrual cycles (where applicable)

Bulimia nervosa involves repeated episodes of binging and purging: eating large amounts of food (everything in the refrigerator) and then purging through self-induced vomiting or use of laxatives or diuretics. In addition (*DSM-IV*):

- Both the binge eating and compensatory behaviors occur, on average, at least twice a week for three months.

- Self-esteem is overly influenced by weight.

- Disturbance does not occur only during periods of anorexia nervosa.

Much research has investigated personality characteristics, psychological issues, family dynamics, and the biological basis of anorexia and bulimia. Anorexia usually requires a multimodal, if not a multidisciplinary, treatment approach. The severe nutritional deficiency causes a multitude of problems that must be addressed medically and which make response to medication treatment alone poor. Indeed, no medication has shown significant consistent benefit in the treatment of anorexia. One theory holds that patients with anorexia become addicted to starvation; it is known that endorphins are released during prolonged fasting. This theory holds that anorectics have a biological vulnerability to becoming addicted to fasting. Studies have shown some benefit of naltrexone (an opiate antagonist) in the treatment of anorexia—the explanation being that it blocks the "high" of fasting and thereby removes the incentive (Luby, Marrazzi, and Kinzie 1987). Other medications *sometimes* helpful include antidepressants, antipsychotics, cyproheptadine, and lithium (see figure 14-A). These drugs can be especially useful when there are coexisting features, for instance antidepressants when depressive features are present.

Bulimia, in contrast, often benefits from treatment with antidepressants (40 to 70 percent respond) and is considered by some to be a depressive variant. All types of antidepressants have proven useful, although it should be remembered that bupropion (Wellbutrin) is contraindicated in eating disorders because of increased incidence of convulsions. Selective serotonin reuptake inhibitors (SSRIs) have been quite effective and, because of their low side effect profile, are often tried first.

Attention Deficit Disorder

Attention deficit disorder first manifests itself in childhood, usually during the first few years of school. It has been called hyperactivity and minimal brain dysfunction

---

Medications for Treating Eating Disorders

Disorder	Medication
Anorexia	Naloxone/ Antidepressants Antipsychotics Cyproheptadine Lithium
Bulimia	Antidepressants (SSRIs, TCAs, or MAOIs), naltrexone, zofran, topiramate

Figure 14-A

---

in the past. The central feature is a difficulty with self-control and self-regulation often accompanied by impulsive behavior. As defined in the *DSM-IV,* attention-deficit/hyperactivity disorder is demonstrated by a patient's meeting the criteria for either inattention or hyperactivity. Inattention is defined as at least six of the following symptoms persisting to a significant degree for at least six months:

Inattention

- Carelessness

- Difficulty sustaining attention

- Not listening

- Failure to follow through on tasks

- Difficulty with organizing activities

- Avoidance of activities requiring prolonged mental effort

- Forgetfulness

- Frequent distraction

- Frequent loss of materials required for activities

Hyperactivity-impulsivity is defined as at least four of the following symptoms persisting to a significant degree for at least six months:

Hyperactivity

- Fidgeting or squirming

- Leaving seat in class

- Inappropriate activity—running, climbing

- Difficulty playing quietly

Impulsivity

- Answering questions before they are completely stated

- Difficulty waiting for turn

Additional criteria for ADD are onset by age 7, symptoms present in two or more situations, and that the behavior causes significant distress or impairment.

Attention deficit disorder is thought to have a neurological basis, as implied in the previous name "minimal brain dysfunction." That name was dropped because the exact "dysfunction" could not be proven and "soft" (equivocal) neurological signs are not always present. Attention deficit disorder has been shown to have significant comorbidity with conduct disorder, depression, bipolar disorder, anxiety disorders, mental retardation, Tourette's syndrome, and borderline personality disorder. It was previously thought that all kids with ADD "grew out of it" during adolescence. Recently, however, a syndrome called residual ADD has been described. This term refers to a persistence of symptoms of ADD into adulthood and is associated with significant impairment, for example, in work performance. Approximately 70 percent of children with ADD go on to experience ADD symptoms in adolescence and adulthood.

The diagnosis of ADD has become a controversial one with slogans like "don't drug our kids" being tossed around. Possibly, it can be said that most children, especially most boys, are a "little ADD." But just as everyone who experiences unhappiness does not have major depression, so, too, not everyone with concentration problems has ADD. At some point the quantitative differences become qualitative differences. Also, many children (and adults) have had the quality of their lives improve significantly with treatment for ADD. Untreated ADD can lead to persistent feelings of failure and inferiority, behavioral problems, and conflict with authority figures. The diagnosis of ADD should be made by a properly trained clinician after a thorough evaluation. There are scales (e.g., the Conners') that are filled out by parents and teachers. There are also computerized tests (e.g., the TOVA) that can objectively measure attention. These objective measures can aid in the evaluation, but they are not sufficient to make the diagnosis.

Medications play an important part in the treatment of ADD. Stimulants are the mainstay of the treatment of ADD: methylphenidate (Ritalin), dextroamphetamine (Dexedrine), and pemoline (Cylert). These differ in their half-lives, with Ritalin having the shortest and Cylert the longest. A warning has recently been issued about Cylert because of reports of sometimes fatal liver toxicity. Thus, it is recommended that it be used only if methylphenidate and dextroamphetamine are ineffective. There is individual variability in response, so that a person who does not respond to one may respond well to another. Other medications can also be effective in the treatment of ADD and may be useful, especially in residual ADD, where substance abuse may be an issue. These include tricyclic antidepressants (especially desipramine), bupropion, venlafaxine, and clonidine. (Note: Desipramine has been shown to be related to several deaths due to cardiac arrhythmias; it must be used with great caution.) There are reports of antipsychotics and lithium being helpful in selected cases, as well.

Self-Mutilation

Self-mutilation refers to deliberate self-injury without the intent to die. It is most commonly encountered in three groups of patients: those with organic disorders (including mental retardation), psychotic disorders, and personality disorders. Self-mutilation is often a clinical issue in patients with severe personality disorders who, for example, repeatedly make lacerations (often fairly superficial) on their wrist or forearm. They may describe that, as they watch the blood flow from the cut, it feels as if some internal tension is flowing out of them.

Recently, there has been growing interest into the possible biological substrate of this type of behavior. Studies have involved the opiate, dopamine, and serotonin systems. It has been shown that endorphins (endogenous opiates) are released by painful stimulation. Opiate antagonists (such as naltrexone) have been helpful in reducing self-injurious behavior (Winchel and Stanley 1991). Self-injurious behavior in animals has been increased by dopamine agonists and decreased by dopamine blockers. Serotonin has also been implicated, partly by the similarity between self-mutilation and some behaviors seen in obsessive-compulsive disorder—irresistible urges to commit an act and the resulting relief from anxiety that follows commission. Selective serotonin reuptake inhibitors have been shown to be somewhat helpful in treating trichotillomania (hair pulling).

A wide variety of medications have been found to sometimes be helpful in self-injurious behavior. Those that have been found to sometimes be helpful in self-injurious behavior in the context of a personality disorder, include MAO inhibitors, SSRIs, carbamazepine, lithium, antipsychotics, and benzodiazepines. The choice of medication should be based on the associated features present. Thus, when depressive features are present, try an SSRI; when there are symptoms of atypical depression and rejection sensitivity, an MAOI; and when psychotic features are present, an antipsychotic. This is an area where there are no clear guidelines for medication use and no guarantee of effectiveness. However, using trial and error, one can often find a drug that has significant benefit.

Sleep Disorders

Sleep disorders may be divided into two main groups: primary and secondary sleep disorders. Primary sleep disorders refer to those disorders of sleep not due to another medical or psychiatric condition. Secondary sleep disorders are those resulting from other conditions. Examples include the early morning awakening of depression and the insomnia of thyrotoxicosis. Our discussion here is limited to the primary sleep disorders, although secondary sleep disorders are referred to throughout the book.

There are three major primary sleep disorders: sleep apnea, nocturnal myoclonus, and restless legs syndrome. All three disorders result in partial arousals that interfere with stage 3 and 4 (deep) sleep. Their main symptom is fatigue or excessive daytime sleepiness and they should always be considered in cases of significant unexplained daytime sleepiness. Diagnosis is made by evaluation (polysomnography) at a sleep laboratory; sometimes the evaluation is performed at home.

Sleep apnea is a disorder characterized by frequent periods of slow or absent breathing. This can be caused by collapse of the throat (obstructive), or failure of the brain to stimulate breathing (central), or, more commonly, a combination of both. This results in frequent arousals and a lack of deep sleep. Those suffering from it may be unaware of the condition, because they may not fully awaken at night. They may be aware only of excessive daytime fatigue. Sleep apnea is associated with loud snoring and obesity and, untreated, may lead to serious medical complications. There are several forms of treatment including surgery and the use of a CPAP (breathing) machine. Most sedative medications are contraindicated in sleep apnea.

Nocturnal myoclonus is a disorder characterized by involuntary jerking movements of the limbs, especially the legs, during sleep. This results in partial arousals and a lack of deep sleep. Nocturnal myoclonus is treated with medication, such as clonazepam.

Restless legs syndrome is a disorder characterized by restlessness of the legs during sleep. It also is treated with medication such as clonazepam, levodopa, pergolide, or bromocripfine.

Obesity

New pharmacological treatments have been developed for the treatment of obesity. They should not be used as the sole treatment for obesity, but can be helpful adjuncts to other forms of treatment such as exercise, dietary restriction, and behavioral modification. Obesity is usually defined as a body mass index (calculated by dividing weight in kilograms by height in meters squared) greater than 30. Phentermine (Fastin, Ionamin) is a stimulant and fenfluramine (Pondimin) is a serotonin agonist. In the past, they were used together ("fen/phen") in the treatment of obesity, but this was discontinued because it caused valvular lesions of the heart. Used separately, they can cause anxiety and insomnia and must be used with extreme caution if taken with antidepressants, especially the SSRIs. Sibutramine is a serotonin and norepinephrine reuptake inhibitor with some demonstrated efficacy (Hanotin et al. 1998). It can cause elevations of heart rate and blood pressure. Orlistat is another new medication for obesity that works by inhibiting the digestion and absorption of fat. It inhibits the enzyme lipase so that about one-third of dietary fat is not absorbed (Drent and van der Veen 1993).

Aggression

Aggression, including irritability, hostility, or violent behavior, is usually a symptom of a psychiatric or neurological disorder. Below is a list of some examples of such disorders:

- ADD
- Antisocial personality disorder
- Borderline personality disorder
- Conduct disorder
- Delirium
- Dementias
- Depression
- Explosive disorder
- Medication-induced aggression
- Mania
- Mental retardation
- Paranoid disorder

- Postconcussion syndrome

- Schizophrenia

- Substance-use disorders

- Temporal lobe epilepsy

In these cases, the preferred strategy is to treat the primary disorder. There have been indications (Fava et al. 1993) that some angry outbursts may be similar to panic attacks, but instead of flight/fear there is fight/anger. It has been shown to be responsive to antidepressant medications. In addition, there are a number of medications listed below that have a somewhat nonspecific antiaggression effect. In choosing a medication it is helpful to choose on the basis of associated features.

Medication Type	Associated Features
- Anticonvulsants (e.g., carbamazepine)	Labile mood, poor impulse control, organicity
- Antipsychotics	Disorganized behavior
- Beta blockers (e.g., propranolol)	Organicity, e.g., dementia
- Buspirone	Organicity
- Clonidine	Anxiety, agitation
- Lithium	Labile mood, impulsivity
- SSRIs	Anger "attacks"

Chronic Pain

Antidepressant medications have been shown to often be helpful in chronic pain syndromes. These medications are effective only for chronic pain and not for acute pain. They help reduce pain and, when combined with narcotic analgesics, potentiate the effects of the narcotic. The cyclic antidepressants are the best studied and have the most supporting evidence. When there is not an accompanying depression, lower than the usual antidepressant doses may be effective. Venlafaxine, because of its similarities to the cyclic antidepressants, is probably effective also. There are a few studies showing the effectiveness of the SSRIs, but some studies that do not.

Part Three

Medications

Part three deals with the different classes of psychopharmaceuticals, including dosage and choice of medication, side effects, and mechanism of action (where and in so far as it has been established). Also covered are precautions for monitoring medication effects and serum levels, and guidelines for educating patients and their families about the effects and side effects of these drugs.

15

Antidepressant Medications

The term *antidepressants* refers to a large, important group of medications used to treat depression. In recent years, they have grown enormously in frequency of prescription and popularity, as well as notoriety. This growth is due to increased awareness of depression and decreased troublesome side effects from the newer agents.

Antidepressants were developed in the 1950s. Iproniazid, an agent used to treat tuberculosis, was inadvertently found to produce an improvement in mood. Ultimately, it was discovered to be an inhibitor of monoamine oxidase (MAO)—an enzyme used to break down catecholamines (dopamine, norepinephrine, and serotonin) in neurons. This led to the development of an entire class of antidepressants: the monoamine oxidase inhibitors, or MAOIs.

At about the same time, the drug imipramine was first produced. It was originally developed as a phenothiazine (antipsychotic), but was found to have antidepressant properties. Soon came amitriptyline, followed later by other "tricyclic" and "heterocyclic" antidepressants.

We now have at least six major groups of antidepressants: cyclic antidepressants, selective serotonin reuptake inhibitors (SSRIs), serotonin and norepinephrine reuptake inhibitors (SNRIs), norepinephrine reuptake inhibitors (NRIs), monoamine oxidase inhibitors (MAOIs), and the atypicals. In addition, sometimes stimulants (such as Ritalin or Dexedrine) are used to treat depression, and there are some reports of the use of buspirone (Buspar).

Despite our knowledge of some of the important mechanisms of action of these medications, we still do not really know how they relieve depression. It is theorized that they start a process that leads to neuro-endocrine effects, e.g., decreased CRF (corticotropin releasing factor) and/or, through intracellular second messengers, to increased BDNF (brain-derived neurotropic factor), leading to improvement (Musselman et al. 1998).

Types of Antidepressant Drugs

Tricyclics

For many years, tricyclic antidepressants (TCAs) and heterocyclics were the mainstay of the treatment of severe depression. The following is a list with their brand names:

Cyclic Antidepressants	
Generic Name	**Brand Name**
Amitriptyline	Elavil
Amoxapine	Asendin
Clomipramine	Anafranil
Desipramine	Norpramin, Pertofrane
Doxepin	Sinequan, Adapin
Imipramine	Tofranil
Maprotiline	Ludiomil
Nortriptyline	Pamelor, Aventyl
Protriptyline	Vivactil
Trazodone	Desyrel
Trimipramine	Surmontil

No antidepressant has been proven consistently superior to another but they do differ significantly in terms of side effects. All of the tricyclics have the same side effects, but in varying degrees. These side effects can be grouped as follows:

- Anticholinergic

- Adrenergic

- Antihistaminic

- Miscellaneous

The tricyclics are considered "dirty" drugs in that they react with a number of receptors besides the one responsible for the therapeutic effect, resulting in a host of side effects (see figure 15-A). Anticholinergic side effects range from unpleasant (dry mouth, dry skin, blurred vision, and constipation) to serious (paralytic ileus, cessation of movement of the intestine, which can lead to intestinal rupture and death; and urinary retention, inability to urinate, which in serious cases can lead to rupture of the bladder). Adrenergic side effects include sweating, sexual dysfunction, and orthostatic hypotension—sudden drop in the blood pressure upon rising

Side Effects of Cyclic Antidepressants

	Anticholinergic	Sedation	Orthostatic
Amitriptyline	++++	++++	+++
Amoxapine	++	+	++
Clomipramine	+++	+++	++
Desipramine	+	+/0	+
Doxepin	++++	++++	+++
Imipramine	++	++	++
Maprotiline	++	++	+++
Nortriptyline	++	++	+
Protripyline	++	++	++
Trazodone	0	+	++
Trimipramine	++	++++	+++

Figure 15-A

Side Effects of SSRI and Atypical Antidepressants

	Anxiety	Sedation	Insomnia	Nausea	Sexual Dysfunction
SSRIs					
Fluoxetine	++	±	++	+	++
Fluvoxamine	±	++	±	++	++
Paroxetine	±	++	±	+	++
Sertraline	+	+	+	++	++
Citalopram	+	0	+	+	+
SNRIs					
Venlafaxine	+	+	+	+	++
Mirtazapine	±	++	±	+	++
NRI					
Reboxetine	+	0	+	+	0
Atypical					
Bupropion	++	±	+	+	0
Nefazodone	±	±	±	+	±

Figure 15-B

and a sensation of lightheadedness. This condition can lead to a fall and, in turn, to fractures, which can have serious medical consequences, especially in the elderly. Antihistaminic effects include sedation and weight gain. Miscellaneous side effects include lowered seizure threshold, cardiac arrhythmia, hepatitis, agranulocytosis, rashes, sweating, anxiety, and elevated heart rate.

Selective Serotonin Reuptake Inhibitors

The SSRIs are a newer class of antidepressants. They have been used widely because they are generally as effective as the tricyclics, but have significantly fewer side effects and are safer in overdosage. The first SSRI on the market was fluoxetine (Prozac). Four newer agents are citalopram (Celexa), fluvoxamine (Luvox), paroxetine (Paxil), and sertraline (Zoloft). They share the same side effects but in varying degrees (see figure 15-B). Unlike the tricyclics, they are relatively "clean," and interact very little with other receptors besides the serotonin 5-HT reuptake receptor. Their side effects tend to be related to increased serotonin activity: nausea, gastrointestinal upset, sweating, anxiety, insomnia, headache, restlessness, and sexual dysfunction. They can have mild anticholinergic side effects and can cause dry mouth, sedation, and blurred vision. Such side effects generally are considerably less than those seen with cyclic antidepressants. After several months of treatment, patients taking SSRIs can develop a syndrome including loss of energy, passivity, decreased pleasure, and decreased libido which resembles, but is not the same as, the depression for which they are being treated. This may, with close patient monitoring, respond to the addition of buproprion or a stimulant such as methylphenidate or modafinil.

Sexual dysfunction, delayed or absent ejaculation in men, and anorgasmia in women, are common SSRI side effects. Decreased libido may also be caused by the SSRIs. These side effects often may be diminished by dose reduction, drug holidays, or the use of other medications as antidotes, such as yohimbine, cyproheptadine, or buproprion.

Another difference between the antidepressants is their half-lives. Paroxetine has a half-life of approximately one day, sertraline one to two days, and fluoxetine seven to ten days. A long half-life is an advantage in maintaining a stable blood level but may be a disadvantage when stopping the medication. It takes six weeks to reach a steady state with fluoxetine.

Serotonin and Norepinephrine Reuptake Inhibitors

The serotonin and norepinephrine reuptake inhibitors (SNRIs) are dual-action antidepressants, affecting both serotonin and norepinephrine. The SNRIs include venlafaxine (Effexor) and mirtazapine (Remeron). Venlafaxine is a blocker of the reuptake of both serotonin and norepinephrine and mirtazapine is an alpha2-adrenoreceptor blocker, producing increased serotonin and norepinephrine activity. Some of the older cyclic antidepressants are also dual-action, but they are not included here because they have many other effects. There is evidence that both venlafaxine and mirtazapine are more effective than the SSRIs in the treatment of severe depression (Clerc et al. 1994; Wheatley et al. 1998). However, both venlafaxine and mirtazapine have additional side effects relative to the SSRIs.

Norepinephrine Reuptake Inhibitors (NRIs)

Reboxetine (Vestra) is a new antidepressant that selectively blocks norepine-phrine reuptake. It is not currently available in the United States but is being used in Europe. Pre-marketing studies suggest it tends to be especially effective at improving energy and cognition. Also, reboxetine has little or no effect on sexual function. On the negative side, it may tend to increase anxiety and can cause hypotension. Other NRIs are slated for release in the United States in the next few years.

Atypical Antidepressants

Bupropion (Wellbutrin) is a relatively new antidepressant with unique proper-ties. Along with mirtazapine (see below), it is one of the antidepressants whose mechanism of action is *not* reuptake inhibition. It appears to work in a complex way to increase noradrenergic activity. In addition, it has weak dopaminergic activity, resulting in some stimulant effect. It has side effects of anxiety and insomnia. It had received much attention because of its tendency to lower the seizure thresholds in patients with eating disorders. However, the newer sustained release formulation (Wellbutrin SR) does not present this problem any more than other antidepressants, if given in doses of 300 mg or less per day. (Note: All antidepressants lower seizure thresholds to a degree.) Bupropion is also one of the most common agents used to augment SSRIs and has an additional positive feature in that it has fewer sexual side effects.

Nefazodone (Serzone), like venlafaxine, is a new antidepressant that affects multiple neurotransmitter systems. Like trazodone, nefazodone is a potent 5-HT2A receptor blocker. In addition, it is both a serotonin and norepinephrine reuptake inhibitor. The most common side effects are nausea, headache, anxiety, sedation, and dizziness. It has been associated with drug interaction, and there is a warning regarding its use with Xanax.

Buspirone (BuSpar) is a medication used mainly for the treatment of anxiety. However, there are several reports of its effectiveness as an antidepressant in higher doses (40–60 mg per day and up). It has the side effects of anxiety (paradoxically), nausea, headache, and dizziness.

Monoamine Oxidase Inhibitors

The MAO inhibitors represent a group of antidepressants now used mainly when other antidepressants have failed for atypical depression, and panic disorder. This is partly because of the risk of a hypertensive reaction. The MAOIs can cause a severe and sudden rise in blood pressure, potentially leading to cerebral hemorrhage or death. Such a reaction can be caused by eating foods high in tyramine content (see figure 15-C) or taking sympathomimetic drugs, such as decongestants or other anti-depressants.[1] Thus, it is recommended that people taking MAOIs wear a medic alert bracelet and seek medical attention immediately at the sign of a hypertensive reac-tion (severe, pounding occipital headache). In one study of 182 people taking MAOIs, 12 hypertensive reactions occurred, with no fatalities, giving a rate of about

---

1. In a study by Bieck and Antonin (1988) 50 percent of patients taking tranylcypromine (Parnate) showed a significant hypertensive reaction from taking 8 mg of tyramine.

Tyramine Contents in Food Products

Food   **Tyramine Content per Serving**

Fish

Lumpfish roe	0.2 mg/50 g
Sliced schmaltz herrring in oil	0.2 mg/50 g
Pickled herring[a]	negligible
Smoked salmon	negligible
Salmon mousse	0.7 mg/30 g

Meat and sausage

Salami	5.6 mg/30 g
Mortadella	5.5 mg/30 g
Air-dried sausage	3.8 mg/30 g
Chicken liver	1.5 mg/30 g
Bologna	1.0 mg/30 g
Aged sausage	0.9 mg/30 g
Smoked meat	0.5 mg/30 g
Corned beef	0.3 mg/30 g
Kielbasa sausage	0.2 mg/30 g

Fruit

Avocado[a]	negligible
Banana[a]	negligible
Banana peel	1.424 mg/banana
Raisins[a]	negligible
Figs[a]	negligible

Other

Marmite concentrated yeast extract	6.45 mg/10 g
Sauerkraut	13.87 mg
Beef bouillon mix	231.25 µg/package
Beef bouillon	102.00 µg/cube
Soy sauce	0.2 mg/10 ml
Yogurt[a]	negligible
Fava beans[a]	negligible
Beer[b]	0.3–1.5 mg
Wine	0–0.5 mg

a Previously thought to be higher in tyramine

b Some types of beer have been recently identified as having dangerously high tyramine content. *See* Tailor, S. A. N., Shulman, K. I., Walker, S. E., Moss, J., and D. Gardner. 1994. "Hypertensive Episode Associated with Phenelzine and Tap Beer—A Aeanalysis of the Role of Pressor Amines in Beer." *Journal of Clinical Psychopharmacology.* 14:5–14.

Source: Shulman et al. 1989.

Figure 15-C

7 percent (Rabkin et al. 1985). In addition to the hypertensive reactions, which are fortunately uncommon, there are a number of other side effects that can be troublesome. These include sedation, insomnia, agitation, confusion, orthostatic symptoms, and edema.

Phenelzine (Nardil) and tranylcypromine (Parnate) are the two most common MAOIs. Two newer MAOIs are being studied to evaluate their clinical use; both have a reduced risk of hypertensive reaction. Selegiline (Deprenyl) is an MAO-B inhibitor (inhibits type B MAO) that is used in the treatment of Parkinson's disease and may be especially useful for treating depression in patients with Parkinson's. Meclobemide, a reversible MAO-A inhibitor, is currently used in Europe and Canada and is not available in this country.

Stimulants

Stimulants have been used as antidepressants for many years, especially dextroamphetamine (Dexedrine) and methylphenidate (Ritalin). They have the side effects of anxiety, insomnia, agitation, and appetite suppression. They can be quite effective antidepressants but are now usually reserved for medically ill patients such as those who have had a stroke and those unresponsive to other antidepressants.

Mechanism of Action

The antidepressants, generally, produce their therapeutic effects by blocking the reuptake of one or more catecholamines (norepinephrine, serotonin, and dopamine), which leads to a decrease (down-regulation) of the number of post-synaptic receptors—generally within seven to twenty-one days, coinciding with the onset of clinical effect (see chapter 3). The MAOIs block monoamine oxidase, which metabolizes the catecholamines stored at the nerve ending of the presynaptic neuron—thereby making more catecholamine available. Stimulants increase the release of catecholamines. Buspirone is a 5-HT IA receptor blocker.

Antidepressants generally produce effects within two to three weeks. Once therapeutic benefit has been obtained, it is important that the patient continue the medication for at least six months. Discontinuing in less than six months is likely to lead to relapse. In treating a patient's first depression, it is reasonable to gradually discontinue the medication after six to twelve months. If the patient has had two or more depressions, it is probably best to continue the medication because the likelihood of recurrence is significant (70 to 80 percent or more). Recent studies have also shown that subsequent depressive episodes may be less responsive to treatment. Therefore, in such cases the best treatment is to prevent relapse by continuation of medication.

Another consideration in the treatment of depression after the initial phase is treating to remission, as opposed to improvement. Most studies showing antidepressant benefit use 50 percent improvement in symptoms (usually 50 percent reduction in the Ham-D score) as the criterion for treatment response. However, people with this level of response still may be significantly depressed. They may feel better, but still be impaired in their social or occupational functioning. Treating to remission (Ham-D score of 7 or less) may require raising the dose of the antidepressant, or augmenting or switching to another antidepressant.

Comparison of Antidepressants

Celexa (citalopram): Advantages: Minimal documented interaction with other drugs.

Minimal sedation/weight gain.

Disadvantages: May cause anxiety initially.

Effexor (venlafaxine): Advantages: Good for severe depression, social anxiety and GAD, and possibly chronic pain.

Disadvantages: May cause hypertension. Increased gastrointestinal side effects.

Paxil (paroxetine): Advantages: Good antianxiety benefit.

Disadvantages: More prone to discontinuation symptoms, weight gain, may interact with other medications.

Prozac (fluoxetine): Advantages: Activating (energizing), long half-life.

Disadvantages: Prone to cause anxiety, may interact with other medications.

Remeron (mirtazapine): Advantages: Good for severe depression, insomnia. Less sexual dysfunction.

Disadvantages: Significant weight gain and sedation.

Serzone (nefazodone): Advantages: Good at reducing anxiety. Fewer sexual side effects.

Disadvantages: Sedating. Prone to medication interactions. Rare reports of liver damage

Vestra (reboxetine):—Advantages: Energizing, less sexual dysfunction, less weight gain: May improve concentration.

Disadvantages: May cause anxiety, hypotension.

Wellbutrin (buproprion): Advantages: Energizing, few sexual side effects, less weight gain.

Disadvantages: May increase anxiety and insomnia. Can cause seizures, especially at doses over 400 mg/day.

Zoloft (sertraline): Advantages: Neither too sedating, nor too prone to cause anxiety.

Disadvantages: More prone to gastrointestinal side effects.

Figure 15-D

Dosages

In order for medications to be effective, they must be taken at an adequate dose (see figure 15-E) for an adequate period of time. There seems to be a threshold effect, with subtherapeutic doses producing little or no benefit. However, achieving an effective dose may be difficult due to side effects.

Antidepressant Doses*

Drug	Dose (mg/day)
Cyclics	
Amitriptyline	75–300
Doxepin	75–300
Imipramine	75–300
Trimipramine	75–300
Clomipramine	75–200
Amoxapine	150–400
Desipramine	75–300
Maprotiline	75–225
Nortriptyline	50–150
Protriptyline	15–60
Trazodone	150–400
SSRIs	
Fluoxetine	20–80
Sertraline	50–200
Paroxetine	20–60
Fluvoxamine	50–300
Citalopam	10–60
Atypical, SNRIs, NRIs	
Bupropion SR	150–300
Mirtazapine	15–45
Nefazodone	100–600
Venlafaxine XR	75–350
Reboxetine	2–8
MAOIs	
Phenelzine	45–90
Tranylcypromine	20–40
Isocarboxazid	20–40

* Doses for children and adolescents: See appendix B.

Figure 15-E

Initially, you will see only side effects. Over the course of one to two weeks, tolerance to side effects will develop and the dosage can be increased. It is always a good idea to start with a very low dose (5–10 mg of fluoxetine or 10–25 mg of nortriptyline), in case the person is particularly sensitive to side effects. One severe reaction to medication can have very destructive consequences for the therapeutic relationship and the willingness to try further medications.

For the SSRIs, nausea can often be managed by taking the medication with a meal. Insomnia may require taking the medication only in the morning and sometimes by taking a sedating medication, like trazodone, at bedtime. Anxiety can be reduced by avoiding caffeine and oral decongestants. Sedation can be reduced by taking the medication at bedtime. Sexual dysfunction often can be improved by adjunctive medications like Viagra or Wellbutrin.

For the tricyclics, dry mouth is common and can be managed by drinking water, chewing gum, or using a synthetic saliva (available at a pharmacy). Constipation can be managed with a stool softener such a Metamucil or DSS. Orthostatic symptoms can be managed by avoiding dehydration, adding salt to the diet, standing up gradually, and holding on to something for a few seconds after standing.

Many more measures can be taken to manage other side effects, but they are beyond the scope of this book. When these measures do not work and the patient complains of troublesome or intolerable side effects, one can decrease the dosage (which may lead to a loss of benefit) or change to another medication, as is addressed in the next section.

Choice of Medication

Choosing an antidepressant involves considering a number of factors. One important consideration is the person's previous response to medication, if any, and his or her family history of response to medication. Another important consideration is the presence of associated symptoms and comorbidity, e.g., does the person have panic attacks, OCD, or PTSD? Consideration should be given to whether the person

Blood Levels of Antidepressants

Drug	Typical Plasma Concentration (mg/ml)
Amitriptyline	100–250
Doxepin	100–250
Imipramine	200–300
Trimipramine	250–300
Clomipramine	200–300
Amoxapine	150–500
Desipramine	100–250
Maprotiline	250–300
Nortriptyline	50–150
Protriptyline	100–250
Trazodone	800–1600
Fluoxetine	200–700
Bupropion	25–100
Sertraline	32–190

Figure 15-F

may have a bipolar disorder, because antidepressant treatment can cause a manic episode in the absence of a mood stabilizer (see chapter 16).

With the possible exception of severe and melancholic depression (for which dual-action antidepressants appear to be more effective) all antidepressants have similar efficacy. So, the next consideration is to minimize undesirable side effects.

Due probably to feelings of hopelessness and pessimism, depressed patients are especially prone to discontinuing medication prematurely. This is particularly the case when they encounter significant side effects. Thus, choosing an antidepressant with minimal side effects becomes a crucial part of ensuring an adequate medication trial. On the other hand, sometimes medication is chosen on the basis of its side effects. Thus, if a patient complains of anxiety and insomnia, you might use a sedating medication. Or, conversely, if the individual complains of lack of energy, you might choose a nonsedating or energizing antidepressant. Many professionals feel that because of their safety, efficacy, and lack of side effects that the SSRIs or one of the newer antidepressants are the first choice in the treatment of depression. Others continue to prescribe TCAs first because of their long record of efficacy and lower cost. Many clinicians prefer the secondary amines (refers to chemical structure) over the tertiary amine tricyclics, because they have fewer side effects. The secondary amines are amoxapine, desipramine, maprotiline, nortriptyline, and protriptyline.

Whichever antidepressant is chosen first, the question of what to try if the first one doesn't work may arise. But what is considered a nonresponse? Before you abandon one medication for another, it is important that the patient experience an "adequate clinical trial." This means adequate time at an adequate dose—at least four weeks, and some studies suggest eight to twelve weeks because there is a small percentage of late responders. But then, what is an adequate dose—the usual dose, such as 20 mg of fluoxetine, or the maximum tolerated dose? (Again, blood levels may help.) Medication compliance must also be considered.

When switching, it probably makes sense to try an antidepressant quite different from the first (see figure 15-G). Special considerations also apply to certain classes of patients when selecting an antidepressant—see figure 15-H.

Phases of Treatment

It is helpful to consider three phases in the treatment of major depression. These are outlined below.

Acute Treatment: Begins with the first dose and extends until the patient is asymptomatic (in good case scenarios, this may be from six to eight weeks).

Continuation Treatment: To avoid acute relapse, it is strongly suggested that patients continue treatment for a minimum of six months beyond the acute phase. Also, recent studies indicate that the patient should be maintained on the *same* dose used during the acute phase. Remember to treat to remission, not just improvement.

Maintenance Treatment: Relapse prevention is an important aspect of treatment, especially in those patients judged to have recurrent episodes (or those at risk for recurrence). Continued (lifelong) treatment provides the best outcome for such individuals. The following guidelines are offered:

1. *First Episode:* At the end of the continuation phase, gradually reduce the dose (over a period of one to two months) and, assuming no return of depressive symptoms, discontinue. Educate the patient to be alert to any

signs of recurrence (e.g., poor sleep, fatigue, etc.) and should this occur, as soon as possible reinstigate treatment.

2. *Second Episode:*

   a. *With "Risk Factors":* which include: family history of mood disorders, first episode occurring prior to the age of 18, and/or most recent episode has severe symptoms: Recommend lifelong medication treatment to prevent recurrence.

   b. *Without "Risk Factors":* Gradually discontinue medications.

3. *Third or Subsequent Episodes:* Recommend lifelong medication treatment.

Treatment-Resistant Depression

Many people are inadequately treated for depression and have minimal positive response, usually due to poor compliance and inadequate trials. However, true *treatment-resistant depression* (TRD) refers to a depression that has failed to respond to adequate trials of two or more antidepressants. As many as 30 percent of people with depression may fall into this category—although it probably is closer to 10 to 20 percent.

A full discussion of the treatment of TRD is beyond the scope of this book, but it will be helpful for you to be familiar with some of the typical strategies used in such cases. The following list should be considered in the treatment of resistant depression, but it is by no means exhaustive:

- Check the diagnosis: Are depressive symptoms due to characterological disorder, medical illness, or psychotic disorder?

- Is it a type of depression that typically is not responsive to medication treatment (such as psychological-reactive depression), so that psychotherapy is instead the treatment of choice?

- Check the dose: Has the medication dose been too low? (It may help to check the blood level.) Has the patient taken the medication as prescribed and for a long enough period of time (at least four to six weeks at adequate dose)? Adequate trials require, if necessary, pushing the dose to upper limits and making sure that the patient has been compliant. Frequently, a failure to fully respond may be due to inadequate compliance.

- Check for substance abuse, especially alcohol.

- Change the medication: Usually you will want to try another class of medication (NE, 5-HT, MAOI). See the algorithm at the end of this chapter as a general guideline for a systematic progression of medication trails.

- Augmentation: The addition of a second medication (referred to as augmentation) often yields a positive response. The strategy is to add a medication with a different mechanism of action to try to get a synergistic effect. There is little scientific evidence to guide us in our choice of augmenting agent, but a survey of clinicians at Harvard (Mischoulon et al. 1999) revealed that the most common medication combination was an SSRI with Wellbutrin. The second most common was an SSRI with Buspar, followed by the addition of Ritalin to an antidepressant. Other augmenting agents

Selective Action of Antidepressant Medications

Generic Name	Brand Name	Norepine-phrine Effects	Serotonin Effects	Monoamine Oxidase Effects	Dopamine Effects
Imipramine	Tofranil	++	+++	0	0
Desipramine	Norpramin	+++++	0	0	0
Amitriptyline	Elavil	+	++++	0	0
Nortriptyline	Aventyl, Pamelor	+++	++	0	0
Protriptyline[a]	Vivactil	++++	+	0	0
Trimipramine[a]	Surmontil	++	++	0	0
Doxepin[a]	Sinequan, Adapin	+++	++	0	0
Maprotiline	Ludiomil	+++++	0	0	0
Amoxapine	Asendin	++++	+	0	0
Venlafaxine	Effexor	++	+++	0	+
Trazodone	Desyrel	0	+++++	0	0
Fluoxetine	Prozac, Sarafem	0	+++++	0	0
Paroxetine	Paxil	+	+++++	0	0
Sertraline	Zoloft	0	+++++	0	0
Bupropion[b]	Wellbutrin	++	0	0	++
Nefazodone	Serzone	+	+++	0	0
Fluvoxamine	Luvox	0	+++++	0	0
Clomipramine	Anafranil	0	+++++	0	0
Mirtazapine	Remeron	+++	+++	0	0
Citalopram	Celexa	0	+++++	0	0
Reboxetine	Vestra	+++++	0	0	0
Isocarboxazid	Marplan	+++	+++	+++++	+++
Phenelzine	Nardil	+++	+++	+++++	+++
Tranylcypromine	Parnate	+++	+++	+++++	+++

a Uncertain, but likely effects

b Atypical antidepressant; uncertain effects but likely to be a dopamine and norepinephrine agonist

Figure 15-G

include lithium, thyroid, the new stimulant medication modafinil (Provigil), and atypical antipsychotics (e.g., olanzapine or risperidone).

- Consider electroconvulsive treatment (ECT) see sidebar at end of chapter, transcranial magnetic stimulation (TMS)*, or vagal nerve stimulation (VNS).

- Never forget psychotherapy.

---

* Currently undergoing clinical trials—considered experimental at this time.

Choice of Antidepressant

Is anxiety a prominent symptom?

If not, and anergia is prominent, try a norepinephrine medication such as buproprion.

If anxiety is prominent, try an SSRI or venlafaxine. If these cause anxiety, try nefazodone or mirtazapine.

If these are not effective, try a different class of antidepressant or tricyclic antidepressant.

If depression is severe, try a dual action antidepressant first, e.g., venlafaxine, mirtazapine, bupropion, or a tricyclic.

If no benefit, and atypical depression, bipolar, or prominent anxiety, consider MAOI.

Figure 15-H

Patient Education

Education of patients about antidepressants has several facets. First, education about the biological aspects of depression is helpful, especially so that they do not view taking medication as a sign of moral weakness. Next, it is important to describe what to expect from the antidepressants: what typical side effects are, that the medication is not habit forming, that a clinical response typically takes two to three weeks to be achieved, that side effects diminish over time, and that other medications can be tried if the first one does not work. For people taking MAOIs, education about foods and medications to avoid is crucial.

The most common cause of medication failure is failure to take enough medication for long enough. Discussion about side effects can be very helpful in helping someone continue the medication long enough to benefit. This can be difficult, because initially there are only side effects and no benefits; only later are there benefits and diminished side effects. Through supportive therapy you can often help your depressed patient to overcome annoyance or distress over side effects (preoccupation with somatic symptoms), discouragement about delayed benefits, and pessimism about the outcome. In these ways, you can help your client to continue in treatment and achieve greater benefit.

Over-the-Counter Options

Two over the counter (OTC) products have been shown to have efficacy in treating depression. The herb, *St. John's Wort*, has research support for effectiveness in treating mild-to-moderate depression. The dosing is 300–600 mg three times a day, and generally daily treatment for a minimum of 6–8 weeks is required before the onset of symptomatic improvement. Two cautions are important to note. First, since the FDA does not regulate herbals there is no guarantee that all products have adequate or standardized amounts of the psychoactive ingredient. Second, St. John's

---

Special Considerations in Choosing an Antidepressant

Patient Type	Medication Choices
Anxious or agitated	Trazodone, nefazodone, paroxetine, mirtazapine, consider tertiary amine TCA or MAOI
Atypical	SSRI or MAOI
Bipolar	Bupropion or MAOI, possibly SSRI Avoid TCA
Child	SSRI
Choices to avoid	
Obesity	TCAs, especially tertiary amines, mirtazapine
Seizure disorder	Bupropion (immediate release)
Cardiac disease	TCAs
Elderly	TCAs
Comorbidity	
OCD	SSRI, clomipramine, venlafaxine, mirtazapine
Panic Disorder	Not bupropion
Chronic pain	TCAs, venlafaxine
Dysthymia	SSRI
High suicide risk	Less toxic antidepressants (fluoxetine, trazodone, paroxetine, sertraline, bupropion, venlafaxine, nefazodone)
Psychotic	Amoxapine, TCA, venlafaxine, possibly SSRI (used with an antipsychotic)
Retarded or anergic	Bupropion, venlafaxine, secondary amine TCA
Severe, recurrent depression	Combined SSRI + TCA or bupropion venlafaxine, mirtazapine TCAs or bupropion alone

Figure 15-I

Wort has been shown to induce liver enzymes and thus presents with significant drug-drug interaction problems. Although this product has few side effects when taken alone, serious drug interactions have been reported when it is combined with other prescription drugs, including antidepressants. Should a patient be taking St. John's Wort and the decision is made to switch treatment to a prescription anti-depressant, a one week wash-out is strongly advised before initiating the new medication.

SAMe (s-adenosyl-methionine) is another OTC product with some research support for effectiveness in treating mild-to-severe depression. The effective dosage range is from 400–1600 mg per day. Onset for symptomatic improvement appears to

ECT: ELECTRO-CONVULSIVE THERAPY

During the late 1930's it was observed that people suffering from both epilepsy and from serious mental illnesses exhibited an interesting phenomenon in the aftermath of a seizure. Often, such individuals would experience a noticeable reduction in psychiatric symptoms after having seizures; the effect would last from a few days to a couple of weeks. Based on this observation, numerous attempts were made to intentionally induce seizures in psychiatric patients who did not otherwise have epilepsy. It was found that the safest way to accomplish this was by delivering an electrical shock to the head. The duration of the shock was a couple of seconds, resulting in a grand mal seizure. It was found that a series of "shock treatments" (generally 9-12, given at a rate of three per week) were required to produce a significant diminution in psychiatric symptoms. Especially since there were no other viable medical treatments for severe mental illness during the 1930's, this new procedure caught on, and was used extensively for the next three decades.

Indiscriminate use of electro-convulsive therapy (ECT) was common in these early days. There were a number of serious complications that accompanied the treatment (e.g. spinal fractures). And the public's view of ECT, characterized in numerous movies, was of an inhumane, horrific, and frightening procedure. During the 1950's it was also gradually became clear that ECT was not especially effective for some types of illnesses (e.g. schizophrenia).

Eventually, clinical experience showed that the best outcomes from ECT were with people with severe mood

Continued

be similar to that seen with the use of prescription antidepressants. At the time of the publication of this book, serious drug-drug interactions have not been reported, therefore caution is warranted until this medication has been more fully evaluated. (Also see chapter 19).

disorders (i.e. very severe depression with melancholic features, psychotic depressions, and severe, acute mania). In more recent times, techniques for administering ECT have changed dramatically. This currently includes the use of powerful muscle relaxers (to prevent severe motor contractions that had been previously encountered) and the use of a general anesthesia; prior to the treatment per se, the patient is fully anesthetized. Serious or persistent side effects now are considered to be rare. However, it is important to note that all patients receiving ECT do experience significant memory problems that continue throughout the treatments and generally for 4-6 weeks after treatments have ended. Cognitive problems persisting after this time are rare.

Although ECT can dramatically and quickly improve mood, on-going medication treatments (antidepressants, antipsychotics in cases of psychotic depressions, and mood stabilizers in cases of mania) are crucial for the prevention of acute relapse.

ECT is often considered a treatment of last resort, but when used with appropriately diagnosed patients, it can be extremely effective and at times, a life-saving. And ECT remains the "gold standard" for severe depressions.

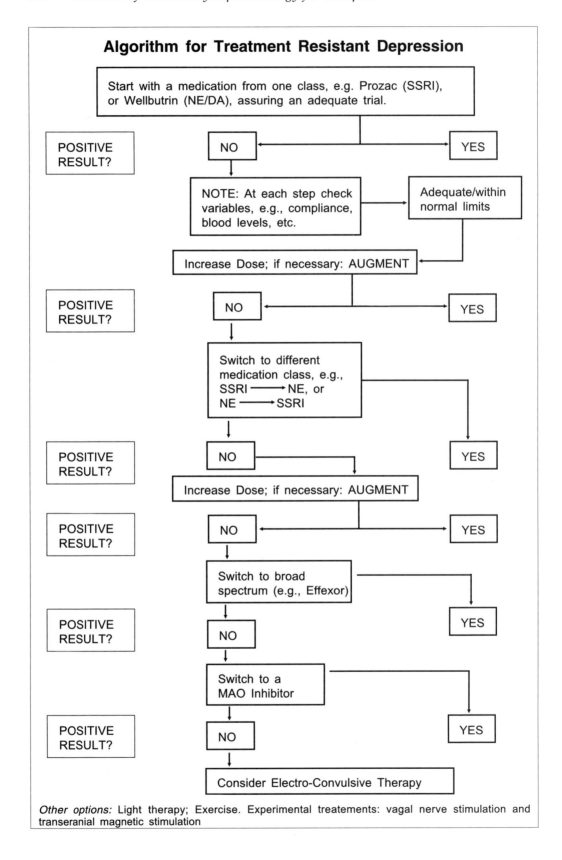

Algorithm for Treatment Resistant Depression

Start with a medication from one class, e.g. Prozac (SSRI), or Wellbutrin (NE/DA), assuring an adequate trial.

POSITIVE RESULT?   NO   YES

NOTE: At each step check variables, e.g., compliance, blood levels, etc.   Adequate/within normal limits

Increase Dose; if necessary: AUGMENT

POSITIVE RESULT?   NO   YES

Switch to different medication class, e.g., SSRI ⟶ NE, or NE ⟶ SSRI

POSITIVE RESULT?   NO   YES

Increase Dose; if necessary: AUGMENT

POSITIVE RESULT?   NO   YES

Switch to broad spectrum (e.g., Effexor)

POSITIVE RESULT?   NO   YES

Switch to a MAO Inhibitor

POSITIVE RESULT?   NO   YES

Consider Electro-Convulsive Therapy

Other options: Light therapy; Exercise. Experimental treatements: vagal nerve stimulation and transeranial magnetic stimulation

16

Mood Stabilizers

For treating bipolar disorder, pharmacotherapy is unquestionably the mainstay of treatment. Although medication options over the last thirty years have grown more plentiful, they also have become more complex. The initial treatment of choice for mania was lithium. The anticonvulsants, carbamazepine and valproic acid (also known as divalproex), also became established as effective agents. For many years medication regimens included one, or a combination, of these three agents.

However, within the last several years, drug selection trends have changed. Routinely, medication regimens include multiple mood stabilizers, concurrent antidepressant therapy, and adjunctive agents, such as benzodiazepines and/or antipsychotics. These emerging patterns of drug use are necessary due to the severity of symptom presentation and the complicated course of illness for many patients. Even with these substantial treatment options, poor response or treatment resistance is not uncommon. In this chapter, we address the well-established mood stabilizers lithium, divalproex, and carbamazepine. A number of newer anticonvulsants are gaining wider use. Although solid evidence supporting their effectiveness is still lacking, because you are likely to encounter their use in your practice, we provide basic information about them.

Special mention is necessary regarding medication treatment for bipolar II. Several clinical questions have arisen. First, is there a difference in responsiveness to the various mood stabilizers between bipolar I and bipolar II? Second, what is the role of antidepressants in bipolar II, especially as monotherapy? Regarding the preferred mood stabilizer in bipolar II, studies are inconclusive, although lithium, carbamazepine, divalproex, and lamotrigine have all been found to be effective. As to the role of antidepressants, few definitive studies have been conducted, but preliminary results suggest that antidepressants may be safe and effective, and may not present a high risk for manic and hypomanic switching.

Although guidelines are not in agreement on antidepressant monotherapy (without a mood stabilizer), some practitioners advocate that many patients do not require a mood stabilizer. Due to the high morbidity and mortality associated with bipolar II, the decision to exclude a mood stabilizer must be made on a case by case basis. Further study is needed to confirm these initial findings and, until such time that clear guidelines exist, medication decisions should be given careful and individual consideration (MacQueen and Young 2001).

Review of Treatment Guidelines

Goldberg (2000) has provided a comprehensive review of recent treatment guidelines for bipolar disorder. Of particular value in this overview are the points of agreement, as well as the areas of controversy, that exist from various expert groups. Published guidelines cited by Goldberg are these:

- American Psychiatric Association's Practice Guidelines for Treatment of Patients with Bipolar Disorder (1994)

- The Expert Consensus Guideline Series (1996, 2000)

- Clinical Practice Guidelines for Bipolar Disorder from the Department of Veteran's Affairs (1999)

- The Texas Medication Algorithm Project (1998)

- The Canadian Network for Mood and Anxiety Treatments (1997)

It is noteworthy that treatment guidelines emphasize not only drug selection, but reasonable sequencing and appropriate combinations. As in other fields of medicine, rational therapeutics should be the cornerstone of prescribing medications. Adhering to basic principles of medication use is particularly important in bipolar disorder. Due to the clinical success of the anticonvulsants, carbamazepine and divalproex, assumptions can be made that each new anticonvulsant will be effective in bipolar disorder. This may, or may not, be borne out. Certainly, first line agents should be used before the use of agents with little or no conclusive evidence of effectiveness.

Lithium

The use of lithium in psychiatry has varied historically. In the nineteenth century, lithium salts were employed in the treatment of anxiety, as well as gout and seizures. The importance of lithium's antimanic actions was indirectly discovered, in 1949, with observations that it produced a calming effect in animals. Human testing in agitated or manic patients followed, with encouraging results. However, lithium's use did not gain acceptance in American medicine until 1970, due to safety concerns following reports of toxicity in cardiac patients who were using lithium chloride as a salt substitute. Lithium is now firmly established as a safe and effective treatment for acute mania and for the prevention of manic-depressive episodes, with response rates in typical bipolar disorder estimated at 60 to 80 percent. However, lithium's mechanism of action remains to be identified. Except for mild cognitive and motor slowing in healthy individuals, lithium does not share the sedating or euphoriant properties of other psychotropics.

Most treatment guidelines consider lithium and divalproex as first line agents. Many physicians select divalproex over lithium because of concerns about side effects and toxicity. Other prescribers prefer lithium, and when therapeutic guidelines are followed, believe it is the most effective agent for many patients. Regardless of the indication, safe and effective use of lithium requires close monitoring of blood levels and management of side effects; this chapter covers those aspects of therapy in detail.

Lithium is the lightest of the solid elements, is widely found in nature, and because of its chemical activity will combine with other ions to form lithium salts (Gennaro 1980). Lithium salts share some, but not all, properties of sodium and potassium. The two therapeutically available forms are lithium carbonate and lithium citrate.

Lithium demonstrates a narrow *therapeutic window*—the therapeutic dose is very close to the toxic dose. (See also "Therapeutic Index" in appendix A.) Consequently, lithium is prescribed not only by dose, and stage of symptoms, but by concentration in the blood (see figure 16-A). Side effects are often indicative of blood level but not always. During acute states, daily doses of 1200 mg to 2400 mg of lithium are required, with most patients needing less after stabilization (600 to 1800 mg per day). Also, as the acute episode resolves, many patients will become more intolerant of side effects, necessitating a dosage reduction. The onset of action of lithium occurs in five to fourteen days, although full stabilization may take up to several months.

Dosage Guidelines for Lithium

Stage	Dosage Range (mg/day)	Serum Level (mEq/l)
Acute mania	1200–2400	0.8–1.5
Maintenance	600–1800	0.6–1.2

Figure 16-A

Side Effects and Their Management

Lithium produces a distinct continuum of side effects which range from relatively benign, transient symptoms to toxicity that can be fatal. The most significant side effects fall into the following categories.

Gastrointestinal

Nausea, vomiting, and diarrhea can occur to varying degrees at any time during treatment. These side effects may appear at the beginning of treatment or upon dosage increases. *However, GI symptoms may also be one of the critical indicators of lithium toxicity.* Obtaining a lithium blood level in response to the appearance of these symptoms is important. After ruling out an elevated lithium level as a cause of GI symptoms, changing from one dosage form to another, especially to a long-acting or liquid preparation, is often helpful. Lithium may also be administered after meals or the total daily dosage may be divided into smaller doses to alleviate the nausea.

Nervous system and neuromuscular

Initial complaints, which usually diminish with time, include headache, lethargy, and muscle weakness. Nearly half of patients experience a fine hand tremor at some time during lithium treatment. For most people, this initial symptom remits; however, for 10 percent of patients, it is a continuing side effect (American Society of Health System Pharmacists 2000). Often the tremor becomes worse when the individual reaches for something. Sustained tremor, at therapeutic levels, can be managed with reassurance, and by limiting stimulants, such as caffeine, which may exacerbate the tremor. Sometimes this tremor is treated with beta blockers, usually propranolol (Inderal).

Not all neurologic side effects are benign; sometimes they are indicators of toxicity. *Worsening of tremor, confusion, stupor, and slurred speech are warning signs that require a lithium blood level to be taken to rule out toxicity.* Severe lithium toxicity can result in seizures, CNS depression, irregular heartbeat, decreased kidney function, coma, or death. Although various emergency measures, including dialysis, can be employed in lithium intoxication, there is no antidote. An episode of severe lithium intoxication will resolve as the drug is eliminated from the body, usually over several days. A small number of patients are left with permanent neurological impairment following acute or chronic dosage excesses.

Endocrine

Thyroid hormones are frequently affected by lithium, but rarely in a clinically significant way. Changes in certain laboratory tests of thyroid function are common but seldom require discontinuation of treatment. The two significant endocrine effects attributed to lithium therapy are clinical hypothyroidism (1-4 percent) and goiter (5 percent) (American Society of Health System Pharmacists 2000). Several potential risk factors have been identified including age, gender (more prevalent in women), and familial history of hypothyroidism (Johnston and Eagles 1999; Kleiner, Altshuler, Hendrick, and Hershman 1999). Several treatment options for hypothyroidism are utilized depending on the clinical situation. Periodic thyroid function monitoring is important, not only from a safety standpoint but to rule out (in the bipolar individual with depressed or mixed-state features), that hypothyroidism is not the cause of symptoms.

Renal

The pharmacokinetics of lithium are important in understanding its kidney-related side effects. Lithium, unlike most other medications, relies only on the kidney for elimination from the body, without any liver metabolism. Therefore, adequate kidney function is critical to safe lithium use. *Interference or alteration in normal kidney functioning can potentially lead to a buildup of lithium.* Lithium use usually should be avoided in the presence of renal disease. Also, since elderly people in general show age-related decreases in kidney function, lithium should be prescribed cautiously and with appropriately reduced dosages.

Additionally, lithium excretion is directly related, in an *inverse* way, to sodium excretion. Conditions leading to excess sodium elimination will cause a corresponding increase in the amount of lithium retained in the body. Excessive sodium loss occurs from diarrhea, vomiting, fever, dehydration, profuse sweating, diuretic medications, and severely salt-restricted diets.

The benign effects of lithium on the kidney will be experienced by the majority of patients as increased thirst (polydipsia) and increased urination (polyuria). To ensure adequate lithium excretion, patients must be advised to maintain fluid intake, even in the presence of polyuria.

Since the inception of its use, there has been debate about the long-term effects of lithium on the kidney. After initiation of treatment, 30-50 percent of patients experience a decrease in the ability of the kidney to concentrate urine. This effect persists in 25 percent of patients after one to two years of treatment (American Society of Health System Pharmacists 2000). Conclusions about whether lithium causes structural changes in the kidney are confounded by findings that such changes occur in bipolar patients independent of lithium treatment (Gitlin 1999). Progressive deterioration in kidney function, although potentially very serious, is a rare occurrence and is likely related to additional factors, such as lithium intoxication, high serum levels, interacting drugs, age, or concurrent medical conditions (Johnson 1998).

Hematological

A benign, reversible increase in white blood cell (WBC) count occurs frequently with lithium treatment. This is clinically nonsignificant and does not require discontinuation of treatment.

Cardiovascular

It is not unusual for lithium to induce some minor changes on electrocardiogram (EKG) studies. However, serious cardiac problems are rare at therapeutic levels.

Dermatological

The more common dermatological effects of lithium treatment are rash and acne-like lesions. Whether to stop lithium therapy is determined by the severity of either of these conditions.

Weight gain

Various mechanisms have been proposed, without conclusion, for this relatively common side effect, estimated at up to 20 pounds in at least 20 percent of patients (Vestergaard, Amdisen, and Schow 1980). Supervised caloric restriction may be helpful.

Teratogenicity

Lithium is contraindicated during pregnancy, especially the first trimester, due to congenital abnormalities, most notably of the heart. In rare situations, it may be necessary to continue lithium treatment in the pregnant patient, with dosage adjustments as necessitated by pregnancy-induced changes in kidney function.

Monitoring blood levels

Laboratory monitoring is necessary throughout lithium treatment to determine a safe and therapeutic dose and to limit side effects. The especially critical times to obtain a lithium level are during initiation, with dosage changes, with breakthrough symptoms, and any time toxicity is suspected (see figure 16-B). In the presence of severe side effects the prescriber will often discontinue lithium, pending laboratory results. Even though side effects and serum levels are not absolutely correlated in all patients, there is a general association (see figure 16-C).

Mechanism of Action

Decades of research have yet to provide a clear understanding of the exact mechanism of action of lithium. Multiple sites of action within the CNS have been

Recommended Lithium Monitoring

Reason	Frequency
Initiation of treatment	Every 3 to 7 days for first several weeks
	Once monthly for 3 to 6 months
Routine	Every 1 to 3 months in stable patient
With dosage change	Within 3 to 5 days
Signs of toxicity	Immediate
Symptoms of mania or depression	Immediate
Addition or discontinuation of interacting meds	Within 3 to 5 days
In presence of medical conditions resulting in dehydration	Immediate
Suspected pregnancy	Immediate

Figure 16-B

identified, none of which fully explain lithium's action on both mania and depression. Since neurotransmitter production, release, and reuptake rely on various ions (sodium, calcium, potassium, and magnesium), lithium's ionic properties may affect neurotransmitter-mediated depression and mania. Another potential mechanism of action of lithium is linked to its ability to stabilize cell membranes, via activity at sodium and potassium channels.

Lithium's benefit in mania may be linked to effects on dopamine and norepinephrine, possibly by preventing dopamine receptor supersensitivity in the manic individual. Additionally, lithium blocks some cocaine- and amphetamine-induced symptoms of mania, which are thought to be mediated by stimulant-related increases in CNS dopamine concentration. The action of lithium on norepinephrine is variable,

Severity of Side Effects

Mild	Moderate	Severe
(Lithium level up to 1.5)	(Lithium level 1.5–2.5)	(Lithium level above 2.5)
Increased thirst	Recurring, persisting or worsening nausea, vomiting, or diarrhea	Decreased urine output
Increased urination		Stupor
Weight gain		Seizure
Nausea, vomiting, diarrhea	Coarse tremor	Cardiovascular collapse
Fine hand tremor	Muscle twitching	Coma, death
Muscle weakness	Confusion	
Drowsiness	Slurred speech	
Lethargy		

Figure 16-C

causing an initial prolonged increase in reuptake, although this effect is not evident with long-term administration (American Society of Hospital Pharmacists 2000).

Lithium's serotonergic activity is postulated to be responsible for its role in preventing depressive episodes of bipolar disorder. Some bipolar patients demonstrate low CNS concentrations of serotonin. Lithium may contribute to serotonin production by increasing the uptake of the tryptophan, a serotonin precursor (American Society of Health System Pharmacists 2000).

Since the early 1990s it has been suggested that lithium's actions inside neuronal cells explain its therapeutic effects, specifically reducing overactivity of second messenger systems (Weber, Saklad, and Kastenholz 1992). Evidence has continued to be gathered supporting that theory, and broadened in scope. Current concepts purport that chronic lithium administration alters function of three signaling pathways, G protein, protein kinase A, and protein kinase C. In addition, it is now postulated that lithium possesses neuroprotective properties. Chronic lithium administration increases the amount of neuroprotective substances in the brain (Manji 2001; Chang 2000). Neuroprotective proteins are thought to protect against the destructive consequences of certain biochemical processes in the brain. For instance, it is postulated that there may be neuro-anatomical changes associated with mood disorders, such as a reduction in CNS neuron quantity and cell volume. Another theory is that glutamate and NDMA receptor activation may result in cellular damage. There is evidence to suggest that the neuro-protective proteins mitigate some of this damage. Although this line of research is relatively new, it holds great promise for maximizing drug therapies, as well as uncovering crucial information regarding the etiology of bipolar disorder.

Anticonvulsants

Two anticonvulsants, carbamazepine (Tegretol) and divalproex (Depakote), have proven mood stabilizing properties. Various treatment guidelines generally agree that divalproex is one of the first line agents for mania. It is believed by some to be the preferred agent for rapid cycling, although this is not a universal recommendation. In mixed mania, divalproex is considered one of the first line agents. Carbamazepine is generally considered a second line agent for mania and a first line agent for mixed mania.

Like lithium, the exact mechanisms of action have yet to be identified for the anticonvulsants. It is noteworthy that divalproex has demonstrated some of the same neuroprotective effects as lithium. Carbamazepine is thought to work by prolonging the inactivation of sodium ion channels or by potentiating the action of GABA, the primary inhibitory neurotransmitter in the CNS. Divalproex appears to work via both of these mechanisms. The newer anticonvulsants have similar properties to carbamazepine and divalproex. In addition they have an effect on glutamate receptors and calcium ion channels (Korn 2000).

Side Effects and Their Management

There are important therapeutic and side effect differences between carbamazepine and divalproex. Side effects are experienced by about 30 percent of patients treated with carbamazepine (Hollister 1992). Central nervous system effects are common, and include sedation, dizziness, drowsiness, blurred vision, and incoordination. Gastrointestinal side effects include nausea, vomiting, diarrhea, and abdominal

Dosage Guidelines for Anticonvulsants

Drug	Dosage Range[a] (mg/day)	Serum Level[b] (mcg/ml)
Carbamazepine	600–1600	4–10+
Divalproex	750–1500	50–100
Gabapentin	300–1800	c
Lamotrigine	50–500	c
Topiramate	50–300	c

a Serum levels are based on established anticonvulsant use. Mood-stabilizing response may fall above or below these values.

b Dosage requirements may be less for patients on multiple psychotropics.

c Serum monitoring may not be necessary.

For doses for children and adolescents: See appendix B.

Figure 16-D

pain, all of which may be alleviated by taking the medication with food or milk. Many of the CNS and GI side effects are often dose related and can be minimized by small dosage increases during titration or dosage reduction. Dermatological side effects can manifest with a red, itching rash or hives; they often necessitate discontinuation of treatment. Carbamazepine should be administered with caution to patients with a history of cardiac problems and liver disease.

Carbamazepine can induce decreases in white blood cell (WBC) count. These changes may be slight, especially during the first few weeks of treatment, and do not absolutely warrant stopping the medication. However, with a significant reduction in WBC or related components, most clinicians will consider discontinuing the medication and further evaluate these hematological changes.

Divalproex is tolerated slightly better than carbamazepine relative to nervous system side effects, notably in fewer complaints of fatigue and dizziness. Gastrointestinal side effects of nausea, vomiting, and indigestion are common, although these are usually transient. Use of sustained-release tablets (Depakote) may reduce these effects. Divalproex can occasionally interfere with the normal blood clotting cycle. Potential liver damage is also possible with valproate, although this effect has primarily been demonstrated in children taking multiple anticonvulsant medications.

Blood level monitoring is required for carbamazepine and divalproex, utilizing therapeutic anticonvulsant ranges (see figure 16-D). While there are not established ranges for antimanic effects, performing routine monitoring will identify potentially toxic levels. Levels should be taken weekly for the first month and every one to three months thereafter. Excessively elevated serum levels (overdoses) of the anticonvulsants are potentially life-threatening. Associated with carbamazepine toxicity are neurologic and cardiac malfunctions, while divalproex overdose may produce somnolence and coma. To promptly achieve therapeutic serum levels of divalproex, a loading dose has been suggested (Keck, McElroy, Tugrul, and Bennett 1993). This strategy employs a rapid titration, based on body weight, over the first one to five days of treatment. Side effect intolerance or potential for drug interactions may limit the application of this regimen.

Two additional anticonvulsants also show efficacy in the treatment of mania: gabapentin and lamotrigine.

Newer Anticonvulsants

Most newer anticonvulsants are in theory, and in practice, considered alternative treatments for bipolar disorder. It is important to note that when these drugs were marketed, they were intended for use in seizure disorders. It was only after they were released that their use in bipolar disorder became established. Some of the drugs may prove to be beneficial, some may not. Some of them have potentially life-threatening side effects associated with their use. Physicians are often faced with treatment-refractory bipolar patients, so it is not uncommon to see the agents listed below prescribed in an attempt to control symptoms. Therapists, by becoming familiar with the current status of supporting literature, can help patients to understand why medication decisions are made by their physicians. A list of some of the newer anticonvulsants and comments as to their documented efficacy in well-controlled studies for bipolar disorder is provided below:

- Lamotrigine (Lamictal): There is some evidence of effectiveness in bipolar depression; recommended in several expert guidelines. Associated with potentially life-threatening side effect of Stevens-Johnson syndrome.

- Gabapentin (Neurontin): Although widely used, recent research concludes there is no evidence to support use as first line or second line agent (Letterman and Markowitz 1999; Pande, Crockatt, Janney, Werth, and Tsaroucha 2000). Primary use in medicine is in seizure disorders and neuropathic pain.

- Topiramate (Topamax): Lack of research to support use at this time. Weight gain as side effect may occur less frequently than with divalproex based on anecdotal and retrospective reports.

- Tiagabine (Gabitril): Lack of research to support use at this time.

- Oxcarbazepine (Trileptal): Structural variant of carbamazepine. Lack of research to support use at this time.

- Felbamate (Felbatol): Use is associated with aplastic anemia and acute hepatic failure. The FDA and the manufacturer warn that use should be reserved only for severe, treatment-refractory seizure disorders.

Atypical Antispsychotics

Antipsychotics, both typical and atypical, have an established role as adjunctive therapy in bipolar disorder. There has been recent interest in whether the atypical antipsychotics might be effective as primary mood stabilizers. There are a number of studies involving clozapine, risperidone, olanzapine, and quetiapine in the treatment of bipolar disorder. At this time, in clinical practice, and until more long-term studies are conducted, the benefits of atypical antipsychotics appear to be as adjuncts, not as primary mood stabilizers (Ghaemi 2000).

Combinations of Medication

Patients with bipolar disorder frequently require multiple medications or changes in therapy. For example, antianxiety agents are helpful in reducing anxiety and agitation, especially in patients who refuse antimanic or antipsychotic agents. Likewise an added antipsychotic is more effective than a mood stabilizer alone in acute manic episodes that include significant psychomotor activity and delusions or hallucinations. Ongoing treatment with antipsychotics after the manic episode is resolved is often not necessary. However, it is not uncommon for a refractory patient to require a combination of mood stabilizers, an antidepressant, and an antipsychotic.

For patients with bipolar depression, the role of antidepressant therapy remains controversial. Certainly there is a risk of triggering a manic switch, but recent concerns have surfaced about whether antidepressants actually can induce rapid cycling. Likewise, length of treatment with antidepressants is debated, ranging from six weeks to six months. Practice patterns are likely to reflect this controversy. As to the choice of antidepressants in bipolar depression, the guidelines are mostly in agreement that bupropion, venlafaxine, or an SSRI are preferred.

Length of Treatment

Patients with bipolar disorder face long-term (lifetime) treatment with medications. Although use of antidepressants and antipsychotics may be limited to specific periods, a mood stabilizer is considered routine maintenance therapy in most patients. Medication-free periods are seldom beneficial and often result in symptom relapse. If evidence continues to mount that mood stabilizers have neuroprotective effects, maintenance treatment becomes even more important to positive outcomes.

Patient Education

Comprehensive patient education is critical in ensuring compliance and in ultimately limiting the devastating effects of bipolar disorder. Perhaps the most difficult fact for the patient to accept is the need for long-term treatment. In addition, patients must become active participants in identifying target symptoms and critical side effects, especially with lithium.

The first year after diagnosis can be an extremely difficult time for the patient and is often marked by treatment noncompliance and relapse. Thus patient education should include a discussion of the serious implications of medication noncompliance. Some individuals may naively (or out of denial) view periodic manic episodes as relatively benign occurrences, when in fact these are times of increased mortality risk. Patients should be informed that recurring manic episodes may increase susceptibility to future episodes. Additionally, some patients may actually become less responsive to mood stabilizer treatment with repeated episodes of mania. The therapist can be instrumental in helping patients recognize that continued medication noncompliance may actually contribute to a progressive worsening of their disorder.

Psychotherapeutic Issues

Professional opinions about lithium vary by discipline and by individual clinician. Some therapists find it easier to support the use of a "natural" substance, whereas others have been influenced by reports of side effects and toxicity. While the acutely manic patient is most often hospitalized, patients with hypomania or cyclothymia may be initiated on medications as outpatients, making the therapist an important part of the stabilization process. In this role, the therapist can assist the patient in assessing response and identifying side effects.

Patients will often resist mood stabilizers because of concerns not only about side effects but about therapeutic effects. What is clinically considered a symptom may be a desired state for the patient: a higher lever of energy, creativity, confidence. It is important to explore with the patient the sense of loss bipolar patients typically feel when valued conditions are diminished. For the bipolar patient, the desire for the manic "high" can be quite strong, not unlike the craving a drug addict experiences during the initial stages of recovery. This analogy may be helpful to patients who are struggling to accept the disease. The therapist can provide support and reassurance by acknowledging that mania is indeed a powerfully reinforcing "intrinsic high," but eventually the longing to be manic will diminish.

Psychotherapy is not only possible but can be very productive with the bipolar patient. Miklowitz (1996), in addressing combined psychotherapy and medication treatment for bipolar disorder, offers a comprehensive and detailed description of two approaches, family psychoeducation and individual therapy. The latter incorporates elements of interpersonal therapy for affective disorders with strategies to stabilize social rhythms. However, the therapist must be skilled at identifying symptoms of hypomania, mania, and depression, and the necessity for medication adjustment referrals. The therapist can be tested especially by the effects of medication noncompliance, when symptoms return and judgment and insight diminish.

Drug therapy is increasingly being advocated for an expanded spectrum of cylic mood symptoms, such as premenstrual syndrome, personality disorders, and temperamental disorders (Jacobsen 1993; Deltito 1993; Akiskal 1996; Akiskal and Bowden 2000). Although these presentations are inherently difficult for the treating clinician, there are no evidence-based guidelines directing medication use. The therapist is likely to encounter patients being treated with mood stabilizers who do not meet the *DSM-IV* criteria for bipolar I, bipolar II, or cylcothymia. As with all medication therapy it is important to identify target symptoms and expected response indicators before these medications are prescribed.

17

Antianxiety Medications

The first benzodiazepine synthesized was chlordiazepoxide (Librium), in 1957. Since then, many others have been developed and are available in the United States. These medications are used both for anxiety (sedatives) and insomnia (hypnotics). Additional uses are as anesthetics and as aids in handling withdrawal from other drugs. Some are used primarily as hypnotics (flurazepam, temazepam, and triazolam), but they differ little, other than by use, from the other benzodiazepines. When benzodiazepines were first developed, they represented a significant improvement over the previously available antianxiety agents: the barbiturates, meprobamate (Equanil, Miltown), tybamate (Tybatran), glutethimide (Doriden), methyprylon (Noludar), and ethchlorvynol (Placidyl). The benzodiazepines had better antianxiety specificity and were much less lethal in overdose.

These medications have been very widely used (and abused) because anxiety and insomnia are very common and because these drugs are very effective and well tolerated. Within twenty to thirty minutes after an oral dose the effects can be felt. Benzodiazepines can cause sedation, slurred speech, incoordination, prolonged response time in higher doses (or when the person is very sensitive to the drug), and sometimes a lessening of inhibitions, as with alcohol.

The main differences between the different drugs are their pharmacodynamics: especially half-life and metabolism (see figure 17-A). Those with a longer half-life tend to build up in the system—even if taken only once a day. Most are metabolized by the liver and therefore can build up in the system when the liver is impaired, as with alcoholic liver disease. The three least dependent on the liver are lorazepam, temazepam, and oxazepam. The ones with a very short half-life (triazolam, midazolam, and, to a lesser degree, lorazepam) can cause anterograde amnesia: loss of memory for a short period after the drug has worn off.

Half-Lives of Benzodiazepines

- More than 24 hours:

    Diazepam
    Chlordiazepoxide
    Flurazepam
    Prazepam
    Clorazepate

- 18–24 hours:

    Clonazepam

- 8–16 hours:

    Temazepam
    Lorazepam
    Alprazolam
    Oxazepam

- Less than 6 hours:

    Triazolam
    Midazolam
    Zaleplon

Figure 17-A

Types of Antianxiety Drugs

Benzodiazepines

The benzodiazepines work by interacting with benzodiazepine receptors, of which there are three types. Most current benzodiazepines show little selectivity for these receptor types; however, those developed in the future may have greater selectivity and possibly less sedation or dependence potential. Benzodiazepine receptors are co-located with GABA receptors, which usually function as presynaptic inhibiting receptors. The benzodiazepine receptors have a high density in the limbic system. Binding of a benzodiazepine at the BZ receptor enhances the effect of GABA and increases the influx of chloride ions (see figure 17-B; also see chapter 8 for a more detailed discussion of the biological basis of anxiety disorders). Figure 17-C gives the dosage range for benzodiazepines.

Atypical Benzodiazepines

There are three new benzodiazepine derivatives being used as hypnotics (see figure 17-C). Estazolam (ProSom) is a triazolobenzodiazepine with a rapid onset of action, intermediate half-life, and no significant active metabolites; thus it does not have a tendency to lead to drug accumulation and daytime sedation. Quazepam (Doral) has the same active metabolite as flurazepam and has similar properties. Zolpidem (Ambien) is a short-acting nonbenzodiazepine of the imidazopyridine class. Some studies suggest it may be associated with less cognitive impairment, and less dependence. This may be due to its greater specificity in interacting preferentially with one of the three BZ receptors. Zaleplon (Sonata) is the newest nonbenzodiazepine hypnotic. It has a very short half-life (one hour) and preliminary studies suggest a low risk. Most benzodiazepines tend to suppress REM sleep and Stage III and IV (delta) sleep (Nishino, Mignot, and Dement 1998), thereby altering "sleep architecture" and producing a less restful sleep. This can lead to daytime fatigue and impaired concentration. However, zolpidem and zaleplon have been shown to have little, if any, effect on sleep architecture and are therefore preferable as hypnotics.

Buspirone

Buspirone is a unique antianxiety agent. It acts at the 5-HT 1A receptor; however, its exact mechanism of action is not fully understood. Buspirone tends to have a delayed onset of action—similar to the antidepressants. A typical starting dose is 5 mg two or three times per day; typically patients require 20–40 mg per day in divided doses (see figure 17-C). Reduced anxiety is seen within one or two weeks.

The advantages of buspirone over benzodiazepines are that it is not associated with tolerance or dependence, it does not interact with other CNS depressants (such as alcohol), and it is not associated with impaired psychomotor function. The drug's disadvantages are its delayed onset of action and that it is not always effective, especially in people who have used benzodiazepines. The most common side effects of buspirone are nausea, dizziness, and, paradoxically, anxiety.

Antihistamines

Certain antihistamines are frequently used in the treatment of anxiety: hydroxyzine (Vistaril, Atarax) and diphenhydramine (Benadryl) (see figure 17-C). They act by blocking histamine receptors in the CNS, causing sedation and thereby reducing anxiety. They can also cause drowsiness and impaired performance. They work within twenty to thirty minutes and last four to six hours. They are not habit-forming, but have the disadvantages that tolerance can develop to their anxiolytic (antianxiety) effects and they tend to have a narrow therapeutic window between reducing anxiety and producing sedation.

Beta Blockers

Beta blockers are medications that act by blocking the effects of norepinephrine at the receptor. They are very effective at reducing the peripheral manifestations of anxiety (increased heart rate, sweating, tremor), but are not very effective at blocking the internal experience of anxiety. They are used very effectively for the treatment of performance anxiety, such as that caused by public speaking. The most commonly used beta blocker is propranolol (Inderal), but atenolol (Tenormin) and several others are also used (see figure 17-C). Beta blockers can cause dizziness and lowered blood pressure (in fact, their main use is as antihypertensives) and can cause depression if used over a long period of time. They have been used with some benefit as

Figure 17-B

adjunctive agents in the treatment of panic disorder. Beta blockers are not habit forming, but should be discontinued slowly to avoid rebound elevation of blood pressure.

Clonidine

Clonidine (Catapres) is an alpha-2 adrenergic agonist, which thereby functions as a presynaptic inhibitor of norepinephrine release. It is usually used to treat hypertension (like the beta blockers) but has been used to treat anxiety disorders with some success. It is also used to treat opiate withdrawal. A typical starting dose is 0.1 mg two to three times daily (see figure 17-C). It is also available as a transdermal patch.

Length of Treatment

Antianxiety medications, especially benzodiazepines, can provide relief of anxiety regardless of the cause: situational stress, hyperthyroidism, or manic excitement (see figure 17-D). Of course, it is crucial to recognize and treat the underlying disorder. The use of benzodiazepines should be avoided until other measures have been tried (such as psychotherapy, relaxation training) or if anxiety is severe.

Benzodiazepines are very safe and effective in the short-term treatment of anxiety. However, prolonged use (over six months) may lead to tolerance and dependence.

Dosages of Antianxiety Agents

Generic Name	Brand Name	Single-Dose Dosage Range (mg)	Usual Dosage Range (mg/day)
Benzodiazepines			
Diazepam	Valium	2–10	4–40
Chlordiazepoxide	Librium	10–50	15–100
Flurazepam	Dalmane	15–60	15–60
Prazepam	Centrax	5–30	20–40
Clorazepate	Tranxene	3.75–15	7.5–60
Clonazepam	Klonopin	1–8	0.5–2
Temazepam	Restoril	15–30	15–60
Lorazepam	Ativan	0.5–2	1.5–6
Alprazolam	Xanax	0.25–2	0.5–6
Oxazepam	Serax	10–30	30–90
Triazolam	Halcion	0.125–0.5	.125–0.5
Midazolam	Versed (injectable only)		
Atypical Benzodiazepines			
Estazolam	ProSom	1.0–2.0	1.0–2.0
Zolpidem	Ambien	5–10	5–10
Zaleplon	Sonata	5–10	5–10
Other Antianxiety Agents			
Buspirone	BuSpar	5–20	10–40
Hydroxyzine	Atarax, Vistaril	10–50	30–200
Diphenhydramine	Benadryl	25–100	75–200
Propranolol	Inderal	10–80	20–160
Atenolol	Tenormin	25–100	25–100
Clonidine	Catapres	0.1–.3	0.2–0.9

For doses for children and adolescents: See appendix B.

Figure 17-C

Indications for Antianxiety Agents

- Adjustment reaction
- Phobic disorders
- Panic disorders
- Generalized anxiety disorder
- Obsessive-compulsive disorder
- Post-traumatic stress disorder
- Psychophysiological disorders related to anxiety (somatization disorder)
- Other disorders with prominent anxiety or agitation

Figure 17-D

There have been several waves of public alarm about the abuse potential of benzodiazepines. Over ten years ago, there was much concern about Valium abuse, as portrayed in the book *I'm Dancing As Fast As I Can* (Gordon 1990). More recently, there has been much concern about abuse of Xanax and memory impairment due to Halcion.

Because of the potential for dependence and abuse, it is best to try to use benzodiazepines only for short-term treatment. (One bad experience with someone who abuses these drugs is enough to make you vow to never prescribe them long-term again.) The problem lies in identifying beforehand that small percentage of people at high risk for abuse. A prior history of substance abuse is, of course, a good predictor, but is not always present. On the other hand, many people take moderate doses of benzodiazepines for years without escalation in dose or any deleterious side effects. And some patients with panic disorder or other anxiety disorders who do not tolerate or respond to other forms of treatment (such as antidepressants or buspirone) do well on long-term maintenance with benzodiazepines without abuse developing. However, long-term benzodiazepine treatment is presently, and probably will remain, controversial.

Benzodiazepine Withdrawal

Minor tranquilizers and sedative-hypnotics are widely used in general medical practice and psychiatry. Although the benzodiazepines as a class are much safer than earlier medications (there is less risk of dependency and abuse, and withdrawal symptoms are generally much less dangerous than with barbiturates), problems do exist when patients begin to reduce doses, especially if they discontinue rapidly or "cold turkey." Benzodiazepine withdrawal syndromes are encountered frequently. They cause considerable patient distress, can be dangerous at times, and are almost always avoidable if the clinician follows the discontinuation guidelines carefully.

When patients are treated daily for more than a few weeks, especially in moderate to high doses, the nervous system adapts to the presence of the drugs (tolerance develops) such that any rapid drop in blood levels of the medication can precipitate a withdrawal syndrome. Symptoms of withdrawal include the following (Smith and Wesson 1983):

Mild to Moderate	Severe
Anxiety	Seizures
Restlessness	High fever
Insomnia	Psychosis
Nightmares	Death

Typically, antianxiety medications with short half-lives (see figure 17-A) are more likely to produce withdrawal symptoms (since the medications are more rapidly eliminated from the system). However, clearly, withdrawal can occur with *all* minor tranquilizers and sedative-hypnotics (with the exception of buspirone and possibly zolpidem, which are chemical compounds unrelated to the benzo-diazepines).

Often anxiety symptoms occur after medications are discontinued. It is some-times difficult to distinguish between anxiety symptoms attributed to withdrawal, per se, and a reemergence of the primary anxiety associated with the original anxiety disorder. One defining feature is that symptoms that continue longer than two weeks tend to indicate the persistence of the underlying disorder. In such cases, discontinu-ation is premature (since the underlying disorder has not yet resolved) and contin-ued treatment is warranted. However, withdrawal symptoms may mimic the anxiety symptoms, especially in panic disorder.

When symptoms are determined to be withdrawal, the medication should be restarted or returned to the dosage level previously used for chronic treatment. Then a *very gradual* withdrawal regime can be initiated, a 5 to 10 percent reduction of the daily dosage per week. With the shorter half-life tranquilizers, often the pace of med-ication discontinuance must be even more gradual; that is, a longer time must be allowed between progressive decreases in dose.

For reasons that are not well understood, many patients find that it is especially difficult to discontinue the very last dose, even if discontinuation has proceeded well up to that point. For example, many patients have problems discontinuing the final dose of alprazolam (for example, 0.25 mg twice a day). It is advisable to not rush this final stage of drug phase out. It may be wise to take an additional month or two to gradually discontinue the medication, or in some cases you may want to consider ongoing treatment with what amounts to microdoses of these medications. If there are no noticeable side effects, there are really no contraindications for prolonged treatment with very low doses of minor tranquilizers.

Finally, severe cases of drug dependence (high doses) are most safely detoxed in the hospital. Phenobarbital is the "gold standard" for severe withdrawal syn-dromes, but pentobarbital or carbamazepine may also be used.

Patient Education

Patients who have been prescribed antianxiety medications should be cautioned about the risk of dependence, the dangers of combining these drugs with alcohol (the story of Karen Ann Quinlan can be helpful in this regard), and the possible impairment of coordination (including driving a car). You may find it helpful to have an agreement with your client that they will use the medications only for a specific length of time, such as one month. Some patients are too quick to ask for antianxiety medications, and some are too reluctant. Both of these represent problems that need to be dealt with. For example, some patients have severe, disabling anxiety or insomnia and need to be encouraged to take antianxiety medications for a short period of time. They need to be reassured that they will not become addicted after a few days of treatment.

Similarly, often people taking buspirone need a lot of encouragement to keep taking the medication long enough to get benefit. This is especially the case for those looking for a "quick fix." Studies show that the benefits of buspirone are still increasing after three to six months of use.

Patients who have been on the medications for some time need to be advised against abrupt discontinuation, which can lead to a severe withdrawal syndrome and possible convulsions. A reduction in dose is likely to lead to a reemergence of the anxiety symptoms for which the person is being treated, such as panic attacks. If this is due only to drug withdrawal, the symptoms usually subside within two weeks. For this reason, as stated above, it is best to taper off benzodiazepine dosage very slowly after prolonged use.

18

Antipsychotic Medications

Antipsychotic medications have truly revolutionized the treatment of psychotic disorders. Their effectiveness is so vastly superior to previous treatments that they have ushered in a new era in the treatment of severe mental illnesses. Chlorpromazine (Thorazine) was first used in 1952 as a postoperative sedative. It was subsequently used as a sedative for psychiatric patients, and it was soon discovered that it had antipsychotic properties. Soon other "phenothiazines" were developed.

When these drugs were first used in clinical settings, the mechanism of action was unknown, although the medications were clearly quite successful in reducing psychotic symptoms. Later research determined that antipsychotic medications acted by producing a chemical blockade of dopamine D2 postsynaptic receptors and that their clinical potency correlated with their degree of dopamine blockade. This led to the dopamine hypothesis of schizophrenia (see chapter 10).

Other, chemically distinct dopamine blockers were then developed, such as thiothixene, haloperidol, loxapine, molindone, and pimozide. All of these antipsychotics are potent dopamine blockers and collectively were called neuroleptics because they inadvertently cause certain neurological side effects (discussed below). More recently, atypical antipsychotic medications have been developed (clozapine risperidone, and others), which are effective antipsychotics yet are weak dopamine blockers and cause minimal neurological side effects. This group, which has revolutionized the treatment of psychosis, is discussed separately below.

Standard Antipsychotics

The phenothiazines and similar antipsychotics can be divided into high-potency and low-potency groups (see figure 18-A). In addition, they can be ranked according to their tendency to produce extrapyramidal symptoms (EPS) versus sedation and anticholinergic side effects (see figure 18-B).

Dosages of Antipsychotic Medication

Generic Name	Brand Name	Dosage Range (mg/day)	Equivalence[a] (mg)
Low Potency			
Chlorpromazine	Thorazine	50–1500	100
Thioridazine	Mellaril	150–800	100
Clozapine[c]	Clozaril	300–900	50
Mesoridazine	Serentil	50–500	50
Quetiapine	Seroquel	300–750	0
Ziprasidone	Geodon	40–160	10
High Potency			
Molindone	Moban	20–225	10
Perphenazine	Trilafon	8–60	10
Loxapine	Loxitane	50–250	10
Trifluoperazine	Stelazine	10–40	5
Fluphenazine	Prolixin[b]	3–45	2
Thiothixene	Navane	10–60	5
Haloperidol	Haldol[b]	2–40	2
Pimozide	Orap	1–10	1
Risperidone[c]	Risperdal	4–16	1–2
Olanzapine[c]	Zyprexa	5–20	1–2
Antiparkinson/ Anticholinergic Drugs			
Trihexyphenidyl	Artane	5–15	
Benztropine mesylate	Cogentin	1–8	
Biperiden	Akineton	2–8	
Amantadine	Symmetrel	100–300	

a Dose required to achieve efficacy of 100 mg chlorpromazine

b Available in time-release IM formulation

c Atypical antipsychotic

For doses for children and adolescents: See appendix B.

Figure 18-A

Side Effects of Antipsychotic Medications

Medication	Sedation	Extrapyramidal[a]	Anticholergenic[b]
Chlorpromazine	++++	++	++++
Thioridazine	++++	+	+++++
Clozapine	++++	0	+++++
Mesoridazine	++++	+	+++++
Molindone	+	+++	+++
Perphenazine	++	+++	++
Loxapine	+	+++	++
Trifluoperazine	+	++++	++
Fluphenazine	+	+++++	++
Thiothixene	+	++++	++
Haloperidol	+	+++++	+
Pimozide	+	+++++	+
Risperidone	+	+	+
Olanzapine	+	+/0	+
Quetiapine	+	+	0
Ziprasidone	+	+/0	++

a Acute: Parkinson's dystonias, akathisia. Does not reflect risk for tardive dyskinesia.
b All neuroleptics may cause tardive dyskinesia.

Figure 18-B

Side Effects and Their Management

All neuroleptics, to a greater or lesser degree, produce the following side effects, which can be classified into five groups.

Extrapyramidal

The neuroleptics produce extrapyramidal side effects due to the blocking of dopamine receptors. In addition to producing a reduction in positive psychotic symptoms by blocking dopamine in the mesolimbic region, they unfortunately produce extrapyramidal symptoms by dopamine blockade in the basal ganglia. There are three types of acute extrapyramidal symptoms: Parkinsonian side effects are those that resemble Parkinson's disease, with slowed movements, decreased facial expression, resting tremor, and a shuffling gait. Dystonic symptoms involve sustained muscle spasms, usually of the neck or shoulder (such as torticollis) and can be quite frightening and painful. Akathisia refers to an intense feeling of restlessness. At times this side effect can be confused with psychotic agitation and thus mistakenly result in the physician increasing the dose of medication which results in increased akathisia. Severe akathisia can be very uncomfortable and is associated with increased noncompliance and increased risk of suicide.

Anticholinergic

Antipsychotic medications block acetylcholine receptors and thereby affect the parasympathetic nervous system. This leads to dry membranes (especially mouth and eyes), blurred vision (especially near vision), intestinal slowing (constipation), difficulty urinating, sedation, and sexual dysfunction. These symptoms may be very mild or, depending on the type of medication, quite severe and disabling.

Antiadrenergic

Antipsychotic medications produce alpha-adrenergic blockade, which leads to orthostatic hypotension. This means that when the person stands up, blood pressure drops precipitously, leading to a transient lightheadedness and potentially a fall and injury.

Tardive dyskinesia

All of the above side effects appear within the first few hours or days of treatment or with increases in dose. In contrast, the tardive dyskinesias (disorders involving involuntary movements) appear late in the course of treatment or when the medication is reduced or discontinued. These movements usually improve slowly over time, but they may persist for years even after the medication is discontinued.

Atypical side effects

As with all medications, certain people may have allergic reactions to antipsychotic medications. Weight gain is a common side effect. Agranulocytosis, a very serious blood disorder, was reported in the past, but it now appears to have been caused by a contaminant in some drug preparations and has not been reported recently. Hepatitis, similarly, has not been reported recently. Since the antipsychotics lower the seizure threshold, they may lead to grand mal seizures. They also interfere with temperature regulation and may lead to hyperthermia, especially when the person exercises during warm weather. Antipsychotics raise prolactin levels and this may cause lactation. Neuroleptic malignant syndrome (NMS) is a rare, but potentially fatal reaction to antipsychotic medication. It is characterized by fever, confusion, and rigidity. If not recognized and treated promptly it can lead to irreversible coma and death.

Symptoms that require immediate medication reevaluation are these:

Side Effects Calling for Medication Reassessment

- Confusion

- Falls

- Inability to urinate

- Prolonged or severe constipation

- Rash

- High fever (may be due to agranulocytosis or NMS)

- Involuntary movements

- Jaundice (yellowish discoloration of skin, including eyes)

- Severe sedation

- Severe restlessness

- Muscle spasm (such as torticollis)

Management

Many of the side effects of antipsychotic medications can be managed so that they are less troublesome to patients. This ensures that patients are more willing to comply in taking them. Some side effects, such as sedation, can be managed by reducing the dose or by switching to a less sedating antipsychotic. (One should always use the lowest effective dose—although determining what dose that is, is not always easy.) Extrapyramidal side effects can be reduced by switching to a less potent (and more sedating) antipsychotic. Additionally, extrapyramidal side effects typically are managed by the addition of an antiparkinsonian drug (such as benztropine, trihexyphenidyl, or biperiden; see figure 18-A). However, these medications also have side effects: dry mouth, blurred vision, and constipation, but are usually fairly well tolerated. Akathisia may be treated with antiparkinsonian drugs, beta blockers (such as propranolol), benzodiazipines, or a combination of these. Usually by adjusting the dose, changing medications, and/or adding adjunctive medications (such as an antiparkinsonian) the side effects of the antipsychotic medications can be reduced to a tolerable level.

Atypical Antipsychotics

In contrast to the neuroleptics, the atypical antipsychotics are strong serotonin (5-HT2A and 5-HT2C) and weak dopamine (D2) blockers. Clozapine is the prototypical agent. It is effective for both positive and negative symptoms and studies have shown that as many as 40 percent of those who have failed to respond to haloperidol and chlorpromazine respond to clozapine.

Clozapine has a very low incidence of extrapyramidal side effects and very few cases of tardive dyskinesia. It is very sedating and has some anticholinergic and antiadrenergic side effects (see Fig. 18-B). Sedation is the most troublesome side effect. Clozapine lowers the seizure threshold and can cause hepatitis. The most serious side effect, however, is a severe blood disorder, agranulocytosis, which has caused several deaths in the United States. These deaths have occurred despite the mandatory weekly monitoring of white blood cell count. (Note: After six months with normal blood counts, monitoring can then take place on a bi-weekly basis.) Clozapine can cost as much as $10,000 per year because of the need for weekly blood tests, although this cost is offset by reduced hospitalizations. Also, there have been a few sudden deaths associated with clozapine, presumably cardiac in nature.

Since the release of clozapine, researchers have sought to develop an atypical antipsychotic without the side effects of clozapine (especially aplastic anemia). As of this writing, four other atypical agents have been released: risperidone, olanzapine, quetiapine, and ziprasidone, and several others may soon be released. These agents vary somewhat in their pharmacological profile and, as a group, may revolutionize the treatment of schizophrenia, and possibly affective psychoses.

The benefits of the atypical antipsychotics include better tolerability by patients, significantly reduced risk of tardive dyskinesia, reduction of negative symptoms, improved cognition and reduced neuro-anatomical changes (enlargement of lateral ventricles). Their use has led to a renewed emphasis on rehabilitation.

Risperidone (Risperdal) was the first atypical after Clozapine. It is a very potent dopamine blocker, with significant risk of causing extrapyramidal side effects, and minimal sedation.

Olanzapine (Zyprexa) has a very low tendency to cause extrapyramidal side effects. However, it is sedating and tends to cause weight gain and problems in carbohydrate metabolism.

Quetiapine (Seroquel) has a low incidence of extrapyramidal side effects. It is sedating and can cause dry mouth.

Ziprasidone (Geodon) is the newest atypical. It is less sedating, causes less weight gain, but can cause extrapyramidal side effects. It also has more effect on cardiac conduction (QT prolongation) than the other atypicals and its use should be avoided in patients with significant cardiovascular disease.

Choice of Medication

The antipsychotic medications tend to be effective in the treatment of psychotic symptoms, regardless of the disorder. They can be effective in substance-induced delusional disorders, delirium, schizophrenia, mania, delusional disorder, and so on. Standard antipsychotics tend to be effective for positive symptoms but do little to improve negative symptoms. The newer, atypical antipsychotics are more effective for negative symptoms although clearly not a panacea since they are successful in only about 30 percent of cases.

The choice of medication is generally based on three factors:

- If an antipsychotic medication has been used with success in the past, generally the same medication is again prescribed.

- The patient's motor state is important to consider. Typically, very agitated patients may be given a more sedating (low-potency) medication, whereas markedly regressed or withdrawn patients will be given a less sedating (high-potency) drug.

- The side effect profile of the drug chosen must be considered in relation to the individual patient (see figure 18-C). For example, in the elderly, drugs high in anticholinergic side effects are likely to increase confusion and memory problems, thus high-potency drugs are often used, such as haloperidol or perphenazine.

Special Considerations in Choosing an Antipsychotic

Patient Type	Medication Choice
Child	Low dose
Elderly	High-potency, low dose or atypical
Anxious or agitated	Zyprexa, Seroquel
Bipolar, manic	Atypical[a]

a Use caution when combining with lithium (may produce encephalopathy).

Figure 18-C

Individual differences in drug metabolism vary considerably, the dosage ranges are quite broad, and thus it is always difficult to know what dose will be required. People are usually started on a low dose and gradually titrated upward depending on clinical response and side effects. In the past, the use of high doses of antipsychotic medications, referred to as *rapid neuroleptization,* was popular. However, more recent studies have shown that moderate doses will produce the same eventual outcome (after ten days) with fewer side effects.

Length of Treatment

All psychotic symptoms do not respond in the same time frame when treated with antipsychotic medications. Typically, severe restlessness, agitation, and marked confusion may subside after a few hours or a few days of treatment. However, longer periods of treatment are generally necessary to resolve symptoms such as delusions, hallucinations, and thought disorder. Some patients may show improvement in these symptoms within a week or two, but in some chronic schizophrenics, many weeks of treatment may be required to gradually reduce these positive symptoms.

The length of treatment also depends on the type of disorder. In substance-induced psychoses, delirium, or brief reactive psychosis, the medication usually can be discontinued after the acute phase. In schizophreniform disorder and atypical psychosis, it is often necessary to continue the medication for six months in order to avoid relapse. As mentioned previously, many studies have shown that discontinuation of medication in schizophrenia is associated with higher relapse rates. The general rule is to continue treating schizophrenics for at least one year following the remission of psychotic symptoms to prevent relapse. However, because of the risk of tardive dyskinesia, this judgment must be based on the patient's prior history and ongoing assessment of emerging side effects. Abnormal movements, which may signal the emergence of TD, should be checked for at least every six months, for example, by using the AIMS scale (see figure 18-D).

Patient Education

Psychotic disorders are always accompanied by significant functional impairment and great personal suffering. A very common problem, especially with schizophrenia, is relapse. Most often, relapse can be traced to noncompliance with the medication regime. Thus patient education becomes a very important part of treatment. Education involves helping patients to recognize prodromal symptoms of their illness (which may necessitate a dosage increase). Often it is helpful to discuss the prodromal period prior to a psychotic episode in detail to emphasize the particular symptoms that may serve as warning signs for that person. It is also vital that both patients and their families be educated about the effects and side effects of antipsychotic medications—particularly tardive dyskinesia—so that side effects can be properly managed. They should be reassured that most side effects can be reduced to tolerable levels.

Helping patients understand the reasons for taking the medication and the need to manage side effects is an important part of ensuring compliance. Education of the patient's spouse and family is also very important in this regard. Often family members are the first to notice a change in the patient's behavior necessitating a

---

AIMS
(Abnormal Involuntary Movement Scale)

Rate the presence of involuntary movements in the following areas according to severity: 1=none, 2=minimal, 3=mild, 4=moderate, 5=severe.

Muscles of facial expression	1 2 3 4 5	
Lips and perioral area	1 2 3 4 5	
Jaw	1 2 3 4 5	
Tongue	1 2 3 4 5	
Upper extremities	1 2 3 4 5	
Lower extremities	1 2 3 4 5	
Trunk	1 2 3 4 5	
Overall severity of abnormal movements	1 2 3 4 5	
Incapacitation due to abnormal movements	1 2 3 4 5	
Distress due to abnormal movements	1 2 3 4 5	
Problems with teeth or dentures	Yes/No	
Usually wears dentures	Yes/No	

Source: U.S. Department of Health, Education, and Welfare

Figure 18-D

medication adjustment. The patient's physician and psychotherapist play a crucial role in helping to educate the patient and in detecting early symptoms of relapse.

Psychotherapeutic Issues

Several issues are important in doing psychotherapy with someone with schizophrenia, where medication compliance is often an issue and where medication noncompliance is usually, eventually, associated with relapse. One goal is to recognize and take measures to minimize side effects. Several studies have shown that akinesia and akathisia are associated with medication noncompliance. Another issue is making the schizophrenic symptoms ego-dystonic to the patient. This may be a long process, involving repeatedly pointing out the ways in which the symptoms are dysfunctional in the patient's life.

Medication may be seen by the patient as intrusive and controlling or, alternatively, as comforting—a transitional, object-like extension of the therapist. Patients will be prone to interpret the medication in psychotic ways, especially when they are more symptomatic (and more in need of medication). When compliance remains a significant problem, consideration may be given to using one of the long-acting injectable forms of the antipsychotics (haloperidol decanoate or fluphenazine decanoate).

19

Over-the-Counter Dietary Supplements and Herbal Products

American consumers spend 4 billion dollars per year on herbal products (Eisenberg, Davis, et al. 1998). More than five-hundred herbs are currently on the market, in a variety of forms, from raw plants to manufactured preparations (Boullata and Nace 2000). The most rapidly growing segment of the market is for products used to treat or prevent psychiatric symptoms, including St. John's Wort, kava kava, ginkgo, and valerian (Beaubrun and Gray 2000). Sales of mood-altering herbals approached the $400 million per year mark in the year 2000 (*Consumer Reports* 2000, p. 60). Worldwide, 80 percent of people use botanical products and an estimated 40 percent of U.S. citizens have turned to "alternative medicines" (LaFrance, Lauterbach, et al. 2000). The therapist is likely to encounter patients who are already taking herbal remedies or who are seeking information about them. Questions about use of these products should be part of the diagnostic workup. This chapter provides an overview of the relevant issues surrounding these products, especially safety, efficacy, and psychosocial implications.

In Germany, the government has attempted to regulate the use of herbal products, and has done so by promoting research, public education, and medical education. However, in the United States, herbal and other over-the-counter (OTC) products are neither approved prior to marketing, nor regulated for efficacy, by the FDA. The only limitation imposed upon the manufacturers of these products is that they cannot advertise that they prevent or treat certain diseases. Claims can be made, however, for use in nondisease conditions or physical functions.

Although some herbal products do have documented effectiveness in treating some psychiatric conditions, their use also can be problematic or even, at times, dangerous due to the following reasons:

- No assurances of strength or potency. Some products have been shown to have absolutely none of the particular substances listed on the label. There are currently no standardization requirements for herbal products.

- Some products have been shown to contain impurities or contaminants, such as arsenic, mercury, and lead. Potent pharmaceutical contaminants have been discovered in these products, such as digitalis and estazolam (Harris 2000).

- Serious adverse reactions can occur with these products and yet safety monitoring is nearly nonexistent. The FDA can request that one of these products be withdrawn from the market, but manufacturers are not required to comply unless consumers are faced with an "imminent hazard."

- Some herbals (most notably St. John's Wort) have significant effects on liver metabolism and they pose dangers of potentially harmful drug-drug interactions. Although some documentation exists regarding drug interactions, there is a relative lack of accurate information available. There is currently no systematic process in place to assess and report drug interactions with herbals. Many products contain multiple ingredients making the precise identification of drug interactions difficult.

- Seventy percent of people in the United States who use herbal products never inform their doctors (LaFrance, Lauterbach, et al. 2000) increasing the likelihood that an adverse reaction or drug interaction will occur and be misidentified.

In addition to the informational and regulatory challenges associated with herbals, the therapist also encounters the psychosocial implications of their use. The following is a summary of the key points offered by Cauffield (2000) and Harris (2000) that are relevant to therapists.

- Some of the demographics of herbal users overlap with those of psychotherapy patients increasing the possibility that issues regarding their use will surface. These characteristics include higher levels of education and income, as well as an association between an interest in alternative therapies and a commitment to personal growth.

- The conditions cited by users of herbals are often chronic, difficult to treat by conventional methods, and associated with complicated lifestyle features. Examples are chronic pain, anxiety, insomnia, depression, fatigue, and memory problems. These are representative of what therapists routinely treat.

- Alternative therapies with an established role in medicine and psychiatry include relaxation techniques, chiropractic care, biofeedback, and hypnosis. Less established is the role of herbal and high dose vitamin regimens. It can be difficult for patients and practitioners to differentiate between these realms when determining a course of treatment. Additionally, while certain alternative therapies are sometimes covered under insurance, herbals are almost always excluded, resulting in higher out-of-pocket costs for the patient.

There are some reputable manufacturers that voluntarily have instituted production standards; and for some products there are accepted clinical trials supporting efficacy. In this chapter we will briefly review those over-the-counter products that have research support documenting efficacy in treating some psychiatric conditions. Of note, many of the legitimate results published are from Germany, or other countries, where standardized products were used in the studies. It is not reasonable to assume that patients or consumers in the United States would experience the same effects by taking nonstandardized products marketed in this country. For a more complete review see Davidson and Connor (2000); Ness, Sherman, and Pan (1999); LaFrance, Lauterbach et. al (2000); and the *PDR for Herbal Medicines* (1998). Please note that all statements made below are based on limited available data and should be considered as only preliminary.

OTC Products with Some Research Documenting Efficacy

Product	Conditions Treated	Usual Adult Daily Dose	Side Effects	Drug-Drug Interactions[a]
St. John's Wort (hypericum perforatum)	Depression	900–1800 mg.	Minimal nausea Insomnia Hypomania/mania Photosensitivity Interference with certain lab tests	Significant[b]
SAM-e (s-adenosyl-methionine)	Depression	400–1600 mg.	GI symptoms Hypomania/mania Serotonin syndrome	Not well established
Kava Kava (piper methysticum)	Anxiety	100–400 mg.	Sedation, ataxia, habit-forming or intoxicating at higher doses; some evidence of liver impairment; may increase depression or suicidality	Moderate[c]

OTC Products That May Be Beneficial

Melatonin	Sleep disturbance	0.5 mg.	Sedation; at higher doses may aggravate depression	Not well established
Ginkgo Biloba	Cognitive impairment	20–240 mg.	GI problems Headache Dizziness Interference with certain lab tests	Not well established[d]

OTC Products That May Increase Psychiatric Symptoms
(Not Recommended)

Product	Intended Effects	Adverse Psychiatric Effects
Yohimbine	Treatment of impotency	↑ Anxiety
Valerian Root	Improve sleep	May aggravate depression May cause excitability

a For details on drug-drug interactions see Ayd (2000); Fugh-Berman (2000).

b Significant due to hepatic enzyme induction. Do not use with: birth control pills, protease inhibitors, immuno-suppressants (e.g., cyclosporine), asthma mediations (e.g., theophylline), SSRIs, MAOI antidepressants, venlafaxine, mirtazapine, tricyclic antidepressants, amphetamines, anticonvulsants, levodopa, warfarin, and digoxin. Other, as yet undiscovered, interactions may also exist.

c May potentiate effects of alcohol, benzodiazepines, barbiturates, and antipsychotics (side effects); adverse effects also seen with cimetidine and levodopa.

d May cause bleeding in people taking aspirin. Do not use with: divalproex, anticoagulants, moderate to high intake of caffeine. May induce seizures.

The Promise of Herbal Remedies

It is important to keep in mind that a number of important and highly effective pharmaceuticals originally were derived from botanic sources. The list includes: poppy (morphine), willow bark (aspirin), belladonna tops (atropine), and foxglove leaf (digitalis). It is certainly reasonable to assume that other botanicals may prove to be safe and effective treatments for certain psychiatric disorders as well.

However, progress in this area is impeded by two significant factors: First, because herbs are not patentable, there is a decreased incentive for pharmaceutical companies to pour the millions of dollars into the type of research that is required to bring prescription drugs to market. The result is a paucity of well-controlled research. Single case reports and testimonials do not constitute solid scientific evidence. For many of the products, the active ingredient or ingredients has not even been determined. The second problem is the lack of oversight by the FDA. This has resulted in misleading claims or outright false advertising. As the philosopher David Hume stated, "Extraordinary claims require extraordinary evidence," and solid research is often lacking in this area. This is especially problematic, as noted above, when it comes to the issue of drug-drug interactions. Medical catastrophes and deaths most surely have occurred when people unknowingly mixed certain herbal products with prescription drugs.

We need to be watchful and cautious as the evidence regarding OTC herbal products (both pro and con) continues to accumulate. And remember, "natural" does not mean safe. Some so-called natural products can, in fact, be deadly.

20

Red Flags: When to Reevaluate

Previous chapters have discussed the diagnostic phase of treatment, in which the clinician makes initial decisions regarding possible referral for medication treatment. We have also outlined basic treatment strategies and medication doses. The nonmedical therapist is crucially involved in monitoring patient response to medications: noting signs of symptomatic improvement, the emergence of adverse effects, and, at times, exacerbation of symptoms. Knowing what to look for and when to direct the patient back to the prescribing physician is an important task. In this chapter, we will address six important conditions or circumstances in which a re-referral is indicated: failure to respond, need for dosage adjustment, unexplained relapse, the onset of new medical conditions, side effect problems, and discontinuation of medication treatment.

Failure to Respond

As noted in earlier chapters, a positive medication response is rarely immediate. Most psychotropic medications require a number of days or weeks to reach adequate blood levels and produce physiologic changes that yield symptomatic improvement. Also, there exists tremendous variability from patient to patient regarding absorption and metabolism of medications, which affects the ultimate response time. Initial doses often must be raised gradually, as tolerance for side effects is achieved and blood levels of the medication approach therapeutic levels.

Critical to appropriate treatment is conducting an *adequate trial*. Adequate trials must assume that the correct diagnosis has been made and the patient has actually taken the medication as prescribed. Beyond this, the two most important variables to consider are dosage and length of treatment. A general rule with all psychotropics is to use the lowest dose that is effective, although at the same time not to undertreat.

The clinician must be willing to increase doses in order to achieve meaningful results, while continuously monitoring for the emergence of side effects.

Generally, if patients have been treated with moderate to high doses of psychotropic medications (or at adequate blood levels) for four or five weeks without noticeable improvement, a re-referral should be made for dosage increase, augmentation, perhaps a change to another class of medication. It is not unusual to encounter patients who have been treated for months (or even years!) on a particular drug or dose without symptomatic improvement. This is not appropriate. Any condition that warrants medication treatment is undoubtedly causing considerable suffering. There is no justifiable reason to mistreat or undertreat for a long period of time without carefully reevaluating the current treatment and making necessary adjustments.

Need for Dosage Adjustment

In addition to patients' failure to respond, therapists commonly encounter situations in which the patient has shown a positive response, but the symptomatic improvement is only partial. Many patients who show partial response can experience enhanced improvement when doses are increased or medications are augmented. In such cases of partial response, a re-referral is warranted.

Unexplained Relapse

Sometimes a patient who has responded well to psychotropic medication treatment will at some point experience emergence of symptoms—even when medications are continued. When this occurs, the clinician should consider the following common reasons:

- Failure to comply with treatment; for example, the patient has not been taking medication as prescribed.

- The patient has started to drink alcohol excessively, which may exacerbate depression or anxiety symptoms and may also interfere with metabolism of the psychotropic medication. Other substance abuse may account for increased symptomatology.

- The patient has experienced a significant increase in psychosocial stressors.

- A medical condition has developed that may contribute to the development of psychiatric symptoms, such as thyroid disease.

- "Breakthrough symptoms": at times the underlying neurochemical disorder or metabolic activity of the individual undergoes a change that results in a reemergence of symptoms. In many cases of breakthrough symptoms, a dosage adjustment (usually an increase in dose) may be successful.

- Tolerance to the drug can develop. This is uncommon; however, there is increasing evidence that some medications work well in early stages of some biologically based mental illnesses but are not as successful in later phases of the illness. For example, lithium is very effective in early episodes of bipolar disorder but is less effective after a number of episodes. This probably does not represent true "tolerance" but rather a change in the underlying pathophysiology or neurochemical substrate.

Onset of New Medical Conditions

A patient may initially be able to tolerate and safely take psychotropic medications; however, the onset of certain physical conditions can change this, necessitating a re-referral. Such conditions include pregnancy, epilepsy, certain types of glaucoma and physiological changes associated with aging and kidney disease. Another time to reevaluate medications is when the patient has an upcoming surgery, since psychotropics can interact with anesthetics administered before or during surgery or could also inhibit the healing process. Likewise, new prescription and over-the-counter medications added to cope with coexisting medical problems can cause drug interaction problems (see appendix C). This is frequently seen in elderly patients, who often have a host of medical problems and take many medications.

Side Effect Problems

All psychotropic medications have side effects to a greater or lesser degree. Some side effects are minor, benign, and transient. Others are quite unpleasant and at times dangerous. Summarized in figure 20-A are the most common side effects associated with the various classes of psychotropic medications. These are classified into three groups:

- Minor or benign: Many of these side effects diminish or disappear with continued treatment as tolerance develops.

- Troublesome side effects: These can cause moderate levels of discomfort and may result in poor compliance.

- Potentially serious side effects: These may cause excessive discomfort and can actually be dangerous.

A re-referral is warranted in cases where side effects are troublesome or potentially serious or when clinical signs of drug toxicity appear (see figure 20-B).

When It Is Time to Discontinue

Once a patient has fully recovered, the question of when to stop medication arises. Often, even if the patient is asymptomatic, an abrupt discontinuation of medications can result in either relapse or withdrawal symptoms. The matter of when to stop is highly individual and depends heavily on three factors:

- The patient's history of previous episodes

- Your assessment of the patient's vulnerability to relapse

- The patient's feelings about discontinuing medications. Figure 20-C provides *very* general guidelines for length of treatment; each case must be evaluated individually.

It is important to note that people treated with benzodiazepines will develop a tolerance to the medication and if it is abruptly discontinued *will* have withdrawal symptoms—some of which can be serious. Slow tapering of doses is required and almost always can be safely accomplished (see "Benzodiazepine Withdrawal" in chapter 17). In general, it is wise to withdraw *all* psychotropic medications gradually,

Side Effects of Psychotropic Medications

Medication Class	Mild or Benign	Troublesome	Potentially Serious
Antidepressants			

Tricyclics	Dry mouth
	Constipation
	Nasal
	    congestion
	Mild sedation
		Oversedation
		Sexual dysfunction
		Weight gain
		Hypotension
		Tremor
		Blurred vision
		Rash
		Urinary
		    retention
			Dizziness or falls,
			    especially in
			    the elderly
			Seizures
			Photosensitivity
			Cardiac
			    arrhythmias
			Mania or
			    hypomania
			Glaucoma
			Urinary retention
			Low white blood
			    cell count
			Fever
			Sudden high fever
			    with jaundice
			Priapism
			High white blood
			    cell count
			Swollen lymph
			    nodes
			Respiratory
			    distress

SSRIs	Sweating Nausea or gas Diarrhea Constipation Dry mouth Sedation	Headache Anxiety Insomnia Weight loss Rash Sexual dysfunction Apathy Amotivation Emotional blunting Weight gain	Mania or hypomania

MAOIs	Headaches
	Dizziness
	Dry mouth
	Constipation
	Nausea
	Diarrhea
		Increased heart
		    rate
		Blurred vision
		Weight gain
		Anxiety
			Low blood
			    pressure
			Falls
			Muscle spasms
			Hallucinations
			Hypertensive crisis
			Mania or
			    hypomania

Figure 20-A

Side Effects of Psychotropic Medications
(continued)

Medication Class	Mild or Benign	Troublesome	Potentially Serious

Antipsychotics	Mild sedation
	Tremor
	Dry mouth
	Blurred vision
	Increased
	  perspiration
	Constipation
	Nasal congestion
		Rigidity
		Sexual
		  dysfunction
		Oversedation
		Low blood
		  pressure
		Extrapyramidal
		  symptoms
		Breast
		  enlargement
			Urinary retention
			High blood pressure
			Severe rigidity,
			  especially with
			  fever, jaundice
			Abnormal
			  movements
			Falls
			Confusion
			Liver toxicity
			Cardiac arrhythmia
			Photosensitivity
			Impaired
			  temperature
			  regulation

Mood Stabilizers			
Lithium	Nausea Tremor	Weight gain Memory problems Sedation Muscle weakness Vomiting Diarrhea	Oversedation Confusion Incoordination
Anticonvulsants	Sedation Nausea Vomiting Headache Tremor	Muscle twitching Rash Blurred vision Dizziness Weight gain	Confusion Urinary retention Bone marrow depression
Antianxiety Agents			

Benzodiazepines	Mild sedation
	Constipation
		Oversedation
		Confusion
		  (especially in
		  the elderly)
		Parodoxical stimulation
			Dizziness or falls
			Low blood pressure

Buspirone	Dizziness Nausea Headaches	Insomnia Nervousness Dysphoria	
Antihistamines	Drowsiness GI upset	Dry mouth Sexual dysfunction Low blood pressure	Difficulty breathing Urinary retention

Figure 20-A *continued*

Signs of Toxicity or Overdose

Antidepressants:[a]

- Oversedation
- Cardiac arrhythmia
- Falls
- Dilated pupils
- Confusion
- Psychosis
- Seizures
- Coma
- Agitation

Lithium:[b]

- Oversedation
- Confusion
- Incoordination
- Seizure
- Coma

Anticonvulsants:

- Oversedation
- Confusion
- Incoordination
- Cardiac arrhythmia

Antipsychotics:

- Oversedation
- Hyperthermia
- Restlessness or agitation
- Seizures
- Rigidity
- Coma
- Falls
- Cardiac arrhythmia
- Confusion

Antianxiety Agents:

- Confusion
- Slurred speech
- Incoordination
- Falls
- Oversedation
- Coma

a Severe tricyclic overdoses oftentimes are fatal. SSRIs, venlafaxine, and bupropion: low degree of toxicity.

b Severe overdoses oftentimes are fatal.

Figure 20-B

for example, antidepressants should be withdrawn gradually over a period of four to six weeks. A re-referral to the prescribing physician is warranted when, in your judgment, it is time to begin discontinuing treatment.

Finally from start to finish, ongoing collaboration and communication between psychotherapist and physician is important. Even at times when no problems exist, you may simply want to update the physician on the patient's progress.

Length of Continued Treatment After
Patient Becomes Asymptomatic

Disorder	Time Frame
Major depression	
First episode	6–12 months
Subsequent episodes	12–36 months or possibly indefinitely
Panic disorder	
First episode	6 months
Subsequent episodes	12–24 months
Psychotic disorder	
Brief psychotic episode (remitting quickly)	3 months
Schizophrenia and schizophreniform disorder	
First episode	12 months
Subsequent episodes	24 months to indefinite
Bipolar disorder	Generally requires ongoing prophylactic treatment
Obsessive-compulsive disorder	6 months[a]
Post-traumatic stress disorder	6 months[a]
Borderline personality disorder	6 months[a]

a The time frame for discontinuing has not been firmly established.

Figure 20-C

Epilogue

On the Horizon

These are exciting times in mental health and the neurosciences—new discoveries are being made each month. As this book goes to press, no less than two dozen new psychotropic medications are in the various phases of prerelease investigation and research. There is great promise for continued breakthroughs: new medications that may provide more safe, effective, and selective treatments for mental disorders.

There have been many advances in psychopharmacology over the past forty years and new treatments that have progressively resulted in decreases in emotional despair in many millions of people suffering from psychiatric disorders. Yet, in closing, we want to strongly underscore the importance of the human relationship in psychiatric treatment. Ultimately, loneliness, alienation, hopelessness, and demoralization are not to be cured with chemicals, but rather must be addressed in the arena of human contact and understanding. This is what psychotherapists do best. And, in collaboration with our medical colleagues, we can make a real difference in the lives of our clients.

Appendix A

Pharmacokinetics

This appendix provides an expanded discussion of the pharmacokinetics of psycho-therapeutic agents presented in chapter 4. It is intended for therapists with a special interest in this area or for those who actively comanage medication-treated patients.

Absorption

Absorption is important not only as the initial step in the pharmacokinetic process, but also as a determinant of a crucial clinical parameter called *bioavailability*, defined as the amount of drug reaching systemic circulation (Winter 1988). The amount of the drug that is bioavailable is usually expressed as a percentage of the administered dose. Medications directly injected into a vein (intravenous) are nearly 100 percent bioavailable, whereas orally administered drugs produce variable patterns of bioavailability. For instance, demonstrated oral bioavailability for some antipsychotics and certain tricyclic antidepressants ranges from 30 to 60 percent (Hollister 1992). Bioavailability may be decreased by a physiological process called the *first-pass effect*, in which a significant amount of the drug is metabolized before reaching the bloodstream. Most tricyclics undergo extensive first-pass metabolism, contributing to their relatively low bioavailability.

The therapist may encounter the clinical ramifications of bioavailability in regard to the issue of generic medications. Bioavailability is the benchmark measurement for determining bioequivalence between brand name and generic products. With many medications, generic formulations meet bioavailability standards and can provide economical alternatives to brand name products. This can be an important issue for psychiatric patients with limited financial resources, who often will simply quit taking their medications because of the expense or will take them sporadically to "make them last longer."

However, absolute bioequivalence is not guaranteed for all generic products. Although the active ingredient may be quantitatively the same as in the brand name product, there may be differences in the manufacturing process or in the physical properties of the final preparation that can affect the rate and extent of drug absorption. From a practical standpoint, the patient may experience a variable or inadequate response from the generic product. Although this does not occur frequently, it is a factor to consider when a patient responds atypically to a drug—especially with medications that have a narrow therapeutic index, such as anticonvulsants and tricyclic antidepressants. Psychotropics with periodic reports of generic unequivalence include nortriptyline and carbamazepine. Advise patients taking these medications to avoid frequent switches from brand to generic preparations and changes between generic manufacturers.

Distribution

Distribution of a medication throughout the body is a two-phase process. Initially, distribution is preferential for organs with a rich supply of blood flow, such as the kidney, liver, heart, and brain. In the second phase, the drug moves into areas with less extensive circulation, such as muscle and fat tissue. In chapter 3 these latter areas of the body are referred to as reservoirs, sometimes called compartments. Eventually (usually within several minutes), equilibrium is established. At equilibrium the process of drug distribution is completed, and the flow of the drug between compartments is relatively stable. When, as for most drugs, equilibrium is reached rapidly, the body as a whole is considered to be a single compartment, and the distribution pattern is referred to as a "single-compartment model." In this case it is assumed that the drug is uniformly distributed throughout the body; in other words, the serum level of the drug is equal to the concentration in organs and tissues.

Some psychotherapeutic medications, however, demonstrate "two-compartment" distribution. In the two-compartment model equilibrium is reached more slowly because of significant movement of the drugs into muscle and fat cells. Also distribution is not uniform throughout the body. Depending on the physical or chemical properties of the drug, and upon the physiological state of the patient, the drug can be unequally distributed between organs and reservoirs. Ultimately, large concentrations of medications can accumulate in deep reservoir areas.

Due to individual physiologic differences, there can be wide variations in effective dosages of the same medication from patient to patient. Also, when a medication is stopped (by either therapeutic plan or noncompliance), complete elimination of the drug does not occur immediately, or even within known half-life parameters. This partially explains why recurrence of psychosis may not immediately appear in the noncompliant schizophrenic and why depressive symptoms reemerge weeks (or days) after an antidepressant is discontinued. (The therapist can help educate the patient as to the potential consequences of medication discontinuation.)

Circulating in the plasma are various proteins to which medications can attach. This process is called protein binding and provides another reservoir area for drugs. Only the unbound or "free" molecules of a drug are able to cross cell membranes and reach an eventual site of action; thus a bound drug is inactive, whereas an unbound drug is active. Most psychotropic medications are bound extensively to serum proteins, usually albumin. Laboratory monitoring results typically indicate a total concentration that includes both bound and unbound drug molecules.

Metabolism

Metabolism (biotransformation) of most drugs primarily occurs through the action of enzymes located predominately in the liver. Metabolic enzymes are also found in the gastrointestinal tract (in bacteria and intestinal tissue), the kidney, the lung, and the placenta. This system, comprised of more than thirty related enzymes, is called the mixed function oxidase (MFO) or cytochrome P450 system. These enzymes are iron-containing proteins, located in the endoplasmic reticulum, that serve to mediate the process of electron and proton transfer during drug metabolism. The intended result of drug metabolism is the transformation of the original compound into one that is more readily eliminated by the kidney. In general, this means converting drugs that are more lipid-soluble to ones that are more water-soluble. The most common enzymes involved in drug metabolism are known by the following designations: 1A2, 2A6, 2C9, 2C19, 2D6, 2E1, and 3A4. The majority of drugs and naturally occurring compounds are metabolized by the CYP3A4 isoenzyme, both in the liver and in the gastrointestinal tract (Benet, Kroetz, and Sheiner 1996; Michalets 1998).

Drug metabolism takes place through a series of chemical reactions, categorized as phase I and phase II. Specific types of phase I reactions are oxidation, reduction, and hydrolysis. Oxidation is the most important type of phase I reaction. Phase I reactions are also called nonsynthetic because the original molecule undergoes degradation via electron loss. Oxygen serves as the electron acceptor. Phase I reactions are likely to yield molecules that are not significantly different than the original, and they commonly have pharmacologic activity. During this oxidative process, highly reactive, or even toxic, free radical compounds may be formed.

Phase II reactions involve the coupling, or conjugation, of the drug molecule with other compounds, such as an amino acid. These reactions are also known as synthetic reactions. Products of phase II reactions are often considerably different than the original and are usually inactive. Many drugs are metabolized sequentially, first by phase I, and then by phase II reactions. Some drugs are metabolized via only phase I or only phase II reactions.

Not all biotransformation reactions result in terminal, deactivated, nontoxic products. There are notable reactive, toxic compounds formed with many routinely used drugs. Examples are the hepatotoxicity seen with the common pain reliever acetaminophen, or nonsteroidal anti-inflammatory agents, such as ibuprofen or isoniazid.

The by-products of metabolism are called metabolites. Compared to the original drug, often called the parent compound, metabolites can be more active, less active, or inactive. As discussed in chapter 4, metabolites may possess similar activity to the original drug. These active metabolites may contribute to the intended effect of the medication. Metabolites can also demonstrate different properties than the parent drug. An example is seen in the substantially longer half-lives that metabolites of some benzodiazepines exhibit compared to the parent compounds, which can potentially lead to drug accumulation.

Metabolic Drug Interactions

The amount and activity of these enzymes are subject to change, especially when medications are co-administered. Significant drug interactions result from metabolic disruptions secondary to multiple medications. The fact that the particular enzymes involved in metabolizing many drugs have not been identified complicates the assessment and management of metabolic drug interactions. The two mechanisms by which enzyme activity is altered are enzyme induction and enzyme inhibition.

Induction takes place when the activity and amount of enzyme are increased. The result is usually a reduced serum concentration of the object drug by the precipitant drug. Another consequence of enzyme induction is the increased formation of toxic metabolites. Enzyme induction can result from a medication, such as carbamazepine (Tegretol), or a condition like smoking. Enzyme induction generally follows a gradual time course for both onset and dissipation. A two-to-three week time period is required for the production of new enzyme and for maximum effect to be achieved. Degradation and elimination of the increased enzymes require a similar, if not longer, period of time.

Inhibition occurs when there is a decrease in either production or activity of enzymes. The latter is usually secondary to enzyme competition at the binding site. This results in an increased serum concentration of the object drug. Such increases can be precipitous, and depending on the drugs involved, can lead to serious side effects and/or toxicity. Enzyme inhibition can result from a medication, such as cimetidine (Tagamet), or from a disease state, such as cirrhosis or hepatitis. Enzyme inhibition can be rapid, occurring within hours.

Anticipating, recognizing, and treating drug interactions present significant challenges in the use of medications, including psychotropics. Drug interactions may produce a range of outcomes, from toxicity to loss of desired effect. Drug interactions involving altered metabolism are the most common, the most widely researched, and present the greatest potential for undesirable medication effects. For example, recent attention has focused on drug interactions with SSRI and newer mixed mechanism antidepressants. These antidepressants present potentially significant capacity to inhibit several key cytochrome P450 enzymes.

Another area of relevance in psychiatric practice are the drug interactive effects of alcohol, which pose unique challenges. With acute ingestion, alcohol competitively blocks metabolic oxidation, and, as such, is considered an enzyme inhibitor. Conversely, with chronic alcohol ingestion, enzyme induction occurs. Additionally, prescribers must take into account the physiological changes associated with chronic alcohol use, such as cirrhotic liver damage which decreases drug metabolizing capacity, or decreased serum albumin, which results in more "free" or active drug being available.

Throughout this book, key drug interactions are addressed. It is important to note, however, that there are real limitations in this field of study. The inherent research and interpretive challenges are described in detail by Greenblatt, von Moltke, Harmatz, and Shader (1998) and summarized below:

- Difficulty in identifying specific cytochrome P450 enzymes due to limitations of in vitro models

- Complexities involved in designing and conducting in vivo pharmacokinetic research studies

- Great interindividual variability in enzyme metabolizing capabilities

- Assessing reliability of reported information

The study of drug interactions, especially those involving metabolism, is a highly complex, rapidly evolving field. Arriving at a clear understanding of clinical implications is greatly challenging to prescribers. Published information should be evaluated critically, especially if it is clearly promotional in nature.

There are several reliable, primary drug interaction resources that physicians and pharmacists routinely consult.

Therapeutic Index

A critical pharmacokinetic parameter that directs safe and effective medication use is the *therapeutic index*. This parameter establishes a quantitative comparison between a drug's effective concentration and its toxic concentration. The closer these measurements are, the narrower the index, and therefore the more care that must be taken in prescribing. Lithium and anticonvulsants, for example, have narrow therapeutic indices.

Appendix B

Pharmacotherapy in Special Populations

Pregnancy

One of the most difficult dilemmas facing physicians is medication management in the psychiatric patient who is pregnant or considering pregnancy. Although therapists will not have to make ultimate prescribing decisions, they will undoubtedly remain involved in the patient's care. The information presented here summarizes general guidelines relevant to psychotropic medication use during pregnancy and nursing.[1]

It is important to remember that absolute data in this area is disturbingly incomplete. Experimental research obviously is limited by ethical restrictions. Animal studies are extensive but their results cannot be assumed to necessarily apply to humans. And, for infrequently prescribed medications, the available observational data are in some cases so limited that conclusions are impossible. Nevertheless, in some patients the risk of not medicating, especially in the presence of psychosis, mania, and severe depression, clearly outweighs the potential hazards to mother and child. The risk factors are these:

Risk Factors Associated with Medications During Pregnancy

- Teratogenesis (malformation of fetus or fetal organs)

- Drug effects on the growing and developing fetus

- Drug effects on labor and delivery

- Residual drug effects on the newborn (neonatal)

---

1. Information from a variety of sources was compiled for this appendix: American Society of Health System Pharmacists 2000; Brown and Bryant 1992; Ereshefsky and Richards 1992; *Facts and Comparisons* 2001; Jann 1992; Jinks and Fuerst 1992; Meyer 1992; Rubin 1992; Snodgrass 1992; Vestal, Montamat, and Nielson 1992.

- Behavioral teratogenesis (long-term effects on the child resulting from drug exposure in utero)

- Pregnancy-induced changes in drug actions

- Drug effects on the breastfed infant

Perhaps of most concern is the possibility of teratogenesis, with the risk being greatest during the period of organ formation (organogenesis) generally considered to be the first trimester. Avoiding medications as much as possible during this time can lower the risk of fetal malformation. However, since most drugs, with very few exceptions, cross the placenta, fetal medication exposure will continue throughout pregnancy. After the first trimester, safety concerns are related to effects on fetal growth and physiology, immediate and long-term effects on the child, and on breast feeding. Figure B-1 provides guidelines for psychotropic medication use in pregnancy and nursing.

Psychotropic Medication Guidelines for Pregnancy

Antidepressants:

- SSRIs and most TCAs not associated with teratogenesis, although extensive studies in humans have not been done. Animal studies with some agents indicate possible adverse effects.
- MAOIs, venlafaxine, and mirtazapine have not been studied extensively.
- Lack of adverse affects noted in animal studies with bupropion.
- Present in breast milk.
- Effects on neonate can include CNS depression, urinary retention.
- Inconclusive data on miscarriage rate

Lithium:

- Established teratogen. First trimester exposure strongly associated with fetal cardiac anomaly.
- For fetal lithium exposure in first trimester, consider cardiac ultrasound to detect presence or absence of malformation.
- If lithium is necessary after first trimester, dosage adjustments are necessary due to pregnancy-induced kidney function changes. Frequent lab monitoring is also required.
- Reductions in lithium dose are required several weeks prior to delivery.
- Neonatal effects include impaired respiration, EKG and heart rate abnormalities, and renal impairment.
- Carbamazepine, clonazepam, and neuroleptics are possible alternatives to lithium.
- Significant concentrations in breast milk. Can cause decreased muscle tone, cyanosis, lethargy in infant. Nursing contraindicated.

Figure B-1

Psychotropic Medication Guidelines for Pregnancy
(continued)

Antipsychotics:
- High-potency agents may be preferred over low-potency agents.
- Establish lowest effective dose possible.
- Potential short-term abnormal neonatal motor activity.
- Possible alternative to lithium in mania.
- Present in breast milk.

Anticonvulsants:
- Carbamazepine is a probable teratogen.
- Valproic acid is an established teratogen.
- Carbamazapine and valproic acid both found in breast milk.

Benzodiazepines:
- Some benzodiazepines have established role in fetal abnormalities. Avoid use in first trimester. May need to taper dose.
- Switch to clonazepam if benzodiazepines absolutely indicated.
- Switch to tricyclic antidepressant for panic disorder if continued medication is required.
- Neonatal CNS depression, drug accumulation, and withdrawal symptoms possible.
- Excreted in breast milk. Produces drowsiness, failure to thrive in infant.

Source: Cohen, Heller, and Rosenbaum 1989; Briggs 1992; Rubin 1992.

Figure B-1 *continued*

Geriatric Patients

Increasingly, our society is composed of greater numbers of elderly individuals, defined as 65 and older. Currently, the elderly constitute nearly 20 percent of the population. Consequently, psychotherapists are faced with diagnostic and treatment dilemmas specific to this population. Presented here are patterns and risks of medication use in the elderly (figure B-2) and age-specific factors contributing to adverse effects (figure B-3). Also discussed are recommended adjustments for use of psychotropics in the geriatric patient.

Prescribing psychotropic medications in a population receiving numerous maintenance medications for medical conditions is inherently difficult. However, we present the following general recommendations to reduce the risk to this group.

Establish diagnosis and target symptoms

Neuroleptics are frequently prescribed for geriatric patients, especially in long-term care facilities. However, these drugs may not be prescribed for psychotic symptoms but may merely be intended to control agitation and anxiety. An alternative to neuroleptics and benzodiazepines is buspirone (BuSpar).

Obtain complete medication history

Elderly people are at higher risk for developing drug-induced psychiatric symptoms from other prescribed medications, such as depression secondary to cardiovascular drugs or delirium and confusion secondary to CNS medications. Frequently, yet another medication is prescribed as a result, without the real cause of symptoms (the medication) having been identified. Also, additive drug effects are common in the elderly. For example, it is important to evaluate the total number of anticholinergic drugs before adding another one, since geriatric patients are especially prone to "anticholinergic delirium." Lastly, multiple medications (such as antihypertensives and diuretics) can increase the possibility of psychotropic-related falls.

Understand age-specific pharmacology

Some benzodiazepines, such as diazepam (Valium), chlordiazepoxide (Librium), and flurazepam (Dalmane), accumulate to a greater degree than others. Benzodiazepines considered to be safer are oxazepam (Serax), lorazepam (Ativan), and temazepam (Restoril). Additionally, the elderly in general are more likely to experience oversedation from benzodiazepines.

The most consistently predicable age-related change in drug response results from the normal decrease in kidney function that accompanies aging. This phenomenon probably contributes to the greatest number of adverse drug reactions in the elderly (Jinks and Fuerst 1992). Safe use of lithium, therefore, becomes particularly difficult. Aggressive serum-level monitoring and assessment of renal function are imperative.

Central nervous system changes are common with aging, including decreased cerebral blood flow, decreased cholinergic function, increased monoamine oxidase activity, and some brain atrophy. The result of these alterations can include the appearance of behavioral changes in the elderly and unpredictable medication response. Therefore, it is advisable to avoid frequent medication changes and not to experiment with medications in the elderly.

Adjust dosage

All psychotropics prescribed to elderly patients should begin with small doses and be titrated slowly. In addition, maintenance doses may sometimes be 30 to 50

Medication Use and Risks in Geriatric Patients

- 30 percent of all prescription drugs are taken by people over 65 years of age.
- 70 percent of older adults self-medicate with over-the-counter products without physician or pharmacist consultation.
- 50 percent of accidental drug-related deaths occur in geriatric patients.
- Adverse drug reactions occur at double the rate in geriatric patients than in other groups.
- Common adverse drug-related effects are hip fractures, cognitive impairment, and neuroleptic-induced parkinsonism.

Figure B-2

Contributing Factors to Adverse Drug Reactions in the Elderly

- Adverse drug reactions are proportional to the number of medications taken.
- Elderly patients often have multiple prescribers without consolidated records.
- Age-related factors increase the likelihood of adverse effects, such as the following:

    Impaired organ function, especially decreased liver metabolism leading to increased medication levels and effects

    Multiple disease states

    Exaggerated therapeutic response to medications

    Increased sensitivity to side effects

- Noncompliance in elderly is common (usually underdosing) and due to:

    Complicated directions

    Hearing and visual impairment

    Cognitive and memory deficits

    Child-resistant packaging

    Cost

Figure B-3

percent lower than in younger patients. The aging person may demonstrate increased receptor or organ sensitivity to medications and there is an age-associated decrease in albumin, resulting in more free (active) drug available.

In general, continuous attention should be paid to reducing the total number of drugs, eliminating duplicative agents, and simplifying the dosing schedule. Also, clearly instruct the patient and his or her spouse and family when medications are discontinued.

Use therapeutic monitoring

Liberally utilize laboratory monitoring capabilities.

Recognize and respond to side effects promptly

Psychotropic side effects that are more pronounced in the elderly are sedation, anticholinergic reactions, extrapyramidal symptoms, delirium, postural hypotension, cardiotoxicity, and cognitive impairments. Constipation is common and particularly troubling in the elderly. Therefore, add anticholinergic agents with caution, and recommend treatment at time of prescribing to prevent potentially serious gastrointestinal effects.

Children and Adolescents

Until very recent times, the research on psychopharmacology for children and adolescents was sparse. Most studies were single case studies or open-label designs

Psychotropic Medication Guidelines for Children and Adolescents

Antidepressants:

- Dosage ranges are based on body weight: See figure B-5.

- If tricyclics are used, EKG should be performed prior to treatment, when dosage reaches 3 mg/kg/day, and when heart rate is greater than 130 beats per minute. Repeat EKG is recommended when maintenance dose is reached, to minimize the possibility of toxicity.

- More free drug is available in children, due to decreased protein binding and high proportion of lean body mass.

- Few established recommendations for MAOIs.

- Fluvoxamine is FDA-approved for use in OCD in children over eight years of age.

- Expanded indications for select other SSRIs pending FDA approval as of May 2001.

Lithium:

- Lithium is accepted as relatively safe in children and adolescents and is tolerated better by them than by adults.

- Starting dose for children is 30 mg/kg/day in divided doses. Starting dose for adolescents is the same as for adults: 900–1200 mg/day.

- Monitor children closely for dehydration, especially during periods of activity, seasonally hot temperatures, and illnesses associated with fever and fluid loss.

- Monitor for hypothyroidism to avoid growth retardation.

- Limited animal evidence demonstrates inhibited bone growth and lithium deposits in immature bones. Therefore, monitor calcium levels and maintain growth charts. For this reason, carbamazepine may be safer in children under age 12.

Anticonvulsants:

- Established anticonvulsant dosage and monitoring guidelines are generally followed for use in pediatric psychiatry.

- Monitor children for appearance of (or worsening of) cognitive and behavioral side effects associated with anticonvulsants. With caramazepine these can include insomnia, irritability, emotional lability, and impaired task performance. With valproic acid observe for excessive drowsiness and (minimal) effect on task performance.

Figure B-4

Psychotropic Medication Guidelines
for Children and Adolescents *(continued)*

Benzodiazepines:

- Although used medically (such as for seizures or during anesthesia) the benzodiazepines are not considered first-line agents for psychiatric symptoms in children.

- Childhood anxiety disorders may respond better to nonpharmacologic therapies. If medications are indicated, imipramine is more often recommended.

- If benzodiazepines are used in children, dosing should be designed to avoid excessive sedation relating to peak concentrations.

- Clonazepam is reported to cause irritability, aggression, and antisocial features in children.

Antipsychotics:

- For many antipsychotics there are established dosing guidelines, based on body weight, for children aged 3 to 12 years. Adult dosages are usually applied to children over 12.

- Phenothiazines should be used cautiously in children with acute illnesses, such as chicken pox, measles, or GI or CNS infections, due to increased susceptiblilty to dystonia and akathisia.

- Neuroleptics may cause an allergic reaction, including breathing difficulties. Use cautiously in childhood asthma.

- Acute dystonic reactions occur more often in children and adolescents than in adults. For younger children, diphenhydramine (Benadryl) is a common treatment, although other anticholinergics may be used.

- Children, but not adolescents, demonstrate shorter half-lives with antipsychotics, and consequently may not be good candidates for once-a-day dosing.

Psychostimulants:

- Dosage guidelines: see Figure B-5

- Give with meals to minimize GI distress and appetite loss.

- Give doses early in the day to avoid insomnia.

- Growth suppression associated with dextroamphetamine and methylphenidate has not been clearly established; if it does occur it is not permanent.

- Pemoline is not considered a first line agent due to risk of life-threatening liver failure

Figure B-4 *continued*

(without placebo or double-blind controls). Historically, there have been significant barriers in the study of medication treatment with children, although recently the FDA has provided incentives for pharmaceutical companies to do better controlled research on psychopharmacology in young people.

Due to the paucity of well-controlled research, the statements made in this section should be considered only as preliminary. What is clear is that children are not simply just like adults, but smaller. They have different rates of metabolism and other physiological responses (affecting the way drugs are absorbed, transformed, and excreted by the body). The nervous system of children is clearly immature and continues to undergo maturation well through the teenage years, and even into the mid-twenties. One recent finding (Emslie, Rush, et al. 1997) underscores this point. Where most adults with major depression begin to show clinical improvement after two to six weeks of treatment with antidepressants, the time to first response in this well-controlled study examining treatment of children and teenagers was eight to twelve weeks. It is clear that lessons learned from treating adults cannot be simply applied to children.

To make matters even more complex, let's consider the following. The immature level of cognitive development makes diagnosis of childhood psychiatric disorders more complicated; many younger children simply do not have the ability to articulate/communicate their symptoms and inner experiences to the clinician. Parents are often (understandably) concerned about drug treatment and may be opposed to the use of medications with their children. Children often are unable to provide true informed consent. Thus, the decision to take medications rests wholly with the parents. An open discussion regarding medications with children (especially after the age of seven) is entirely appropriate, although often not done.

Other problems exist as well. Many emotional symptoms in children are in response to significant situational stresses (e.g., child abuse, witnessing domestic violence or parental conflict) and may be best addressed with psychotherapy (not drugs). And, finally, often what parents may strive for is behavioral control. Sometimes medications can achieve this, but at the expense of the child (e.g., creating excessive sedation).

It is very important, however, to stress that a number of major psychiatric disorders do begin in childhood or early adolescence (e.g., schizophrenia, OCD, bipolar disorder, ADHD, to mention a few). Furthermore, in many instances, appropriate medication treatment may not only reduce suffering in these young people it may also help to prevent the worsening of the clinical picture (i.e., some disorders become progressively more severe without treatment, e.g., schizophrenia, bipolar disorder). Finally, some children will, unfortunately, be experiencing the first signs of what can become a lifelong psychiatric disorder. Their first experience with medication treatment (whether positive or negative) can certainly set the tone for all later treatment. If they are treated appropriately, with respect and careful attention to side effect management, the experience can have a very positive impact on attitudes regarding psychiatric treatment. Conversely, a bad experience may set the stage for a lifetime of poor compliance and thus less than optimal response to treatment.

Figures B-4 and B-5 provide summary recommendations for psychopharmacology with younger patients. Please be advised that most psychiatric medications are not FDA-approved for use with children; however, in clinical practice there is widespread use. By providing guidelines about dosing of psychotropic medications in children and adolescents, we are not espousing the widespread use of these agents in children. As we note throughout our book, it is our firm belief that all medications should be prescribed based on specific target symptoms and evidence to support use, with frequent monitoring. The controversy surrounding the use of psychotropic medications in children is strongly argued by both opponents and proponents. It is noteworthy that much of the historical debate surrounding psychotropic medications in children focused on ADHD. The controversy has extended now to include depression and anxiety disorders. Patent extensions are being sought by pharmaceutical manufacturers to obtain FDA-approved indications for expanded use in children, thereby extending patent rights by several more years.

Patients with Unusual Medication Metabolism

The emerging fields of pharmacogenetics and psychopharmacogenetics attempt to identify variations in drug response attributable to genetic or ethnic factors. The most commonly encountered alterations in drug reactions are exaggerated response, novel drug effects, and lack of effectiveness (Meyer 1992). The dynamics and kinetics of drugs in the body are determined by genetically mediated patterns of protein structures, receptor sensitivities, and enzyme activity. We present current findings in this area, acknowledging that information is likely to expand rapidly in the future.

Pharmacogenetic research parallels the worldwide efforts directed toward the Human Genome Project. Three genetic variations have been studied widely involving the specific enzymes CYP2D6, CYP2C19, and CYP2C9 (Katzung 2000). Differences in the activity of these enzymes result in two distinct patterns of drug disposition, either an increase or a decrease in metabolism. Individuals with these capacities are termed "extensive metabolizers" and "poor metabolizers," respectively.

Note that these metabolic alterations apply only to the drugs metabolized by those particular enzymes. Most people will not be aware if they have altered drug metabolism until they are exposed to a given drug and experience an out of the ordinary response. Poor metabolizers may be at risk for exaggerated or unexpected side effects at normal dosages. Extensive metabolizers may experience a less than expected response to standard dosages of a given medication. Extensive metabolizers are also at risk for the buildup of intermediate toxic metabolites (see Appendix A for a discussion of metabolic phases).

In Caucasians, 5-10 percent of individuals are poor metabolizers due to CYP2D6 deficiency, compared to 1-3 percent of African-Americans and Asians (Michalets 1998; Vandel, Haffen, Vandel, Bonin, Nezelof, Sechter, et al. 1999).Up to one-third of Ethiopian and Saudi Arabian individuals may display the ultrarapid metabolizing capability of CYP2D6 (Katzung 2001). Due to CYP2C19 deficiencies, 3 to 5 percent of Caucasians and 18 to 23 percent of Japanese individuals are poor metabolizers. Precise information relative to ethnic distribution of CYP2C9 deficiencies have yet to be identified. An interesting finding by Yamazaki (2000) was that although total P450 content is higher in Caucasians than in the Japanese, the relative percentages of each enzyme type is consistent.

Another metabolic process, involving a step called acetylation, can be impaired based on genetic predisposition. About 50 percent of African-Americans and Caucasian-Americans are poor acetylators. Distribution of fast and slow acetylators within and between other ethnic groups is the subject of ongoing study and reports vary widely, especially within Asian subgroups.

Psychotropic Medication Guidelines: Children and Adolescents

Medications	Total Daily Dose	Daily (weight adjusted)
Antidepressants		
Prozac*	5–40 mg	0.25–0.75 mg/kg
Zoloft*	25–200 mg	1.5–3.0 mg/kg
Paxil*	10–30 mg	0.25–0.75 mg/kg
Celexa*	5–40 mg	0.25–0.75 mg/kg
Wellbutrin	50-300 mg	3–6 mg/kg
Serzone	50-400 mg	1–8 mg/kg
Effexor	37.5–150 mg	1–3 mg/kg
Anti-Obsessional		
SSRIs*	see above	see above
Luvox	50–300 mg	1.5–4.5 mg/kg
Anafranil	25–300 mg	2–5 mg/kg
Antianxiety		
BuSpar	5–40 mg	0.5–1.0 mg/kg
Klonopin	0.5–6 mg	0.02–0.1 mg/kg
Xanax	0.5–6 mg	0.02–0.1 mg/kg
Ativan	0.5–6 mg	0.04–0.15 mg/kg
Antipsychotics		
Zyprexa	5–20 mg	1–3 mg/kg
Risperdal	0.5–16 mg	0.1–0.5 mg/kg
Seroquel	25–400 mg	3 -6 mg/kg
Clozaril	25–400 mg	3–6 mg/kg
Mood Stabilizers		
Lithium	300–2100 mg	blood levels
Depakote	250–1500 mg	blood levels
Tegretol	200–1000 mg	blood levels
Lamictal	200–500 mg	1–10 mg/kg
Neuronotin	300–1200 mg	10 mg/kg
Topamax	50–400 mg	3–6 mg/kg
Stimulants		
Dex/amphet	5–40 mg	0.3–1.5 mg/kg
Ritalin, etc.	5–60 mg	1–2 mg/kg
Cylert	37.5–150 mg	1–3 mg/kg
Other		
Clonidine	0.025–0.6 mg	0.001–0.01 mg/kg
Inderal	20–160 mg	2–4 mg/kg
Benadryl	10–25 mg	0.5 mg/kg

Weight Conversion: Weight in pounds/2.2 = kg

This list includes only selected medications (those commonly used). It should serve as a reference only and not as a guide for prescribing. In addition, most of the aforementioned drugs, although commonly used in clinical practice, are not FDA approved for treatment with children.

Figure B-5

Appendix C

Psychotropic Drug Interactions

This appendix provides a quick reference guide to frequent and significant drug interactions between psychotropic medications. These tables are not absolute. Interactive effects will vary from person to person. In some instances an individual may experience the full range of symptoms presented here, while others may demonstrate only one or two symptoms from a range of possible effects.

Also note that the potential for an interaction between drugs does not preclude their concurrent use. Certain combinations are routinely prescribed without problems in many patients (as with lithium and antipsychotics), whereas others are contraindicated due to the severity of the interaction (for example, MAOIs and SSRIs). *However, whenever psychiatric medications are coadministered, the additive potential of central nervous system depression and anticholinergic effects must be considered.*

Information from a variety of sources was compiled for this appendix: American Society of Health System Pharmacists 2000; *Facts and Comparisons* 2001; Hansten and Horn 1993; Nemeroff, DeVane, and Pollock 1996; Flockhart 1996; von Moltke, Greenblatt, Harmatz, and Shader 1994; Watsky and Salzman 1991.

Tricyclic Antidepressant (TCA) Interactions

Drug	Effect of Interaction
Cimetidine (Tagamet)	Increased TCA levels, enhanced TCA response, TCA toxicity
Bupropion (Wellbutrin)	Increased TCA levels, enhanced TCA response, TCA toxicity
SSRIs	Increased TCA levels, enhanced TCA response, TCA toxicity
Propoxyphene (Darvon, Darvocet)	

Anticonvulsants
  Carbamazepine (Tegretol)
  Phenytoin (Dilantin)
  Barbiturates (phenobarbital)
	Decreased TCA levels, diminished TCA response

MAOIs—**contraindicated with TCA,** especially with imipramine and clomipramine; trazodone may be used cautiously with MAOIs	Increased TCA levels; syndrome of excitation, very high temperature, mania, seizures, coma, **death**
Clonidine (Catapres) Guanethidine (Ismelin)	Decreased antihypertensive effect of clonidine and guanethidine
Quinidine	Increased TCA levels, TCA-induced cardiac conduction prolongation
Antipsychotics	Increased TCA levels
Lithium	May worsen lithium tremor, increased TCA effect
Quinolones	Risk of life-threatening cardiac arrhythmias

Figure C-1

Selective Serotonin Reuptake Inhibitor (SSRI) Interactions

Drug	Effect of Interaction
MAOIs—**contraindicated with SSRIs**	Serotonergic syndrome with symptoms of fever, tremor, muscular rigidity, seizure, coma, **death**
TCAs	Increased TCA levels (*may be significant, doubled or greater*), enhanced TCA response, TCA toxicity
Carbamazepine (Tegretol)	Increased carbamazepine levels
Lithium	Increased lithium levels, possible neurotoxicity (confusion, dizziness, tremor, muscle stiffness, incoordination)
L-tryptophan	Headache, nausea, restlessness, agitation, sweating

Anorexiants
   phentermine
   sibutramine
	Serotonergic syndrome

Benzodiazepines (BZ)	Increased BZ levels
Phenytoin (Dilantin)	Increased phenytoin levels
Beta blockers	Decreased heart rate, decreased blood pressure
Cyproheptadine (Periactin)	Decreased antidepressant effect
Oral anticoagulants	Increased bleeding risk
Antispychotics	Increased antipsychotic level/side effects
Barbiturates	Decreased SSRI level
Cimetidine (Tagamet)	Increased SSRI level
Non-sedating antihistamines	Cardiotoxicity
Antiarrythmics (Type IC)	Cardiotoxicity
St. John's Wort	May produce serotonin syndrome
Sumatriptan	Weakness, exaggerated reflexes, and uncoordination
Anticoagulants	Increased effect of anticoagulant, risk for bleeding

Note: Certain interactions with the SSRIs are assumed to occur with all medications in this category. For instance, all SSRIs should be avoided with MAOIs. However, interactions involving metabolic pathways, such as with carbamazepine, may be more likely with one SSRI than with others, since not all SSRIs are metabolized identically. As each new antidepressant, with serotonergic or mixed activity, becomes available, new drug interaction information is collected. Similarities and differences between specific SSRI antidepressants and all interacting drugs are beyond the scope of this reference.

Figure C-2

Monoamine Oxidase Inhibitor (MAOI) Interactions

Drug	Effect of Interaction
Amphetamines—**contraindicated with MAOIs** Methylphenidate (Ritalin)—**contraindicated with MAOIs**	Seriously elevated blood pressure (hypertensive crisis), elevated temperature, seizures, cerebral hemorrhage, **death**
Ephedrine[a]—**contraindicated with MAOIs** Pseudoephedrine[b]—**contraindicated with MAOIs** Phenylephrine[b]—**contraindicated with MAOIs** Phenylpropanolamine[c]—**contraindicated with MAOIs**	Seriously elevated blood pressure (hypertensive crisis), elevated temperature, seizures, cerebral hemorrhage, **death**
L-dopa—**contraindicated with MAOIs**	Seriously elevated blood pressure (hypertensive crisis), elevated temperature, seizures, cerebral hemorrhage, **death**
Buspirone (BuSpar)—**contraindicated with MAOIs**	Seriously elevated blood pressure (hypertensive crisis), elevated temperature, seizures, cerebral hemorrhage, **death**
Dextromethorphan[d]	Nausea, elevated temperature, low blood pressure, agitation, seizures, coma
Meperidine (Demerol)—**contraindicated with MAOIs**	Severe reactions with symptoms of hypertension, muscular rigidity, coma, **death**
TCAs (especially imipramine and clomipramine)—**contraindicated with MAOIs** (trazodone may be used cautiously with MAOIs)	Increased TCA levels; syndrome of excitation, very high temperature, mania, seizures, coma, **death**
Serotonin specific reuptake inhibitors (SSRIs)—**contraindicated with MAOIs**	Serotonergic syndrome with symptoms of fever, tremor, muscular rigidity, seizure, coma, **death**
L-tryptophan	Hyperthermia, confusion, disorientation, agitation
Bupropion—**contraindicated with MAOIs**	Seriously elevated blood pressure (hypertensive crisis), elevated temperature, seizures, cerebral hemorrhage, **death**
Nefazodone—**contraindicated with MAOIs**	Serotonergic syndrome with symptoms of fever, tremors, muscular rigidity, seizure, coma, **death**
Sumatriptan	Increased levels of sumatriptan. Risk for serious cardiac side effects
Venlafaxine—**contraindicated with MAOIs**	Seriously elevated blood pressure (hypertensive crisis), elevated temperature, seizures, cerebral hemorrhage, **death**

a Common ingredient in over-the-counter allergy/asthma products
b Common ingredient in over-the-counter cold/allergy products
c Common ingredient in over-the-counter cold/allergy products and nonprescription diet aids
d Common ingredient in over-the-counter cough syrups

Figure C-3

Lithium Interactions

Drug	Effect of Interaction
Diuretics, especially thiazides	Increased lithium levels, lithium toxicity

Nonsteroidal anti-inflammatory agents
    Ibuprofen (Motrin, Advil, Nuprin)
    Naproxen (Naprosyn)
    Indomethacin (Indocin)
    Piroxicam (Feldene)
	Increased lithium levels, lithium toxicity

Angiotensin converting enzyme inhibitors
    Captopril (Capoten)
    Enalapril (Vasotec)
    Lisinopril (Zestril, Prinivil)
	Increased lithium levels, lithium toxicity

Metronidazole (Flagyl)	Increased lithium levels, lithium toxicity

Calcium channel blockers
    Verapamil (Calan, Isoptin)
    Diltiazem (Cardizem)
	Increased or decreased lithium levels, neurotoxicity (weakness, incoordination, muscle stiffness, abnormal movements, psychosis)

Antipsychotics	Neurotoxicity (delirium, seizures, encephalopathy) or increased extrapyramidal symptoms
Carbamazepine (Tegretol)	Neurotoxicity (*not* associated with increase in lithium level)
TCAs	Possible worsening of lithium tremor, increased TCA effect
SSRIs	Increased lithium levels, possible neurotoxicity (confusion, dizziness, tremor, muscle stiffness, incoordination)
Theophylline Caffeine	Decreased lithium levels
Sodium chloride (high doses) Sodium bicarbonate (high doses)	Decreased lithium levels

Figure C-4

Antipsychotic Interactions

Drug	Effect of Interaction
Amphetamines	Increased psychosis
Anticonvulsants Carbamazepine (Tegretol) Phenobarbital	Decreased antipsychotic levels, increased sedation
Meperidine (Demerol)	Hypotension, lethargy
L-dopa	Decreased effectiveness of L-dopa in parkinsonism
Isoniazid (INH)	Liver toxicity, encephalitis
Anesthetics	Hypotension
Lithium	Neurotoxicity (delirium seizures, encephalopathy) or increased extrapyramidal symptoms
TCAs	Increased TCA levels
Beta blockers	Increased levels of both drugs, hypotension
SSRIs	Increased antipsychotic level/side effects

Figure C-5

Anticonvulsants: Carbamazepine (CBZ) and Divalproex

Drug	Effect of Interaction
Bupropion	CBZ decreases bupropion levels
Cyclosporine	CBZ decreases cyclosporine levels
Isoniazid	Increased CBZ levels
Nefazodone	Increased CBZ levels
Cimetidine	Increased divalproex levels
Erythromycin	Increased divalproex levels
TCAs	Divalproex increases TCA levels
Zidovudine	Divalproex increases zidovudine levels
Cimetidine (Tagamet) Calcium channel blockers Verapamil (Calan, Isoptin) Diltiazem (Cardizem) Fluoxetine (Prozac) Propoxyphene (Darvon, Darvocet) Erythromycin and related antibiotics	Increased CBZ levels, CBZ toxicity (drowsiness, dizziness, nausea, vomiting, blurred vision, slurred speech, cardiac problems)
Other anticonvulsants, Phenytoin (Dilantin), Phenobarbital	Increased or decreased CBZ and VA levels, increased or decreased levels of other anticonvulsants
Aspirin	Increased VA levels
TCAs Anticoagulants, Antipsychotics, Theophylline, Oral contraceptives, Doxycycline	CBZ decreases serum levels, diminished effect of listed drugs
Lithium	Neurotoxicity with lithium and CBZ (*not* associated with increase in lithium level)

Figure C-6

Benzodiazepine Interactions

Drug	Effect of Interaction
Disulfiram (Antabuse) Cimetidine (Tagamet) Isoniazid (INH) Oral contraceptives	Increased benzodiazepine levels
Alcohol, CNS depressants (narcotics, barbiturates)	Potentiate CNS depression
L-dopa	Decreased effectiveness of L-dopa in parkinsonism
Bupropion (Wellbutrin)	Abrupt benzodiazepine withdrawal increases seizure risk

Figure C-7

Miscellaneous Drug Interactions

Interactive Combination	Effect of Interaction
Bupropion (Wellbutrin) and benzodiazepines	Abrupt benzodiazepine withdrawal increases seizure risk
Bupropion (Wellbutrin) and L-dopa	Excitability, restlessness, tremor, nausea, vomiting
Buspirone (BuSpar) and MAOIs—**contraindicated**	Seriously elevated blood pressure (hypertensive crisis), elevated temperature, seizures, cerebral hemorrhage, **death**
St. John's Wort	May be dangerous
Bupropion and TCAs	Increased TCA effect
Bupropion and ritonavir	Increased bupropion levels
Bupropion and carbamazepine	Decreased bupropion levels
Bupropion and MAOIs contraindicated	Seriously elevated blood pressure (hypertensive crisis), elevated temperature, seizures, cerebral hemorrhage, **death**
Bupropion duplicative products (Wellbutrin and Zyban)	Significantly elevated bupropion levels
Buspirone and nefazodone	Significant elevations in levels of both drugs. Effects include dizziness and drowsiness.

Figure C-8

Nefazodone Interactions

Drug	Effect of Interaction
Sibutramine	Serotonin syndrome with symptoms of irritability, tremors, altered consciousness
Trazodone	Serotonin syndrome, as above
Benzodiazepines	Significant elevations in serum levels of some benzodiazepines
Buspirone	Significant elevations in levels of both drugs. Effects include dizziness and drowsiness.
Carbamazepine	Increased CBZ levels
Lipid Lowering Drugs Atorvastatin Lovastatin Simvastatin	Increased levels of lipid lowering drugs. Increased side effects: myositis and rhabdomyolysis
MAOIs—contraindicated	Serotonergic syndrome with symptoms of fever, tremors, muscular rigidity, coma, **death**

Figure C-9

Venlafaxine Interactions

Drug	Effect of Interaction
Cimetidine	Increased venlafaxine levels
MAOIs—contraindicated	seriously elevated blood pressure (hypertensive crisis), elevated temperature, seizures, cerebral hemorrhage, **death**
TCAs	Venlafaxine may increase serum levels of some TCAs
Trazodone	Serotonin syndrome with symptoms of irritability, tremor, altered consciousness

Figure C-10

Appendix D

Differentiating Psychotropic Side Effects from Psychiatric Symptoms

In this appendix we discuss a potentially problematic area: the identification of, and response to, psychotropic-induced side effects. The most obvious danger of failing to accurately differentiate medication side effects from a disease process is the possibility that one might increase the dose of the very medication responsible for the the side effects. Similarly, unwarranted diagnoses may be assigned or unnecessary medications added.

At times, making this distinction is nearly impossible. Not only is the clinician required to separate strikingly similar medication side effects and psychiatric symptomatology, but the patient may be only marginally able to give a useful subjective description.

Akathisia Versus Agitation Associated with Worsening Anxiety or Psychosis

Akathisia, the compulsion to be in motion, may present with a variety of associated symptoms. Patients often experience an inability to remain still, pace, tap their feet while sitting, and shift their weight while standing. Along a continuum, mild akathisia may appear as increasing or emerging anxiety, and when more severe, may be mistaken for worsening psychosis.

Akathisia secondary to neuroleptics is more common in younger patients or with high-potency agents. The onset of akathisia can follow a variable course, appearing either early in treatment or up to several months later. Especially if the patient is not receiving anticholinergics, the possibility of medication-induced akathisia should be considered before more neuroleptic is administered. If symptoms diminish in response to anticholinergics, it is probably akathisia. If symptoms resolve with additional neuroleptic, it is more likely disease exacerbation. In some patients, response to anticholinergics is inadequate, requiring adding, or changing to, a benzodiazepine or beta blocker. In these cases, the patient will usually report a "physical" restlessness as opposed to "emotional" anxiety or agitation.

Akathisia has also been reported with the SSRIs, especially fluoxetine, and with the tricyclic antidepressants. Failure to recognize antidepressant-induced akathisia may lead to unnecessary prescribing of antianxiety agents or neuroleptics.

Excessive Anticholinergic Effects Versus Psychosis

An acute onset of primary organic symptoms may signal anticholinergic delirium, with associated mental status changes of confusion, disorientation, and tactile or visual hallucinations. Physiologic indicators include dry mucous membranes, increased heart rate, and dilated pupils. Recovery usually occurs within several days following discontinuation of the suspected anticholinergic drug, but occasionally this syndrome may last up to two weeks. Elderly people are especially prone to anticholinergic overload.

Drug treatment of anticholinergic delirium is typically not recommended, although benzodiazepines can be used to treat severe agitation. Neuroleptics, with their anticholinergic properties, are relatively contraindicated.

Parkinsonian Side Effects Versus Depression

Neuroleptic-induced parkinsonian side effects are characterized by the triad of tremor, muscle stiffness, and slowness of motion. For the most part, these physical indicators are relatively easy to identify. The tremor, which is somewhat coarse and may include classic "pill-rolling," is worse at rest, and is distinguishable from the fine, intention tremor of lithium. Muscle stiffness or rigidity is notable for the increased resistance to passive movement ("cogwheeling").

The absence of movement (akinesia) does not occur as frequently as slowed movement (bradykinesia). Moderate to severe bradykinesia includes postural abnormalities of shuffling gait, stooped appearance, and feeling off balance. Drooling and slowed, nonexpressive speech are also common. It is the mildly bradykinetic patient, without noticeable tremor or rigidity, whose presentation can mimic a depressive mood disorder. Overall, the slowed motion, lack of facial expression, apathy, and social withdrawal present markedly similar to depression. A careful evaluation should be made to determine the presence of associated parkinsonian characteristics before revising a diagnosis or initiating an antidepressant.

Acute Dystonia Versus Tardive Dyskinesia

Dystonic reactions occur within hours or days of initiating treatment with (or increasing the dose of) a neuroleptic. Tardive dyskinesia (TD) presents with a more insidious onset and is associated with long-term neuroleptic treatment. Figure D-1 summarizes the characteristics of acute dystonia and TD.

Acute Dystonia Versus Tardive Dyskinesia

Acute Dystonia

Fixed upward gaze
(oculogyric crisis)
Neck twisting (torticollis)
Arching of the head
backward (opisthotonos)
Clenched jaw or "lockjaw"
(trismus)
Facial grimacing due to
involuntary muscle contraction
Difficulty swallowing
Difficulty breathing
(larynogospasm)

Tardive Dyskinesia

Abnormal, involuntary, rhythmic
movements of the mouth, tongue,
and lips, including protruding
tongue, worm-like tongue
movements, mouth puckering, lip
smacking, and chewing motions
Irregular, purposeless, involuntary
quick movements of the extremities,
flailing or jerky in appearance
Continuous, writhing movements of
extremities, including trunk or pelvis

Figure D-1

Not only is there no effective treatment for TD, but administration of anticholinergics is likely to worsen the symptoms. Therefore, the differential diagnosis of these two syndromes is critically important.

Antidepressant Toxicity Versus Worsening or Reemerging Depression

Symptoms of depression that reappear, or are slow to resolve with antidepressant treatment, may be explained by several factors, including noncompliance and poor therapeutic response requiring a medication change. Consideration should also be given to medication-related CNS toxicity. The most obvious of these symptoms that are also diagnostic of depression are irritability, confusion, memory impairment, anxiety, agitation, and lethargy. In determining a differential diagnosis, the clinician can assess for the physiologic symptoms of antidepressant toxicity (as described in chapters 15 and 19) and utilize laboratory monitoring for antidepressant blood levels.

A small percent of patients treated with SSRIs for more than six months will report a reemergence of what are experienced as depressive symptoms. A close review of the clinical status will reveal that many of the previously reported depressive symptoms continue, in fact, to be well controlled by the antidepressant. However, what can develop are symptoms of apathy, low motivation, and emotional blunting (e.g., an inability to cry). One hypothesis is that the chronic effect of increased serotonin action in the CNS is to gradually inhibit dopamine neurons in the frontal cortex (inhibitory serotonin receptors are found on dopamine cell bodies). This dopaminergic hypometabolic state has been demonstrated on metabolic brain scans (Hoehn-Saric 1990). This phenomenon also may be responsible for the rare occurrence of emotional disinhibition, sometimes seen with chronic SSRI treatment.

This condition, which should be distinguished from primary depressive illness, can be eliminated by the discontinuation of the SSRI, or oftentimes it is resolved by the co-administration of a dopamine agonist (e.g., bupropion).

Appendix E

Neurocognitive Mental Status Exam

Figure E-1 is a short exam that can be administered to patients as an aid in making a diagnosis. Notes on each question appear below. For a more comprehensive review of a neurologically based mental status exam, the reader is referred to an excellent text: *The Mental Status Examination in Neurology* (Strub and Black 1985).

Notes on the Use of the Brief Neurocognitive Mental Status Exam

1. *Behavioral observations*

    a. Look for signs of drowsiness or fluctuating degrees of alertness.

    b. This may be formally tested by administering a digit span test or by careful observation during the interview.

    c. Make note of slurred speech or word-finding problems.

    d. Watch for unsteady gait and poor gross motor coordination.

2. *Orientation*—ask: "What is the date (month, day, year) and what time of day is it now?" "Can you tell me where you are right now? Please be specific." Ask the patient to identify relatives who have accompanied him or her.

3. *Recent memory*—present three items and ask for immediate recall. Then after a period of five minutes ask the patient to again recall the three items. Most normal adults should be able to recall three items. Inability to do so may suggest recent memory problems. A second trial may be conducted later in the interview.

Brief Neurocognitive Mental Status Exam

Name _____ Age _____ Date _____

Level of education _____ Occupation_____

Onset of symptoms _____

Medications _____

1. Behavioral observations

    a. Level of awakeness/alertness _____

    b. Signs of impaired attention or distractibility _____

    c. Quality of speech _____

    d. Gait _____

2. Orientation: Time _____ Place _____ Person _____

3. Recent memory (three-item recall with five-minute delay)

    Trial A: House, Orange, Robert _____

    Trial B: Petunia, Buick, Wind _____

4. Calculations: 100 – 93 – 86 – 79 – 72 – 65 – 58 – 51 _____

5. Reproduction of cross _____ cube _____

6. Thinking/Speech: Coherent? _____ Relevant? _____

Figure E-1

4. *Calculations*—ask the patient to begin with the number 100 and subtract 7 from this number, then subtract 7 again, and so forth. This test provides a rough measure of concentration.

5. *Reproduction of cross and cube*—present stimulus illustrations shown below. You can copy them onto a 3-by-5-inch, unlined, white index card. Allow the patient to copy the designs one at a time onto a blank sheet of paper. Drawing performance can be compared to samples (see figure E-2) to derive rough estimates of the patient's constructional ability.

6. *Thinking/Speech*—note the presence of incoherent or irrelevant speech.

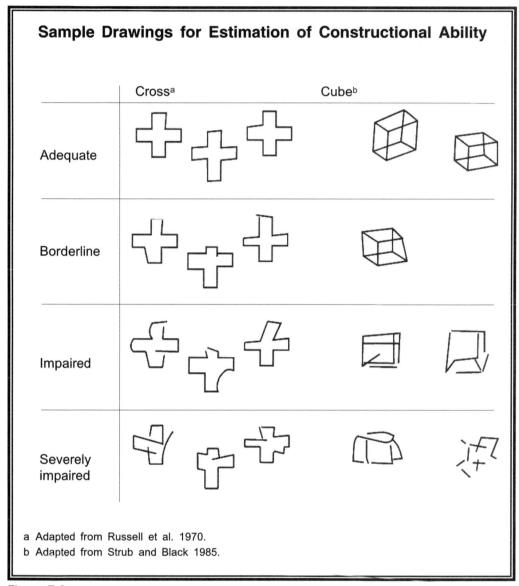

Sample Drawings for Estimation of Constructional Ability

	Cross[a]	Cube[b]
Adequate		
Borderline		
Impaired		
Severely impaired		

a Adapted from Russell et al. 1970.
b Adapted from Strub and Black 1985.

Figure E-2

Appendix F

Trade Versus Generic Drug Names: A Quick Reference

The following tables will enable you to quickly find the corresponding generic or trade name of a medication when you know only one of its names.

Trade to Generic

Trade Name	Generic Name	Trade Name	Generic Name
Adderall	Amphetamine combination	Nardil	Phenelzine
		Navane	Thiothixene
Akineton	Biperiden	Neurontin	Gabapentin
Ambien	Zolpidem	Norpramin	Desipramine
Anafranil	Clomipramine	Orap	Pimozide
Artane	Trihexyphenidyl	Pamelor	Nortriptyline
Asendin	Amoxapine	Parnate	Tranylcypromine
Atarax	Hydroxyzine HCl	Paxil	Paroxetine
Ativan	Lorazepam	Paxipam	Halazepam
Aventyl	Nortriptyline	Permitil	Fluphenazine
Benadryl	Diphenhydramine	Prolixin	Fluphenazine
BuSpar	Buspirone	ProSom	Estazolam
Catapres	Clonidine	Prozac	Fluoxetine
Celexa	citalopram	Remeron	Mirtazapine
Centrax	Prazepam	Restoril	Temazepam
Clozaril	Clozapine	Risperdal	Risperidone
Cogentin	Benztropine	Ritalin	Methylphenidate
Concerta	Methylphenidate sustained release	Sarafem	Fluoxetine
		Serax	Oxazepam
Cylert	Pemoline	Serentil	Mesoridazine
Dalmane	Flurazepam	Seroquel	Quetiapine
Depakene	Valproic acid	Serzone	Nefazodone
Depakote	Divalproex	Sinequan	Doxepin
Desyrel	Trazodone	Sonata	Zaleplon
Dexedrine	Dextroamphetaìmine	Stelazine	Trifluoperazine
Doral	Quazepam	Surmontil	Trimipramine
Effexor XR	Venlafaxine extended release	Symmetrel	Amantadine
		Taractan	Chlorprothixene
Elavil	Amitriptyline	Tegretol	Carbamazepine
Eldepryl	Selegiline (deprenyl)	Tegretol XR	Carbamazepine extended release
Eskalith	Lithium carbonate		
Eskalith CR	Lithium carbonate controlled release	Tenex	Guanfacine
		Tenormin	Atenolol
Gabitril	Tiagabine	Thorazine	Chlorpromazine
Geodon	Ziprasidone	Tindal	Acetophenazine
Halcion	Triazolam	Tofranil	Imipramine
Haldol	Haloperidol	Topamax	Topiramate
Inderal	Propranolol	Tranxene	Clorazepate
Klonopin	Clonazepam	Trilafon	Perphenazine
Lamictal	Lamotrigine	Trileptal	Oxcarbazepine
Librium	Chlordiazepoxide	Valium	Diazepam
Lithobid	Lithium carbonate slow release	Versed	Midazolam
		Vestra	Reboxetine
Lithonate	Lithium carbonate	Vistaril	Hydroxyzine pamoate
Lithotabs	Lithium carbonate	Vivactil	Protriptyline
Loxitane	Loxapine	Wellbutrin	Bupropion
Ludiomil	Maprotiline	Wellbutrin SR	Bupropion sustained release
Luvox	Fluvoxamine		
Marplan	Isocarboxazid	Xanax	Alprazolam
Mellaril	Thioridazine	Zoloft	Sertraline
Metadate ER	Methylphenidate extended release	Zyprex	Olanzapine
Moban	Molindone		

Generic to Trade

Generic Name	Trade Name
Acetophenazine	Tindal
Alprazolam	Xanax
Amantadine	Symmetrel
Amitriptyline	Elavil
Amoxapine	Asendin
Amphetamine combination	Adderall
Atenolol	Tenormin
Benztropine	Cogentin
Biperiden	Akineton
Bupropion	Wellbutrin
Bupropion sustained release	Wellbutrin SR
Buspirone	BuSpar
Carbamazepine	Tegretol
Carbamazepine extended release	Tegretol XR
Chlordiazepoxide	Librium
Chlorpromazine	Thorazine
Citalopram	Celexa
Clomipramine	Anafranil
Clonazepam	Klonopin
Clonidine	Catapres
Clorazepate	Tranxene
Clozapine	Clozaril
d- and l-amphetamine	Adderall
Desipramine	Norpramin
Dextroamphetamine	Dexedrine
Diazepam	Valium
Diphenhydramine	Benadryl
Divalproex	Depakote
Doxepin	Sinequan
Estazolam	ProSom
Fluoxetine	Serafem
Fluphenazine	Prolixin, Permitil
Flurazepam	Dalmane
Fluoxetine	Prozac
Fluvoxamine	Luvox
Gabapentin	Neurontin
Guanfacine	Tenex
Halazepam	Paxipam
Haloperidol	Haldol
Hydroxyzine HCl	Atarax
Hydroxyzine pamoate	Vistaril
Imipramine	Tofranil
Isocarboxazid	Marplan
Lamotrigine	Lamictal
Lithium carbonate	Lithotabs, Lithonate, Eskalith

Generic Name	Trade Name
Lithium carbonate, long acting	Eskalith CR, Lithobid
Lorazepam	Ativan
Loxapine	Loxitane
Maprotiline	Ludiomil
Mesoridazine	Serentil
Methylphenidate sustained release	Concerta
Methylphenidate extended release	Metadate ER
Midazolam	Versed
Mirtazpine	Remeron
Molindone	Moban
Nefazodone	Serzone
Nortriptyline	Pamelor, Aventyl
Olanzapine	Zyprexa
Oxazepam	Serax
Oxcarbazepine	Trileptal
Paroxetine	Paxil
Pemoline	Cylert
Perphenazine	Trilafon
Phenelzine	Nardil
Pimozide	Orap
Prazepam	Centrax
Propranolol	Inderal
Protriptyline	Vivactil
Quazepam	Doral
Quetiapine	Seroquel
Reboxetine	Vestra
Risperidone	Risperdal
Selegeline (deprenyl)	Eldepryl
Sertraline	Zoloft
Temazepam	Restoril
Thioridazine	Mellaril
Thiothixene	Navane
Tiagabine	Gabitril
Topiramate	Topamax
Tranylcypromine	Parnate
Trazodone	Desyrel
Triazolam	Halcion
Trifluoperazine	Stelazine
Trihexyphenidyl	Artane
Trimipramine	Surmontil
Valproic acid	Depakene
Venlafaxine	Effexor
Venlafaxine extended release	Effexor XR
Zaleplon	Geodon
Ziprasidone	Zeldex
Zolpidem	Ambien

Appendix G

Books for Patients About Medication Treatment

Depression

Lift Your Mood Now, by J. Preston. Oakland, Calif.: New Harbinger Publications, 2001.

You Can Beat Depression: A Guide To Recovery, Third Edition, by J. Preston. San Luis Obispo, Calif.: Impact Publishers, 2001.

The Depression Workbook, by Mary Ellen Copeland. Oakland, Calif.: New Harbinger Publications, 2002.

Bipolar Disorder

A Brilliant Madness: Living with Manic-Depressive Illness, by Patty Duke, Mary Lou Pinckert, and Gloria Hochman. New York: Bantam, 1993.

An Unquiet Mind, by Kay Redfield Jamison. New York: Alfred A. Knopf, 1995.

Touched with Fire: Manic-Depressive Illness and the Artistic Temperament, by Kay Redfield Jamison. New York: The Free Press, 1993.

Bipolar Disorder: A Guide for Patients and Families, by Francis Mark Mondimore. Baltimore, Maryland: Johns Hopkins University Press, 1999.

Anxiety

The Anxiety and Phobia Workbook, Second Edition, by Edmund Bourne. Oakland, Calif.: New Harbinger Publications, 2000.

Psychosis

Coping with Schizophrenia: A Guide for Families, by Kim T. Mueser, Ph.D., and Susan Gingerich, M.S.W. Oakland, Calif.: New Harbinger Publications, 1994.

Alzheimer's Disease

The 36-Hour Day, by N. L. Mace and P. V. Rabins. New York: Warner Books, 1981.

Obsessive-Compulsive Disorder

The Boy Who Couldn't Stop Washing, by J. Rapoport. New York: Signet Books, 1989.
When Once Is Not Enough, by Gail Steketee and Kerrin White. Oakland, Calif.: New Harbinger Publications, 1990.

Attention Deficit Disorder

Attention-Deficit Hyperactivity Disorder, by Russell Barkley and Kevin Murphy. New York: Guilford Publications, 1998.

Borderline Personality Disorder

I Hate You—Don't Leave Me, by J. Kreisman and H. Kraus. Los Angeles: Price Stern Publishers, 1989.
Stop Walking on Eggshells: Taking Your Life Back When Someone You Care About Has Borderline Personality Disorder, by Paul T. Mason and Randi Kreger. Oakland, Calif.: New Harbinger Publications, 1998.

Medications and Psychotherapy

Make Every Session Count, by J. Preston, N. Varzos, and D. Liebert. Oakland, Calif.: New Harbinger Publications, 1998.

References

Agras, S. 1985. *Panic: Facing Fears, Phobias, and Anxiety.* New York: W. H. Freeman.

Akiskal, H. S. 1996. The prevalent clinical spectrum of bipolar disorders: beyond DSM-IV. *Journal of Clinical Psychopharmacology* 16:(Suppl)4S–14S.

Akiskal, H. S., and C. L. Bowden. 2000. The spectrum of bipolarity. Symposium conducted at the American Psychiatric Association 153rd Annual Meeting, Chicago, Ill. May.

Akiskal, H. S., and R. E. Weise. 1992. The clinical spectrum of so-called "minor" depressions. *American Journal of Psychotherapy.* 46:9–22.

American Psychiatric Association. Practice guideline for the treatment of patients with bipolar disorder. 1994. *American Journal of Psychiatry* 15:(Suppl)1–36.

———. 1994. Practice guidelines for treatment of patients with bipolar disorder. *American Journal of Psychiatry* 151:(Suppl)1–35.

American Society of Health System Pharmacists. 2000. *American Hospital Formulary Service Drug Information.* Bethseda, Md.: American Society of Health System Pharmacists.

Arndt, S., R. J. Alliger, and N. C. Andreasen. 1991. The distinction of positive and negative symptoms. The failure of a two-dimensional model. *British Journal of Psychiatry* 158:340–345.

Atshuler, L. L., R. M. Post, G. S. Leverich, K. Mikalauskas, A. Rosoff, and L. Ackerman. 1995. Antidepressant-induced mania and cycle acceleration: A controvery revisited. *American Journal of Psychiatry* 152:1130–8.

Avis, H. 1998. *Drugs and Life.* New York: McGraw-Hill Higher Education.

Ayd, F. J. 2000. Evaluating interactions between herbal and psychoactive medications. *Psychiatric Times,* December, p. 45-47.

Ballenger, J. C., and R. M. Post. 1980. Carbamazepine in manic-depressive illness: A new treatment. *American Journal of Psychiatry.* 137:782–790.

Baron, M., N. Risch, R. Hamburger, B. Mandel, S. Kushner, M. Newman, D. Drumer, and R. Belmaker. 1987. Genetic linkage between X-chromosome markers and bipolar affective illness. *Nature* 326:289–292.

Barnes, N. M., and T. Sharp. 1999. A review of central 5-HT receptors and their function. *Neuropharmacology* 38:1083–1152.

Bauer, M. S., A. M. Callahan, C. Jampala, F. Petty, M. Sajatovic, V. Schaefer, et al. 1999. Clinical practice guidelines for bipolar disorder from the Department of Veterans' Affairs. *Journal of Clinical Psychiatry* 60:9–21.

Baxter, L. R. 1991. PET studies of cerebral function in major depression and obsessive-compulsive disorder: The emerging profrontal cortex consensus. *Annals of Clinical Psychiatry* 3:103–09.

Baxter, L. R., J. M. Schwartz, K. S. Bergman, M. P. Szuba, B. H. Guze, J. C. Marriotta, A. Alazvaki, C. E. Selin, H. K. Feung, P. Munford, and M. E. Phelps. 1992. Caudate glucose metabolic rate changes with both drug and behavior therapy for obsessive-compulsive disorder. *Archives of General Psychiatry* 49:681–689.

Beardsley, R. S., G. J. Gardocki, D. B. Larsen, and J. Hidalgo. 1988. Prescribing of psychotropic medication by primary care physicians and psychiatrists. *Archives of General Psychiatry* 45:1117–1119.

Beasley, C. M., and B. E. Dornseif. 1991. Fluoxetine and suicide: A meta-analysis of controlled trials of treatment of depression. *British Medical Journal* 303:685–692.

Beaubrun, G., and G. E. Gary. 2000. A review of herbal medicines for psychiatric disorders. *Psychiatric Services* 51(9):1130–1134.

Beck, A. T. 1976. *Cognitive Therapy and the Emotional Disorders.* New York: International Universities Press.

Beitman, B. D., and G. L. Klerman, eds. 1991. *Integrating Pharmacotherapy and Psychotherapy.* Washington, D.C.: American Psychiatric Press.

Bender, K. J., ed. 1993. Narcotic antagonist for alcoholism. *Psychotropics* 13:6–8.

Benet, L. Z., D. L. Kroetz, and L. B. Sheiner. 1996. Pharmacokinetics: The dynamics of drug absorption, distribution and elimination. In *Goodman and Gilman's: The Pharmacological Basis of Therapeutics.* J. G. Hardman, L. E. Limbird, P. B. Molinoff, R. W. Ruddon, and A. G. Gilman, eds. New York: McGraw-Hill.

Benet, L. Z., J. R. Mitchell, and L. B. Sherner. 1990a. General principles. In *Goodman & Gilman's: The Pharmacological Basis of Therapeutics.* A. G. Gilman, T. W. Rall, A. S. Nies, and P. Taylor, eds. New York: Pergamon Press.

———. 1990b. Pharmacokinetics: The dynamics of drug absorption, distribution and elimination. In *Goodman & Gilman's: The pharmacological Basis of Therapeutics.* A. G. Gilman, T. W. Rall, A. S. Nies, and P. Taylor, eds. New York: Pergamon Press.

Berigan, T. R., and A. Holzgang. 1995. Valproate as an alternative in post-traumatic stress disorder: A case report. *Military Medicine* 160(6):318.

Bhalla, U. S., and R. Iyengar. 1999. Emergent properties of networks of biological signaling pathways. *Science* 283:381–387.

Bieck, P. R., and K. Antonin. 1988. Oral tyramine pressor test and the safety of monoamine oxidase inhibitor drugs: Comparison of brofaromine and tranylcypromine in healthy subjects. *Journal of Clinical Psychopharmacology* 8:237–45.

Bleuler, M. 1968. Prognosis of schizophrenic psychoses: A summary of personal research. In *The Schizophrenias.* F. Flach, ed. New York: Norton.

Bly, R. 1990. *Iron John.* Reading, Mass: Addison-Wesley Publishing.

Bochus, S. E., and J. E. Kleinman. 1996. The neuropathology of schizophrenia. *Journal of Clinical Psychiatry* 57:(Suppl)72–83.

Boullata, J. I., and A. M. Nace. 2000. Safety issues with herbal medicine. *Pharmacotherapy* 20:257–269.

Bourne, H. R., and M. von Zastrow. 2001. Drug receptors and pharmacodynamics. In *Basic and Clinical Pharmacology.* B. G. Katzung, ed. New York: McGraw-Hill.

Bowlby, J. 1986. *Attachment and Loss.* New Your: Basic Books

Bowden, C. L. 1996. Role of newer medications for bipolar disorder. *Journal of Clinical Psychopharmacology* 16:(Suppl)48S–55S.

Bowden, C. L., A. M. Brugger, A. C. Swann, J. R. Calabrese, P. G. Janicak, F. Petty, S. C. Dilsaver, J. M. Davis, A. J. Rush, J. G. Small, E. S. Garza-Trevino, S. C. Risch, P. J. Goodnick, and D. D. Morris. 1994. Efficacy of divalproex vs. lithium, placebo in the treatment of mania. *Journal of the American Medical Association* 271:918–924.

Bowes, M. 2001. OCD: Will immunotherapy succeed where other approaches have failed? *Neuropsychiatry Reviews* 2:1-25.

Brady, K., et al. 2000. Efficacy and safety of sertraline treatment of post-traumatic stress disorder: A randomized controlled trial. *JAMA* 283:1837-1844.

Brenner, R., et al. 2000. Comparison of an extract of hypericum (LI-160) and sertraline in the treatment of depression: A double-blind randomized pilot study. *Clinical Therapeutics* 22:411-419.

Briggs, G. G. 1992. Drugs in pregnancy and lactation. In *Applied Therapeutics: The Clinical Use of Drugs,* 5th ed. M. A. Koda-Kimble, L. Y. Young, W. A. Kradjan, and B. J. Guglielmo, eds. Vancouver, Wash.: Applied Therapeutics.

Brotman, A. 1992. *Practical Reviews in Psychiatry* (audiotape). Birmingham, Ala.: Educational Reviews.

Brown, C. S., and S. G. Bryant. 1992. Major depressive disorders. In *Applied Therapeutics: The Clinical Use of Drugs,* 5th ed. M. A. Koda-Kimble, L. Y. Young, W. A. Kradjan, and B. J. Guglielmo, eds. Vancouver, Wash.: Applied Therapeutics.

Brown, S. A., and M. A. Schuckit. 1988. Changes in depression among abstinent alcoholics. *Journal of the Study of Alcoholism* 49:412–417.

Burton, T. M. 1991. Antidepression drug of Eli Lilly loses sales after attack by sect. *Wall Street Journal,* April 19, A1–A2.

Calabrese, J. R., S. H. Fatemi, M. Kujawa, and M. J. Woyshville. 1996. Predictors of response to mood stabilizers. *Journal of Clinical Psychopharmacology* 16:(Suppl)24S–31S.

Calabrese, J. R., S. E. Kimmel, M. J. Woyshville, D. J. Rapport, C. J. Faust, P. A. Thompson, and H. Y. Meltzer. 1996. Clozapine for treatment-refractory mania. *American Journal of Psychiatry* 153:759–764.

Calabrese, J. R., and M. Woyshville. 1995. A medication algorithm for treatment of bipolar rapid cycling? *Journal of Clinical Psychiatry* 56:(Suppl)11–18.

Carlson, G. A., and F. K. Goodwin. 1973. The stages of mania. *Archives of General Psychiatry* 28: 221–228.

Carpenter, W. T., T. E. Hanlon, D. W. Heinrichs, A. T. Summerfelt, B. Kirkpatrick. J. Levine, and R. W. Buchanan. 1990. Continuous versus targeted medication in schizophrenic outpatients: Outcome results. *American Journal of Psychiatry* 147:1138–1148.

Cauffield, J. S. 2000. The psychosocial aspects of complementary and alternative medicine. *Pharmacotherapy* 20:1289–1294.

Chang, D. M. 2000. Lithium as a neuroprotective drug in vivo and in vitro: Mechanisms and implications. *International Journal of Neuropsychopharmacology* 3:(Suppl)S11.

Clerc, G. E., P. Ruimy, and J. Verdeau-Palles. 1994. A double-blind comparison of venlafaxine and fluoxetine in patients hospitalized for major depression and melancholia. *International Journal of Clinical Psychopharmacology* 9:139–143.

Clothier, J., A. C. Swann, and T. Freeman. 1992. Dysphoric mania. *Journal of Clinical Psychopharmacology* 12:(Suppl)13S–22S.

Coccaro, E. F. 1998. Clinical outcome of psychopharmacologic treatment of borderline and schizotypal personality disordered subjects. *Journal of Clinical Psychiatry* 59(Suppl):130–135.

Cohen, L. S., V. L. Heller, and J. F. Rosenbaum. 1989. Treatment guidelines for psychotropic drug use in pregnancy. *Psychosomatics* 30:25–33.

Connor, K. M., et al. 1999. Fluoxetine in post-traumatic stress disorder: Randomized, double-blind study. *British Journal of Psychiatry* 175:17–22.

Consumer Reports. 2000. Emotional aspirin? Consumer report. December, p. 60–62.

Cornelius, J. R., P. H. Soloff, J. M. Perel, and R. F. Ulrich. 1991. A preliminary trial of fluoxetine in refractory borderline patients. *Journal of Clinical Psychopharmacology* 11:116–20.

Cowdry, R. W., and D. L. Gardner. 1988. Pharmacotherapy of borderline personality disorder. *Archives of General Psychiatry* 45:111–19.

Cowley, G., K. Springer, E. A. Leonard, K. Robins, and J. Gorden. 1990. The promise of Prozac. *Newsweek* March 26. 38–41.

Crutchfield, J., J. Farmer, N. H. Packard, and R. Shaw. 1986. Chaos. *Scientific American* 255:46–57.

Daro, D. 1989. *The Most Frequently "Asked About" Issues Regarding Child Abuse and Neglect.* Toledo, Ohio: NCE Foundation for the Prevention of Child Abuse.

Davidson, J., H. Kudler, R. Smith, S. L. Mahorney, S. Lipper, E. Hammett, W. B. Saunders, and J. O. Cavenar. 1990. Treatment of PTSD with amitriptyline and placebo. *Archives of General Psychiatry* 47:259–66.

Davidson, J., S. Roth, and E. Newman. 1991. Fluoxetine in post-traumatic stress disorder. *Journal of Traumatic Stress* 4:419–23.

Davidson, J. R. T., and K. M. Connor. 2000. *Herbs for the Mind: What Science Tells Us About Nature's Remedies for Depression, Stress, Memory Loss and Insomnia.* New York: Guilford Press.

Davis, K. L., M. S. Buchsbaum, L. Shihabuddin, J. Spiegel-Cohen, M. Metzger, E. Frescska, et al. 1998. Ventricular enlargement in poor-outcome schizophrenia. *Biological Psychiatry* 43:783–793.

Davis, K., R. Kahn, G. Ko, and M. Davidson. 1991. Dopamine in schizophrenia: A review and reconceptualization. *American Journal of Psychiatry.* 148:1474–84.

Deckert, G. 1985. Advances in neuro-biology. Paper presented at Continuing Education Advanced Psychiatric Update, San Francisco, Calif.

Deltito, J. A. 1993. The effect of valproate on bipolar spectrum temperamental disorders. *Journal of Clinical Psychiatry* 54:301–04.

Devlin, M. J., S. Z. Yanovski, and G. T. Wilson. 2000. Obesity: What mental health professionals need to know. *American Journal of Psychiatry* 157:854–866.

Dilsaver, S. C., A. C. Swann, A. M. Shoaib, T. C. Bowers, and M. T. Halle. 1993. Depressive mania associated with non-response to antimanic agents. *American Journal of Psychiatry* 150:1548–51.

Drent, M. L., and E. A. van der Veen. 1993. Lipase inhibition: A novel concept in the treatment of obesity. *International Journal of Obesity and Related Metabolic Disorders* 17:241-244.

DSM-IV Draft Criteria. 1993. Washington D.C.: American Psychiatric Association.

Eisenberg, D. M., R. B. Davis, S. L. Ettner, S. Appel, S. Wilkey, M. Van Rompay, and R. C. Kessler. 1998. Trends in alternative medicine use in the United States, 1990-1997. *Journal of the American Medical Association* 280:1569-1575.

Emslie, G. J., A. J. Rush, et al. 1997. A double-blind randomized, placebo-controlled trial of fluoxetine in children and adolescents with depression. *Archives of General Psychiatry* 54:1031–1037.

Ereshefsky, L., and A. L. Richards. 1992. Psychoses. In *Applied Therapeutics: The Clinical Use of Drugs*, 5th ed. M. A. Koda-Kimble, L. Y. Young, W. A. Kradjan, B. J. Guglielmo, eds. Vancouver: Wash.: Applied Therapeutics.

Evans, D. L., M. J. Byerly, and R. A. Greer. 1995. Secondary mania: diagnosis and treatment. *Journal of Clinical Psychiatry* 56:(Suppl)31–7.

Eysenck, H. J. 1965. The effects of psychotherapy: An evaluation. *Journal of Consulting Psychology* 16:319–24.

Facts and Comparisons. 1993. St. Louis, Mo.: Facts and Comparisons.

Fava, M., K. I. Anderson, and J. Rusenbaum. 1993. Are thynoleptic responsive anger attacks a discrete clinical syndrome? *Psychosouratics* 34(4).

Fava, M., and J. F. Rosenbaum. 1991. Suicidality and fluoxetine: Is there a relationship? *Journal of Clinical Psychiatry*. 52:108–111.

Fesler, F. A. 1991. Valporate in combat-related post-traumatic stress disorder. *Journal of Clinical Psychiatry* 52:361–364.

Flockhart, D. A. 1996. Drug interactions, cardiac toxicity and terfenadine: From bench to clinic? *Journal of Clinical Psychopharmacology* 16:101–02.

Forster, P. L., et al. 1995. Lithium for irritability in post-traumatic stress disorder. *Journal of Traumatic Stress* 8:143-149.

Frances, A. J. 1989. *Borderline Personality Disorder* (audiotape). New York: Guilford Publications.

Frances, A. J., D. A. Kahn, D. Carpenter, J. P. Docherty, and S. L. Donovan. 1998. The expert consensus guidelines for treating depression in bipolar disorder. *Canadian Journal of Psychiatry* 59 (Suppl): 73-79.

Frances, A. J., and P. H. Soloff. 1988. Treating the borderline patient with low-dose neuroleptics. *Hospital and Community Psychiatry* 39:246–48.

Frank, J. D. 1973. *Persuasion and Healing*, 2nd ed. Baltimore: Johns Hopkins University Press.

Freud, S. 1895. Project for a scientific psychology, in vol. 1 of *The Standard Edition of the Complete Psychological Works of Sigmund Freud*, J. Strachey, ed. London: Hogarth Press, 1953.

———. 1917. Mourning and melancholia. In vol. 14 of *The Standard Edition of the Complete Psychological Works of Sigmund Freud*. London: Hogarth Press, 1957.

Fugh-Berman, A. 2000. Herb-drug interactions. *Lancet* 355:134.

Gabbard, G. O. 2000. A neurobiologically informed perspective on psychotherapy. *British Journal of Psychiatry* 177:117–122.

Gardner, D. L., and R. W. Cowdry. 1986. Positive effects of carbamazepine on behavioral dyscontrol in borderline personality disorder. *American Journal of Psychiatry* 143:519–22.

Garlow, S. J., D. L. Musselman, and C. B. Nemeroff. 1999. The neurochemistry of mood disorders clinical studies. In *Neurobiology of Mental Illness*. D. S. Charney, E. J. Nester, and B. S. Bunney, eds. New York: Oxford University Press.

Gelenberg, A. J., and S. C. Schoonover. 1991. Bipolar disorder. In *The Practitioner's Guide to Psychoactive Drugs*, 3rd ed. A. J. Gelenberg, E. L. Bassuk, and S. C. Schoonover, eds. New York: Plenum.

Gennaro, A. R. 1980. Inorganic pharmaceutical chemistry. In *Remington's Pharmaceutical Sciences*, 16th ed. A. Osol, ed. Easton, Penn.: Mack.

George, A., and P. H. Soloff. 1986. Schizotypal symptoms in patients with borderline personality disorder. *American Journal of Psychiatry* 143:212–15.

Ghaemi, S. N. 2000. New treatments for bipolar disorder: The role of atypical neuroleptic agents. *Journal of Clinical Psychiatry* 61:(Suppl)33–42.

Glazener, F. S. 1992. Adverse drug reactions. In *Melmon and Morrelli's Clinical Pharmacology: Basic Principles in Therapeutics*, 3rd ed. D. W. Nierenberg, ed. New York: McGraw-Hill.

Gilbert, D. A., K. Z. Altshuler, W. V. Rago, S. P. Shon, M. L. Crimson, M. G. Toprac, et al. 1998. Texas medication algorithm project: Definitions, rationale, and methods to develop medication algorithms. *Journal of Clinical Psychiatry* 59:345–351.

Gitlin, M. J. 1999. Lithium and the kidney: an updated review. *Drug Safety* 20:2331–2343.

———. 1993. Pharmacotherapy of personality disorders: conceptual framework and lineal strategies. *Journal of Clinical Psychopharmacology* 13(5):343–353.

Goldberg, J. F., M. Harrow, and L. S. Grossman. 1995. Course and outcome in bipolar affective disorder: a longitudinal follow-up study. *American Journal of Psychiatry* 152:379–84.

Goldberg, J. F. 2000. Treatment guidelines: Current and future management of bipolar disorder. *Journal of Clinical Psychiatry* 61:(Suppl)12–18.

Goldberg, S. C., S. C. Schulz, P. M. Schulz, R. J. Resnick, R. M. Hamer, and R. O. Friedel. 1986. Borderline and schizotypal personality disorders treated with low dose thiothixene vs. placebo. *Archives of General Psychiatry* 43:680–686.

Goodman, A. 1991. Organic unit theory: The mind-body problem revisited. *American Journal of Psychiatry* 148:553–563.

Goodwin, F. K., and K. R. Jamison. 1990. *Manic Depressive Illness*. New York: Oxford University Press.

Gordon, B. 1990. *I'm Dancing As Fast As I Can*. New York: Bantam.

Gottschalk, A., M. S. Bauer, and P. C. Whybrow. 1995. Evidence of chaotic mood variation in bipolar disorder. *Archives of General Psychiatry* 52:947–959.

Greenblatt, D. J., L. L. von Moltke, J. S. Harmatz, and R. I. Shader. 1998. Drug interactions with newer antidepressants: Role of human cytochromes P450. *Journal of Clinical Psychiatry* 1998:(Suppl)19–27.

Gur, R. E., P. Cowell, B. I. Turetsky, N. Gallacher, T. Cannon, W. Bilker, et al. 1998. A follow-up magnetic resonance imaging study of schizophrenia: Relationship of neuroanatomical changes to clinical and neurobehavioral measures. *Archives of General Psychiatry* 55:145–152.

Hall, R., M. Popkin, R. Devaul, L. Fairlace, and S. Stickney. 1978. Physical illness presenting as psychiatric disease. *Archives of General Psychiatry* 35:1315–20.

Hammer, M., et al. 1997. Buspirone potential of antidepressants in the treatment of PTSD. *Depression and Anxiety* 5:137–139.

Hanotin, C., F. Thomas, S. P. Jones, E. Leutenegger, and P. Drourin. 1998. A comparison of sibutramine and dexfenfluramine in the treatment of obesity. *Obesity Research* 6:285–291.

Hansten, P. D., and J. R. Horn. 1990. Drug interaction mechanisms and clinical characteristics. In *Drug Interactions and Updates*. Vancouver, Wash.: Applied Therapeutics.

———. 1993. Drug interactions and updates. Vancouver, Wash.: Applied Therapeutics.

Harlow, H. F., and M. K. Harlow. 1971. Psychopathology in monkeys. In *Experimental psychopathology*. H. D. Kimmal, ed. New York: Academic Press.

Harvey, P. D., and R. S. E. Keefe. 2001. Studies of cognitive changes in patients with schizophrenia following novel antipsychotic treatment. *American Journal of Psychiatry* 158:176–184.

Harris, I. M. 2000. Regulatory and ethical issues with dietary suppements. *Pharmacotherapy* 20:1295–1302.

Hidalgo, R. B., and J. R. Davidson. 2000. Selective serotonin reuptake inhibitors in P.T.S.D. *Journal of Psychopharmacology* 14(1):70–76.

Hidalgo, R. B., et al. 1999. Nefazodore in P.T.S.D.: Results from six open-label trials. *International Clinical Psychopharmacology* 14(2):61–68.

Hirschfeld, R. M., and F. K. Goodwin. 1988. Mood disorders. In *The American Psychiatric Press Textbook of Psychiatry*. J. A. Talbott, R. E. Hales, and S. C. Yudofsky, eds. Washington, D.C.: American Psychiatric Press.

Hoehn-Saric, R., et al. 1990. Apathy and indifference in patients on fluvoxamine and Fluoxetine. *Journal of Clinical Psychopharmacology* 10:343–345.

Hoffman, R. E., and T. H. McGlashan. 1997. Synaptic elimination, neurodevelopment, and the mechanism of hallucinated "voices" in schizophrenia. *American Journal of Psychiatry* 154:1683–1689.

Hollander, E., and J. Rosen. 2000. Impulsivity. *Journal of Psychopharmcology* 14:S39–S44.

Hollister, L. E. 1992. Psychiatric disorders. In *Melmon and Morrelli's Clinical Pharmacology: Basic Principles in Therapeutics*, 3rd ed. K. L. Melmon, H. F. Morrelli, B. B. Hoffman, and D. W. Nierenberg, eds. New York: McGraw-Hill.

Hori, A. 1998. Pharmacotherapy for personality disorders. *Clinical Neuroscience* 52(1):13–19.

Horowitz, M. J. 1976. *Stress Response Syndromes*. New York: Jason Aronson.

Hyman, S. E., and E. J. Nestler. 1996. Initiation and adaptation: A paradigm for understanding psychotropic drug action. *American Journal of Psychiatry* 153(2):151–162.

Jacobsen, F. M. 1993. Low-dose valproate: A new treatment for cyclothymia, mild rapid cycling disorders and premenstrual syndrome. *Journal of Clinical Psychiatry* 54:229–34.

Jann, M. W. 1992. Anxiety. In *Applied Therapeutics: The Clinical Use of Drugs*, 5th ed. M. A. Koda-Kimble, L. Y. Young, W. A. Kradjan, and B. J. Guglielmo, eds. Vancouver, Wash.: Applied Therapeutics.

Jaskiw, G. E., and D. R. Weinberger. 1992. Dopamine and schizophrenia—a cortically corrective perspective. *Seminars in the Neurosciences* 4:179–188.

Javitt, D., and S. Zukin. 1991. Recent advances in the phencyclidine model of schizophrenia. *American Journal of Psychiatry* 148:1301–1307.

Jinks, M. J., and R. H. Fuerst. 1992. Geriatric therapy. In *Applied Therapeutics: The Clinical Use of Drugs*, 5th ed. M. A. Koda-Kimble, L. Y. Young, W. A. Kradjan, and B. J. Guglielmo, eds. Vancouver, Wash.: Applied Therapeutics.

Johnson, G. 1998. Lithium—early development, toxicity and renal function. *Neuropsychopharmacology* 19: 200–205.

Johnston, A. M., and J. M. Eagles. 1999. Lithium associated clinical hypothyroidism: Prevalence and risk factors. *British Journal of Psychiatry* 175:336–339.

Joseph, S. 1997. *Personality Disorders: New Symptom-Focused Only Therapy*. New York: Haworth Press.

Kane, J. M. 1990. Treatment programme and long-term outcome in chronic schizophrenia. *Acta Psychiatrica Scandinavica* 82:(Suppl)358:151–157.

Kapfhamner, H. P., and H. Hippius. 1998. Pharmacotherapy in personality disorders. *Journal of Personality Disorders* 12(3):277–288.

Katzung, B. G. 2001. Basic principles. In *Basic and Clinical Pharmacology*. B. G. Katzung, ed. New York: McGraw-Hill.

Keck, P. E., and S. L. McElroy. 1996. Outcome in the pharmacologic treatment of bipolar disorder. *Journal of Clinical Psychopharmacology* 16:(Suppl)15S–23S.

Keck, P. E., S. L. McElroy, K. C. Tugrul, and J. A. Bennett. 1993. Valproate oral loading in the treatment of acute mania. *Journal of Clinical Psychiatry* 54:305–08.

Keller, M. B., P. Lavori, W. Coryell, J. Endicott, and T. I. Mueller. 1993. Bipolar I: A five-year prospective follow-up. *Journal of Nervous and Mental Disease* 181:238–45.

Kelsoe, J. R., M. A. Spence, E. Loetscher, M. Foguet, A. D. Sadovnick, R. A. Remick, et al. 2001. A genome survey indicates a possible susceptibility locus for bipolar disorder on chromosome 22. *Proceedings of the National Academy of Science USA* 98:585–590.

Kety, S. S. 1975. Progress toward an understanding of the biological substrates of schizophrenia. In *Genetic Research in Psychiatry*, R. R. Fieve et al., eds. Baltimore: Johns Hopkins University Press.

Kety, S. S., D. Rosenthal, T. H. Wender, and F. Schulsinger. 1971. Mental illness in the biological and adoptive families of adopted schizophrenics. *American Journal of Psychiatry* 128:302–306.

Kleiner, J., L. Altshuler, V. Hendrick, and J. M. Hershman. 1999. Lithium-induced subclinical hypothyroidism: Review of the literature and guidelines for treatment. *Journal of Clinical Psychiatry* 60:249–255.

Klerman, G. L., M. M. Weissman, B. J. Rounsaville, and E. Chevron. 1984. *Interpersonal Psychotherapy of Depression*. New York: Basic Books.

Koran, L., H. Sox, K. Marton, S. Moltzen, H. Kraemer, T. Kelsey, L. Levin, K. Imai, T. Rose, and S. Chandra. 1989. Medical evaluation of psychiatric patients: I. Results in a state mental health system. *Archives of General Psychiatry* 46:733–740.

Knoll, J. L., IV, D. L. Garver, J. E. Ramberg, S. J. Kingsbury, D. Croissant, and B. McDermott. 1998. Heterogeneity of the psychoses: Is there a neurodegenerative psychosis? *Schizophrenia Bulletin* 24:365–379.

Korn, M. 2000. Developments in the treatment of bipolar disorder. Symposium conducted at the 23rd Annual Congress of the Collegium Internationale Neuro-Psychopharmacologicum. July.

Kraemer, G. W., M. H. Ebert, and S. R. Lake. 1984. Hypersensitivity to d-amphetamine several years after early social deprivation in rhesus monkeys. *Psychopharmacology* 82:266–271.

Kraepelin, E. 1921. *Textbook of Psychiatry*, 7th ed. (abstracted). Translated by Diefendorf. London: MacMillan 1907.

Kramer, A. M. 2000. New advances in the use of lithium. Symposium conducted at the 23rd Annual Congress of the Collegium Internationale Neuro-Psychopharmacologicum. July 2000.

Kramer, P. D. 1993. *Listening to Prozac*. New York: Viking.

Krashin, D., and E. W. Oates 1999. Risperidone as an adjunct therapy for post-traumatic stress disorder. *Military Medicine* 164(8):605–606.

Kupfer, D. J., L. L. Carpenter, and E. Frank. 1988. Possible role of antidepressants in precipitating mania and hypomania in recurrent depression. *American Journal of Psychiatry* 145:804–808.

LaFrance, W. C., E. C., Lauterbach, et al. 2000. The use of herbal alternative medicines in neuropsychiatry. *Journal of Neuropsychiatry and Clinical Neurosciences* 12:177–192.

Langtry, H. D., and P. Benfield. 1990. Zolpidem: A review of its pharmacodynamic and pharmacokinetic properties and therapeutic potential. *Drug* 40:291–313.

Le Doux, J. 1996. *The Emotional Brain*. New York: Simon and Schuster.

Letterman, L, and J. S. Markowitz. 1999. Gabapentin: A review of published experience in the treatment of bipolar disorder and other psychiatric conditions. *Pharmacotherapy* 19:565–572.

Lewis, T., F. Amini, and R. Lennon. 2000. *A General Theory of Love*. New York: Random House.

Liddle, P. F., T. R. E. Barnes, D. Morris, and S. Haque. 1989. Three syndromes in chronic schizophrenia. *British Journal of Psychiatry* 155:(Suppl 7)119–122.

Liebowitz, M. R., and D. F. Klein. 1979. Hysteroid-dysphoria. *Psychiatric Clinics of North America* 2:555–575.

———. 1981. Interrelationships of hysteroid-dysphoria and borderline personality disorder. *Psychiatric Clinics of North America* 4:67–87.

Lieberman, J. A. 1999. Is schizophrenia a neurodegenerative disorder? A clinical and neurobiological perspective. *Biological Psychiatry* 46:729–739A

Lieberman, J. A., J. M. Alvir, A. Koreen, S. Geisler, M. Chakos, B. Sheitman, and M. Woerner. 1996. Psychobiologic correlates of treatment response in schizophrenia. *Neuropsychopharmacology* 14:13S–21S.

Loebel, A. D., J. A. Lieberman, J. M. J. Alvir, D. I. Mayerhoff, S. H. Geisler, and S. R. Szymanski. 1992. Duration of psychosis and outcome in first episode schizophrenia. *American Journal of Psychiatry* 149:1183–1188.

Luby, E. D., J. S. Gottlieb, B. D. Cohen, G. Rosenbaum, and E. F. Domino. 1962. Model psychoses and schizophrenia. *American Journal of Psychiatry* 119:61–67.

Luby, E. D., M. A. Marrazzi, and J. Kinzie 1987. Letter to the editor. *Journal of Clinical Psychopharmacology* 7:52–53.

Mahler, M., et al. 1975. *The Psychological Birth of the Human Infant: Symbiosis and Individuation.* New York: Basic Books

Malaspina, O., H. M. Quitkin, and C. A. Kaufmann. 1992. Epidemiology and genetics of neuropsychiatric disorders. In *The American Psychiatric Press Textbook of Neuropsychiatry.* S. C. Yudofsky and R. E. Hales, eds. Washington, D.C.: American Psychiatric Press.

MacQueen, G. M., and L. Trevor Young. 2001. Bipolar II disorder: Symptoms, course and response to treatment. *Psychiatric Services* 52:358–361.

Manji, H. K. 2001. The neurobiology of bipolar disorder. *The Economics of Neuroscience* 3:37-44.

Manji, H. K., and R. H. Lennox. 2000. The nature of bipolar disorder. *Journal of Clinical Psychiatry* 61:(Suppl)42–57.

Manji, H. K., and W. Z. Potter. 1997. Monoaminergic mechanisms. In: *Biological Models and Their Clinical Application.* R. T. Joffe and L. T. Young, eds. New York: Marcel Dekker.

Manji, H. K., G. J. Moore, G. Rajkowska, and G. Chen. 2000. Neuroplasticity and cellular resilience in mood disorders. *Molecular Psychiatry* 5:578–593.

Markovitz, P. J., et al. 1991. Fluoxetine in the treatment of borderline and schizotypal personality disorders. *American Journal of Psychiatry* 148(8):1064–1067.

Markovitz, P. J., J. R. Calabrese, S. C. Schulz, et al. 1991. Fluoxetine in the treatment of borderline and schizotypal personality disorders. *American Journal of Psychiatry* 148:1064–1067.

Marneros, A. 2001. Expanding the group of bipolar disorders. *Journal of Affective Disorders* 62:39–44.

Mayberg, H. S. 1997. Limbic-cortical dysregulation. *The Neuropsychiatry of Limbic and Subcortical Disorders* Washington, D.C.: American Psychiatric Press. 167-177.

McCann, U. et al. 1994. Dexfenfluramine and serotonin neurotoxicity: Further preclinical evidence that clinical caution is indicated. *Pharmacological Experimental Therapy* 269(2):792–798.

McCullough, J. P. 2000. *Treatment for Chronic Depression.* New York: Guilford Press.

McElroy, S. L., P. E. Keck, H. G. Pope, J. I. Hudson, G. L. Faedda, and A. C. Swann. 1992. Clinical and research implications of the diagnosis of dysphoric or mixed mania or hyppomania. *American Journal of Psychiatry* 149:1633–1644.

Menninger, K. 1963. *The Vital Balance.* New York: Viking.

Meyer, U. A. 1992. Drugs in special patient groups: Clinical importance of genetics in drug effects. In *Melmon and Morrelli's clinical pharmacology: Basic Principles in Therapeutics,* 3rd ed. K. L. Melmon, H. F. Morrelli, B. B. Hoffman, and D. W. Nierenberg, eds. New York: McGraw-Hill.

Michaels, R. 1992. *Principles of Psychodynamic Psychotherapy.* Glendale, Calif.: Audio Digest Psychiatry 20:13.

Michalets, E. L. 1998. Update: Clinically significant cytochrome P-450 drug interactions. *Pharmacotherpy* 18:84–112.

Miklowitz, D. J. 1996. Psychotherapy in combination with drug treatment for bipolar disorder. *Journal of Clinical Psychopharmacology* 16:(Suppl)56S–66S.

Mischoulon, D., et al. 1999. Strategies for augmentation of SSRI treatment: A survey of an academic psychopharmacology practice. *Harvard Review of Psychiatry* 6:322–326.

Moleman, P., et al. 1999. Psychopharmacological treatment of personality disorders: A review. In *Treatment of Personality Disorders.* New York: Kluwer Academic/Plenum Publishers. 207–227.

Musselman, D. L., C. DeBattista, K. I. Nathan, C. D. Kilts, A. F. Schatzberg, and C. B. Nemeroff. 1998. Biology of mood disorders. In *Textbook of Psychopharmacology,* A. F. Schatzberg and C. B. Nemeroff 2nd ed. eds., 549–588.

Nagy, L. M., C. A. Morgan, S. M. Southwick, and D. S. Charney. 1993. Open prospective trial of fluoxetine for post-traumatic stress disorder. *Journal of Clinical Psychopharmacology* 13:107–13.

Nemeroff, C. B., C. L. DeVane, and B. G. Pollock. 1996. Newer antidepressants and the cytochrome P450 system. *American Journal of Psychiatry* 153:311–320.

Nemeroff, C. B. 1997. The role of early adverse life events in the etiology of depression and post-traumatic stress disorder. Focus on CRF. *Annals of the New York Academy of Sciences* 821:194–207.

Ness, J., F. T. Sherman, and C. X. Pan. 1999. Alternative medicine: What data says about common herbal therapies. *Geriatrics* 54(10):33–38.

Nester, P. G., M. E. Shenton, R. W. McCarley, et al. 1993. Neuropsychological correlates of MRI temporal lobe abnormalities in schizophrenia. *American Journal of Psychiatry* 150:1849–1855.

Nishino, S., E. Mignot, and W. C. Dement. 1998. Sedative-hypnotics. In *Textbook of Psychopharmacology*, 2nd ed. A. F. Schatzberg and C. B. Nemeroff, eds. 487–502.

Norden, M. J. 1989. Fluoxetine in borderline personality disorder. Progress in *Neuropsychopharmacological Biological Psychiatry* 13:885–893.

———. 1989. Is there an effective drug treatment for borderline personality disorder? *Harvard Mental Health Letter* 6:8.

Nurnberger, J. I., and T. Foroud. 2000. Genetics of bipolar affective disorder. *Current Psychiatry Reports* 2:147–157.

Pande, A. C., J. G. Crockatt, C. A. Janney, J. L. Werth, and G. Tsaroucha. 2000. Gabapentin in bipolar disorder: A placebo-controlled trial of adjunctive therapy. Gabapentin bipolar disorder study group. *Bipolar Disorder* 2:249–255.

Pazzaglia, P. J., R. M. Post, T. A. Ketter, M. S. George, and L. B. Marangell. 1993. Preliminary controlled trial of nimopidine in ultra-rapid cycling affective dysregulation. *Psychiatry Research* 49:257–273.

PDR. 1998. *PDR for Herbal Medicines*. Montvale, NJ. Medical Economics 6.

Pinsker, H., I. Kupfermann, V. Castellucci, and E. Kandel. 1970. Habituation and dishabituation of the gill-withdrawal reflex in Aplysia. *Science* 167:1740–1742.

Pollock, V. E. 1992. Meta-analysis of subjective sensitivity to alcohol in sons of alcoholics. *American Journal of Psychiatry* 149:1534–1538.

Post, R. M., S. R. B. Weiss, and G. S. Leverich. 1994. Recurrent affective disorder: Roots in developmental neurobiology and illness progression based on changes in gene expression. *Development and Psychopathology* 6:781–813.

Post, R. M., S. R. B. Weiss, and O. Chuang. 1992. Mechanisms of action of anticonvulsants in affective disorders: Comparisons with lithium. *Journal of Clinical Psychopharmacology* 12:23S–35S.

Post, R. M., S. R. B. Weiss, and J. Leverich. 1994. Recurrent affective disorder: Roots in developmental neurobiology and illness progression based on change in gene expression. *Development and Psychopathology* 6:781–813.

Post, R. M., and S. R. B. Weiss. 1997. Emergent properties of neural systems: How focal molecular neurobiological alterations can affect behavior. *Development and Psychopathology* 9:907–929.

Potash, J. B., and J. R. DePaulo. 2000. Searching high and low: a review of the genetics of bipolar disorder. *Bipolar Disorder* 2:8–26

Preston, J. D. 1997. *Shorter Term Treatments for Borderline Personality Disorders*. Oakland, Calif.: New Harbinger Publications.

———. 1993. *Depression and Anxiety Management* (audiotape). Oakland, Calif.: New Harbinger Publications.

Rabkin, J. G., F. M. Quitkin, P. McGrath, W. Harrison, and E. Tricamo. 1985. Adverse reactions to monoamine oxidase inhibitors, part II: Treatment correlates and clinical management. *Journal of Clinical Psychopharmacology* 5:2–9.

Rapoport, J. L. 1991. Recent advances in obsessive-compulsive disorder. *Neuropsychopharmacology* 5:1–10.

Ricaurte, G. A., et al. 1991. Dexfenfluramine neurotoxicity in brains of non-human primates. *Lancet* 338:1487–1488.

Robertson, M. M., and J. S. Stern. 1997. The Gilles de la Tourette syndrome. *Critical Reviews in Neurobiology* 11:1-19.

Rosenthal, J., A. Strauss, L. Minkoff, and A. Winston. 1986. Identifying lithium-responsive bipolar depressed patients using nuclear magnetic resonance. *American Journal of Psychiatry* 143:779–780.

Rubin, P. C. 1992. Drugs in special patient groups: Pregnancy and nursing. In *Melmon and Morrelli's Clinical Pharmacology: Basic Principles in Therapeutics*, 3rd ed. K. L. Melmon, H. F. Morrelli, B. B. Hoffman, and D. W. Nierenberg, eds. New York: McGraw-Hill.

Russell, E. W., C. Neuringer, and G. Goldstein. 1970. *Assessment of Brain Damage: A Neuropsychological Key Approach*. New York: Wiley.

Sachs, G. S. 1996. Bipolar mood disorder: practical strategies for acute and maintenance phase treatment. *Journal of Clinical Psychopharmacology* 16:(Suppl)32S–47S.

Sachs, G. S., D. J. Printz, D. A. Kahn, D. Carpenter, and J. P. Doherty. 2000. The expert consensus guideline series: Medication treatment of bipolar disorder. *Postgraduate Medicine* 4(Special):1–104.

Sackett, G. P. 1965. Effects of rearing conditions on the behavior of the rhesus monkey. *Child Development* 36:855–868.

Safer, D. J., and J. M. Krager. 1992. Effect of a media blitz and a threatened lawsuit on stimulant treatment. *JAMA* 268:1004–1007.

Salzman, C., A. N. Wolfson, A. Schatzberg, et al. 1995. Effect of fluoxetine on anger in symptomatic volunteers with borderline personality disorder. *Journal of Clinical Psychopharmacology* 15(1):23–29.

Sapolsky, R. M. 1994. *Why Zebras Don't Get Ulcers.* New York: W. H. Freeman & Company.

———. 1996. Glucocorticoids and atrophy of the human hippocampus. *Science* 273:749–775.

Schatzberg, A. F., and J. J. Schildkraut. 1995. Recent studies on norepinephrine systems in mood disorders. In *Psychopharmacology. The Fourth Generation of Progress.* F. E. Bloom and D. J. Kupfer, eds. New York: Raven Press.

Schou, M. 1997. Forty years of lithium treatment. *Archives of General Psychiatry* 54:9–13.

Schuckit, M. A., E. Gold, and C. Risch. 1987. Serum prolactin levels in sons of alcoholics and control subjects. *American Journal of Psychiatry* 144:854–859.

Schuckit, M. A., M. Irwin, and S. A. Brown. 1990. The history of anxiety symptoms among 171 primary alcoholics. *Journal of the Study of Alcoholism* 51:34–41.

Schulz, S. C., et al. 1999. Olanzapine safety and efficacy in patients with borderline personality disorder and comorbid dysthymia. *Biological Psychiatry* 46(10):1429–1435.

Seligman, M. E. P. 1990. *Learned Optimism.* New York: Pocket Books

Sharma, V., L. N. Yatham, D. R. Haslam, P. H. Silverstone, S. V. Parikh, R. Matte, et al. 1997. Continuation and prophylactic treatment of bipolar disorder. *Canadian Journal of Psychiatry* 42(Suppl):92S–100S.

Shimoda, K., T. Minowada, T. Noguchi, and S. Takahashi. 1993. Interindividual variations of desmethylation and hydroxylation of clomipramine in an Oriental psychiatric population. *Journal of Clinical Psychopharmacology* 13:181–188.

Shulman, K. I., S. E. Walker, S. MacKenzie, and S. Knowles. 1989. Dietary restriction, tyramine, and the use of monoamine oxidase inhibitors. *Journal of Clinical Psychopharmacology* 9:397–402.

Smith, D. E., and D. R. Wesson. 1983. Benzodiazepine dependency syndromes. *Journal of Psychoactive Drugs* 15:85–95.

Smith, S. S., B. F. O'Hara, A. M. Persico, D. A. Gorelick, D. B. Newlin, D. Vlahov, L. Solomon, R. Pickens, and G. R. Uhl. 1992. Genetic vulnerability to drug abuse. *Archives of General Psychiatry* 49:723–727.

Snodgrass, W. R. 1992. Drugs in special patient groups: Neonates and children. In *Melmon and Morrelli's Clinical Pharmacology: Basic Principles in Therapeutics*, 3rd ed. K. L. Melmon, H. F. Morrelli, B. B. Hoffman, and D. W. Nierenberg, eds. New York: McGraw-Hill.

Snyder, S. H., and C. D. Ferris. 2000. Novel neurotransmitters and their neuropsychiatric relevance. *American Journal of Psychiatry* 157:1738–1751.

Soares, J. C. 2000. Recent advances in the treatment of bipolar mania, depression and mixed states, and rapid cycling. *International Clinical Psychopharmacology* 15:183–196.

Soares, J. C., and J. J. Mann. 1997. The anatomy of mood disorders: review of structural neuroimaging studies. *Biological Psychiatry* 41:86–106

Soloff, P. H., A. George, R. S. Nathan, P. M. Schulz, R. F. Ulrich, and J. M. Perel. 1986. Progress in psychopharmacology of borderline disorders. *Archives of General Psychiatry* 43:691–697.

Solomon, D. A., G. J. Keitner, J. W. Miller, M. T. Shea, and M. B. Keller. 1995. Course of illness and maintenance treatments for patients with bipolar disorder. *Journal of Clinical Psychiatry* 56:5–13.

Spiegel, R., and H. J. Aebi. 1989. *Psychopharmacology: An Introduction.* Chichester, U.K.: John Wiley and Sons.

Stein, D. J., et al. 2000. Selective serotonin reuptake inhibitors in the treatment of post-traumatic stress disorder: A meta-analysis of randomized controlled trials. *International Journal of Clinical Psychopharmacology* 15:S-31–S-39.

Stern, E., D. A. Silbersweig, K. Chee, A. Holmes, M. M. Robertson, M. Trimble, et al. 2000. A functional neuroanatomy of tics in Tourette Syndrome. *Archives of General Psychiatry* 57:741–748.

Stewart, J. W., F. J. Quitkin, and D. F. Klein. 1992. The pharmacotherapy of minor depression. *American Journal of Psychotherapy* 46:23–36.

Stoll, A. L., P. V. Mayer, M. Kolbrener, E. Goldstein, B. Suplit, J. Lucier, B. M. Cohen, and M. Tohen. 1994. Antidepressant-associated mania: A controlled comparison with spontaneous mania. *American Journal of Psychiatry* 151:1642–1645.

Stone, M. H. 1988. Toward a psychobiological theory of borderline disorder. *Dissociation* 1:2–15.

Stoudemire, A., R. Frank, N. Hedemark, M. Kamlet, and D. Blazer. 1986. The economic burden of depression. *General Hospital Psychiatry* 8:387–394.

Strub, R. L., and F. W. Black. 1985. *The Mental Status Examination in Neurology*, 2nd ed. Philadelphia: F. A. Davis.

Sutherland, S. M., and J. R. Davidson. 1994. Pharmacotherapy for P.T.S.D. *Psychiatric Clinics of North America* 17:409–423.

Swann, A. C. 1995. Mixed or dysphoric manic states: psychopathology and treatment. *Journal of Clinical Psychiatry* 56:(Suppl)6–10.

Taylor, R. L. 1990. *Distinguishing Psychological from Organic Disorders*. New York: Springer Publishing.

Teicher, M. H., C. Glod, and J. O. Cole. 1990. Emergence of intense suicidal preoccupation during fluoxetine treatment. *American Journal of Psychiatry* 147:207–210.

Terr, L. C. 1991. Childhood traumas: An outline and overview. *American Journal of Psychiatry* 148:10–20.

Thoenen, H. 1995. Neurotropins and neural plasticity. *Science* 270:593–598.

Tsuang, M. T., and S. V. Faraone. 1990. *The Genetics of Mood Disorders*. Baltimore: Johns Hopkins University Press.

Tsuang, M. T., and S. V. Faraone. 1990. *The Genetics of Mood Disorders*. Baltimore: Johns Hopkins University Press.

Tsuang, M. T., W. Stone, and S. V. Faraone. 2000. Toward reformulating the diagnosis of schizophrenia. *Journal of Psychiatry* 157:1041–1050.

Turnbull, G. J. 1998. A review of post-traumatic stress disorder: Part II. *Treatment Injury* 29:169–175.

Turner, S. 1999. Place of pharmacotherapy in post-traumatic stress disorder. *Lancet* 354:1404–1405.

Ulenhuth, E. H., H. DeWit, M. B. Balter, C. E. Johanson, and G. D. Mellinger. 1988. Risks and benefits of long term benzodiazepine use. *Journal of Clinical Psychopharmacology* 8:161–167.

van der Kolk, B. A. 1987. *Psychological Trauma*. Washington, D. C.: American Psychiatric Press.

van der Kolk, B. A., et al. 1994. Fluoxetine in post-traumatic stress disorder. *Journal of Clinical Psychiatry* 55:517–522.

Vandel, P., E. Haffen, S. Vandel, B. Bonin, S. Nezelof, D. Sechter, et al. 1999. Pharmacokinetics and disposition: Drug extrapyramidal side effects. CYP2D6 genotypes and phenotypes. *European Journal of Clinical Pharmacology* 55:659–665.

Vestal, R. E., S. C. Montamat, and C. P. Nielson. 1992. Drugs in special patient groups: The elderly. In *Melmon and Morrelli's Clinical Pharmacology: Basic Principles in Therapeutics*, 3rd ed. K. L. Melmon, H. F. Morrelli, B. B. Hoffman, and D. W. Nierenberg, eds. New York: McGraw-Hill.

Vestergaard, P., A. Amdisen, and M. Schow. 1980. Clinically significant side effects of lithium treatment. *Acta Psychiatrica Scandinavica* 62:193–200.

von Moltke, L. L., D. J. Greenblatt, J. S. Harmatz, and R. I. Shader. 1994. Cytochromes in psychopharmacology. *Journal of Clinical Psychopharmacology* 14:1–4.

Ward, N. 1992. Psychopharmacology update. Pharmaceutical company presentation, Sacramento, Calif.

Watsky, E. J., and C. Salzman. 1991. Psychotropic drug interactions. *Hospital and Community Psychiatry* 42:247–256.

Weber, S. S., S. R. Saklad, and K. V. Kastenholz. 1992. Bipolar affective disorders. In *Applied Therapeutics: The Clinical Use of Drugs*, 5th ed. M. A. Koda-Kimble, L. Y. Young, W. A. Kradjan, and B. J. Guglielmo, eds. Vancouver, Wash.: Applied Therapeutics.

Weinberger, D. R. 1996. On the plausibility of "the neurodevelopmental hypothesis" of schizophrenia. *Neuropsychopharmacology* 14:15–115.

Weinberger, D. R., K. F. Berman, R. Suddath, and E. F. Torrey. 1992. Evidence of dysfunction of a prefrontal-limbic network in schizophrenia: A magnetic resonance imaging and regional cerebral blood flow study of discordant monozygotic twins. *American Journal of Psychiatry* 149:890–897.

Weiss, J., H. I. Glazer, and L. A. Pohorecky. 1976. Coping behavior and neurochemical changes in rats: An alternative explanation for the original "learned helplessness" experiments. In *Animal Models in Human Psychobiology*, G. Servan and A. Kling, eds. New York: Plenum Press.

Wells, G. B., et al. 1991. Buspirone in the treatment of post-traumatic stress disorder. *Pharmacotherapy* 11: 340–343.

Weng, G., U. S. Bhalla, and R. Iyengar. 1999. Complexity in biological signaling systems. *Science* 284: 92–96.

Wheatley, D. P., M. van Moffaert, L. Timmerman, and C. M. E. Kremer. 1998. Mirtazapine: Efficacy and tolerability in comparison with fluoxetine in patients with moderate to severe major depressive disorder. *Journal of Clinical Psychiatry* 59:306–312.

Willner, P. 1995. Dopaminergic mechanisms in depression and mania. In *Psychopharmacology. The Fourth Generation of Progress*. F. E. Bloom and D. J. Kupfer, eds. New York: Raven Press.

Winchel, R. M., and M. Stanley. 1991. Self-injurious behavior: A review of the behavior and biology of self-mutilation. *American Journal of Psychiatry* 148:306–317.

Winter, M. E. 1988. *Basic Clinical Pharmacokinetics*. Vancouver, Wash.: Applied Therapeutics.

Yamazaki, H. 2000. Roles of human cytochrome P450 enzymes involved in drug metabolism and toxicological studies. *Yakugaku Zasshi* 120:1347–1357.

Young, J. Z. 1987. *Philosophy and the Brain*. Oxford: Oxford University Press.

Zisook, S., et al. 1999. PTSD following bereavement. *Annals of Clinical Psychiatry* 10(4):157–163.

Index

A

abnormal involuntary movements, 207, 208
absorption of medications, 44-45, 223-224
acetylcholine, 39
action potential, 28
acute dystonia, 248-249
acute organic brain syndromes, 64
acute treatment phase, 173
ADD. *See* attention deficit disorder
adenosine, 31
adenosine triphosphate (ATP), 33
adolescents: medication guidelines for,
    234-235, 238; risk factors in medicating,
    233-237
adverse effects. *See* side effects
affective disorders. *See* depressive disorders
affective regulation, 135
age-specific pharmacology, 232
aggression, 158-159
agitation, 247-248
agonist, 51, 58
agoraphobia, 99, 105, 109
agranulocytosis, 204
AIMS scale, 207, 208
akathisia, 203, 205, 208, 247-248
akinesia, 208
Alcoholics Anonymous (AA), 111
alcoholism, 147-148; biological basis for,
    147-148; depression and, 72; diagnosis of,
    60-62; disorders associated with, 148;
    treatment of, 148; unexplained relapse
    and, 214. *See also* substance abuse
Alexander, Franz, 17
allergic reactions, 49
Alzheimer's disease, 260
amantadine, 149

American Psychiatric Association (APA), 10
amino acids, 31
amphetamines, 149
amygdala, 103
angry-impulsive borderline personality, 140
anorexia nervosa, 114, 154
antagonist, 51, 58
antiadrenergic side effects, 204
antianxiety medications, 193-200; anxiety dis-
    orders and, 107-110; borderline
    personality disorders and, 142; child and
    adolescent use of, 238; dosages
    of, 197; educating patients about, 199-200;
    length of treatment with, 196,
    198-199; mechanism of action of, 194, 196;
    side effects of, 193, 217;
    signs of toxicity or overdose, 218; types
    of, 194-196; withdrawal
    symptoms from, 198-199. *See also* anxiety
    disorders
anticholinergic side effects, 201, 204, 248
anticonvulsants, 187-189; aggressive behavior
    and, 159; blood level monitoring of, 188;
    child and adolescent use of, 234; dosage
    guidelines for, 188; drug interactions
    with, 244; newer forms of, 189; preg-
    nancy risks and, 231; side effects of,
    187-189, 217; signs of toxicity or over-
    dose, 218 antidepressant medications,
    163-180; anxiety disorders and, 109, 110;
    atypical, 167; blood levels of, 172; bor-
    derline personality disorders and, 142;
    child and adolescent use of, 234, 238;
    choosing, 172-173, 176, 177;   chronic
    pain and, 159; comparison of, 170; cyclic,
    164; development of, 163; dosages of,

170-172; eating disorders and, 154; educating patients about, 176; mechanism of action for, 169; monoamine oxidase inhibitors, 163, 167, 169; norepinephrine reuptake inhibitors, 167; obsessive-compulsive disorder and, 116-117; over-the-counter options as, 176-178; patient type and, 177; phases of treatment with, 173-174; post-traumatic stress disorder and, 135; pregnancy risks and, 230; schizophrenia and, 127; selective action of, 82, 175; selective serotonin reuptake inhibitors, 163, 166; serotonin and norepinephrine reuptake inhibitors, 163, 166; side effects of, 164, 165, 166, 171-172, 216; signs of toxicity or overdose, 218; toxicity effects from, 249; treatment-resistant depression and, 174-175, 180; tricyclic, 164-169; types of, 81, 163. *See also* depressive disorders

antihistamines, 195, 217

anti-obsessional medications, 116-117; 5-HT antidepressants, 116; child and adolescent guidelines for, 238

antipanic medications, 110

antiparkinsonian medications, 127, 202

antipsychotic medications, 201-208; aggressive behavior and, 159; atypical, 189, 205-206; child and adolescent use of, 235, 238; choosing, 206-207; dopamine receptors and, 124, 125; dosages of, 202; drug interactions with, 244; educating patients about, 207-208; length of treatment with, 207; managing side effects from, 205; mechanism of action of, 201; post-traumatic stress disorder and, 137; pregnancy risks and, 231; psychotic depressions and, 75; reassessing prescriptions for, 204-205; schizophrenia and, 127-128; side effects of, 203-205, 217; signs of toxicity or overdose, 218; standard, 201-205. *See also* psychotic disorders

anxiety: akathisia vs., 247-248; books for patients about, 259; drugs that cause, 106; medical disorders and, 100, 105, 106, 109-110; panic vs., 97-98; stress reactions and, 99, 109

anxiety disorders, 97-112; agoraphobia, 99, 105, 109; biologic theories of, 100-104; diagnosis of, 97-100; educating patients about, 199-200; etiology of, 100-107; facts about, 99; generalized anxiety disorder, 99, 104, 107-109; length of treatment for, 196, 198-199; medications for, 107-110, 193-200; neurotic anxiety, 100, 106-107, 110; over-the-counter products for, 211; panic disorder, 100, 107, 108, 110-111; patients medicated for, 24; phobias, 99, 104-105, 109; psychotherapy for, 109, 110, 111; quick reference to, 112; symptoms of, 98; treatments for, 107-111, 193-200;

types of, 98-100. *See also* antianxiety medications

aplastic anemia, 205

Aplysia study, 18

atenolol, 195

attachment compulsion, 134-135

attention deficit disorder (ADD), 154-156; books for patients about, 260; symptoms of, 155; Tourette's syndrome and, 153; treatments for, 156

atypical antidepressants, 167; dosages of, 171; side effects of, 165, 167

atypical antipsychotics, 189, 205-206

atypical benzodiazepines, 194-195

atypical depressions, 74, 77

atypical side effects, 204-205

autonomic nervous system, 39, 40

Axis I and II disorders (DSM-IV), 57-60, 61

axons, 27

B

barbiturates, 193

basal ganglia, 115

behavioral treatments, 19; for obsessive-compulsive disorder, 115-116; for phobias, 109

benzodiazepines, 194; anxiety disorders and, 102, 108, 109, 110, 193; atypical, 194-195; bipolar disorders and, 181; borderline personality disorders and, 142; child and adolescent use of, 235; drug interactions with, 245; GABA receptor interactions, 194, 196; half-lives of, 194; history of, 7; length of treatment with, 196, 198-199; mechanism of action of, 194, 196; post-traumatic stress disorder and, 137; pregnancy risks and, 231; schizophrenia and, 127; side effects of, 193, 217; withdrawal symptoms from, 198-199

beta blockers, 195-196; aggressive behavior and, 159

bioavailability, 223

biogenic amines, 30

biological factors: alcoholism and, 147-148; anxiety disorders and, 100-104; bipolar disorders and, 92-94; borderline personality disorders and, 141, 142; depressive disorders and, 71, 73-74; personality traits and, 61; psychiatric disorders and, 40-41; psychological functioning and, 16-20; schizophrenia and, 124-127; stress and, 134-137

biological psychiatry: history of, 4-13; managed care dilemma in, 11-12; reasons for learning about, 13-14

biotransformation, 46-47, 225

bipolar disorders, 85-95; bipolar I disorder, 88-89; bipolar II disorder, 89-90; books for patients about, 259; cyclothymia, 90-91; diagnosis of, 85-87; disorders not otherwise specified, 91; drugs inducing mania in, 89; educating patients about,

190, 259; etiology of, 92-94; facts about, 76; length of treatment for, 190, 219; medical conditions associated with, 87; medications for, 94, 181-191; model for expanded spectrum of, 91-92; psychotherapy for, 94, 191; quick reference to, 95; rapid cycling, 91; stages of acute mania, 86; treatments for, 94, 181-191. *See also* mood stabilizers

blocking, 51

blood-brain barrier, 44, 51

books for patients, 259-260

borderline personality disorders, 139-143; books for patients about, 260; diagnosis of, 139-141; etiology of, 141-142; facts about, 140; length of treatment for, 219; medications for, 142; quick reference to, 143; symptoms of, 140; treatments for, 142

brain: acute organic syndromes of, 64; biological functioning of, 16; chronic organic syndromes of, 65; information processing by, 38; psychological functions of, 37; psychological trauma and, 134-137; psychopathology and, 37, 40-41; schizophrenia and, 124; structures of, 35-40

brain imaging techniques, 11-12

breakthrough symptoms, 214

brief reactive psychosis, 121

brief therapy, 110

bromocriptine, 149

bulimia nervosa, 154

bupropion, 167, 170; anxiety disorders and, 111n; drug interactions with, 245; nicotine dependence and, 151

buspirone, 195; antiaggression effect of, 159; anxiety disorders and, 108-109, 195, 217; depressive disorders and, 167; drug interactions with, 245

C

caffeine: content in common substances, 63; diagnosing use of, 62; overuse of, 151

calcium signaling theory, 93

carbamazepine, 187-188, 244

cardiovascular effects, 185

catatonic schizophrenia, 122

catecholamine theory, 93

cellular resiliency, 93-94

central nervous system, 39, 44

chaotic attractor theory, 92

Charcot, Jean-Martin, 4

child abuse and neglect: anxiety disorders and, 104; post-traumatic stress disorder and, 134

children: medication guidelines for, 234-235, 238; risk factors in medicating, 233-237

chlordiazepoxide, 7, 193

chloride ion channels, 102, 103

chlorpromazine, 6, 201

chronic pain, 159

citalopram, 166, 170

clinical depression, 70

clonidine, 159, 196

clozapine, 205

cocaine, 149

cognitive functioning: medical disorders and, 64-65; mental status exam of, 251-254

compliance, 11, 208, 214

conduction, 29

continuation treatment phase, 173

corticotropin releasing factor (CRF), 30, 79

countertransference issues, 25

CPAP (breathing) machine, 157

CT scans, 124

cyclic antidepressants: dosages of, 171; generic and brand names of, 164; side effects of, 165

cyclothymia, 90-91

D

delusional disorder, 121

dementia praecox, 121-122

dendrites, 27

dendritic spines, 27

dependent patients, 24

depression: antidepressant toxicity vs., 249; bipolar disorder and, 88; books for patients about, 259; causes of, 72, 78-80; grief and, 70; Parkinsonian side effects vs., 248; treatment-resistant, 174-175, 180

depressive disorders, 69-84; atypical depressions, 74; biological depressions, 71, 73-74; clinical depressions, 70; diagnosis of, 69-70; educating patients about, 176; electroconvulsive therapy for, 175, 178-179; etiology of, 78-80; facts about, 71; length of treatment for, 219; major unipolar depressions, 70-75; medications for, 74-75, 81-83, 163-176; minor depressions, 76-77; monoamine hypothesis of, 79-80, 81; over-the-counter products for, 176-178, 211; patients medicated for, 25; phases of treatment for, 173-174; physiological consequences of, 80-81; postpartum depression, 78; premenstrual dysphoric disorder, 77-78; psychotherapy for, 83, 175; psychotic depressions, 75; quick reference to, 84; reactive depressions, 71; reactive-biological depressions, 74; resistant to treatment, 174-175, 180; seasonal affective disorder, 77; symptoms of, 71, 73, 76, 84; treatments for, 81-83, 163-176. *See also* antidepressant medications

dermatological effects, 185, 188

dextroamphetamine, 156, 169

diagnosis: of anxiety disorders, 97-100; of Axis I and II disorders, 57-60, 61; of bipolar disorders, 85-87; of borderline personality disorders, 139-141; of depressive disorders, 69-70; of obsessive-compulsive disorder, 113-114; of physical illness, 62-67; of post-traumatic

stress disorder, 133-134; of psychotic disorders, 120-123; of schizophrenia, 121-123; of substance abuse, 60-62, 145-147
Diagnostic and Statistical Manual of Mental Disorders (DSM-IV), 4; Axis I and II disorders, 57-60, 61
differential diagnosis, 58. *See also* diagnosis
diphenhydramine, 195
discontinuance syndrome, 49
discontinuing medications, 215, 218
disorganized schizophrenia, 122
distribution of medications, 45-46, 224
disulfiram, 148
divalproex, 182, 187-188, 244
dopamine: atypical antipsychotics and, 205; depressive disorders and, 80; stimulant abuse and, 149-150
dopamine model of schizophrenia, 124-126
dosages: of antianxiety medications, 197; of anticonvulsants, 188; of antidepressants, 170-172; of antipsychotics, 202; for children and adolescents, 238; of lithium, 183; of mood stabilizers, 183, 188; need for adjusting, 214, 232-233; of OTC products, 211
double depression, 76
down-regulation, 32
drugs: anxiety caused by, 106; broad definition of, 43; depression caused by, 72, 79; interactions between, 49-50, 225-227, 239-246; mania caused by, 89; recreational use of, 60-62; trade vs. generic names of, 255-257; withdrawal symptoms from, 198-199. *See also* medications; substance abuse
D-serine, 31
dysregulation, 16, 92
dysthymia, 76
dystonic symptoms, 203, 248-249

E
eating disorders, 154, 155
educating patients. *See* patient education
egodystonic symptoms, 58
egosystonic symptoms, 58
elderly patients, 231-233
electroconvulsive treatment (ECT), 5, 6, 175, 178-179
enantiomers, 31
endocrine effects, 184
endogenomorphic depressions, 74
endoplasmic reticulum, 34
endorphins, 30, 157
enkephalins, 30
environmental factors, 18
enzyme induction and inhibition, 226
estazolam, 194
ethchlorvynol, 193
etiology, 57-67; of anxiety disorders, 100-107; of bipolar disorders, 92-94; of borderline personality disorders, 141-142; of depressive disorders, 72, 78-80; of

obsessive-compulsive disorder, 114-115; of post-traumatic stress disorder, 134-137; of psychotic disorders, 124-127; of schizophrenia, 124-127
excretion of medications, 47-48
extrapyramidal symptoms (EPS), 201, 203, 205

F
fasting, 154
Federal Drug Administration (FDA), 10
felbamate, 189
fenfluramine, 158
fetal development, 229-230
fight-or-flight response, 38-39, 101
first-pass effect, 223
flashbacks, 135-136
fluoxetine, 166, 170; controversy about, 9-10; intrusive symptoms and, 135
fluvoxamine, 166
Frances, Allan, 139
Frank, Jerome, 23
Freud, Sigmund, 5, 69, 100
frontal cortex, 115, 116

G
gabapentin, 189
gamma amino butyric acid (GABA), 31, 194, 196
gastrointestinal effects, 183, 187-188
gene expression, 33-34
generalized anxiety disorder (GAD), 99; biological factors in, 104; treatments for, 107-109
generic names of medications, 255-257
genetic factors: alcoholism and, 147; bipolar disorder and, 94; depression and, 79; mental illness and, 7; schizophrenia and, 124
geriatric patients, 231-233
ginkgo biloba, 211
glucocorticoid receptors (GR), 39
glutamate, 31
glutethimide, 193
glycine, 31
goiter, 184
G-protein mediated second messenger system, 32, 33
grand mal seizures, 178, 204
grief, 69-70

H
half-life of medications, 47, 194
hallucinogens, 151
hand tremors, 183-184
hematological effects, 185, 188
hepatitis, 204
herbal remedies, 209-212; antidepressant, 176-177; documented benefits of, 211; guidelines for therapists, 210; need for research on, 212; problems with, 209-210
heroin, 150
heterocyclic antidepressants, 164

hippocampus, 39
Hippocrates, 16
history: of biological psychiatry, 4; of patient
    medication use, 232
homeostasis, 32
Horowitz, Mardi, 131
human genome, 34
Human Genome Project, 237
Hume, David, 212
hydroxyzine, 195
hyperactivity, 155
hyperarousal, 135
hyperthermia, 204
hypnotics, 193, 194
hypomania, 85-86
hypothalamic-pituitary-adrenal (HPA) axis,
    38-39, 93, 104
hypothalamic-pituitary-thyroid (HPT) axis,
    39
hypothalamus, 35, 38-39
hypothyroidism, 184
hysteroid-dysphoric borderline personality,
    140

I
idiosyncratic effects, 49
illness. *See* medical disorders
I'm Dancing As Fast As I Can (Gordon), 198
imipramine, 6, 163
impulse-control disorders (ICDs), 114
impulsivity, 155
inattention, 155
induced psychotic disorder, 121
induction, 226
inhalants, 151
inhibition, 226
insomnia, 109, 193
insulin shock, 5
integrated approaches, 4
interactions, drug, 49-50, 225-227, 239-246;
    anticonvulsants, 244; antipsychotics, 244;
    benzodiazepine, 245; lithium, 243;
    monoamine oxidase inhibitors, 242;
    nefazodone, 246; selective serotonin
    reuptake inhibitors, 241; tricyclic antide-
    pressants, 240; venlafaxine, 246
intoxication, 146
intrusive symptoms, 135-136
ion-channel mediated process, 32
ionic actions, 32
iproniazid, 6, 163

K
kava kava, 211
kidney function, 47, 184-185
kindling, 19, 92, 136
Klein, Donald, 140
Kraepelin, Emil, 4, 5, 92
Kramer, Peter, 60

L
lamotrigine, 189
L-dopa, 149

learned helplessness, 18
learning disorders, 153
Librium, 7, 193
ligands, 28, 51
light therapy, 77
limbic system, 36; anxiety disorders and,
    101-102, 104; depressive disorders and, 80
Lindeman, Eric, 131
linophilic drugs, 51
Listening to Prozac (Kramer), 60
lithium, 182-187; aggressive behavior and,
    159; blood level monitoring of, 183, 185,
    186; child and adolescent use of, 234;
    dosage guidelines for, 183; drug interac-
    tions with, 243; history of psychiatric use
    of, 182; mechanism of action for, 185-187;
    pregnancy risks and, 185, 230; schizo-
    phrenia and, 127; side effects of, 183-185,
    186, 217; signs of toxicity or overdose,
    218; treatment guidelines for, 182-183
lithium carbonate, 7
liver function, 188, 210
locus coeruleus (LC), 101, 103, 108
lorazepam, 193
LSD (lysergic acid diethylamide), 151

M
maintenance treatment phase, 173
major unipolar depressions, 70-75; atypical
    depressions, 74; biological depressions,
    71, 73-74; efficacy of medications for,
    74-75; length of treatment for, 219;
    phases of treatment for, 173-174; reactive
    depressions, 71; reactive-biological
    depressions, 71, 73-74; resistant to treat-
    ment, 174-175
malaria therapy, 5
managed care, 11-12
mania: diagnosis of, 85-86; drugs causative
    of, 89; medical conditions associated
    with, 87; stages of acute, 86; treatments
    for, 181
manic-depressive illness. *See* bipolar
    disorders
MAOIs. *See* monoamine oxidase inhibitors
meclobemide, 169
medical disorders, 62-67; anxiety associated
    with, 100, 105, 106, 109-110; checklists for
    diagnosing, 65-66; cognitive functioning
    and, 64-65; depression caused by, 72, 79;
    mania and, 87; neurochemistry and, 67;
    onset of new conditions and, 215; physi-
    cal symptoms indicative of, 66; psychiat-
    ric disorders due to, 62-64; psychotic
    disorders caused by, 120-121
medications: absorption of, 44-45, 224;
    antianxiety, 193-200; antidepressant,
    163-180; antipsychotic, 201-208; argu-
    ments in favor of, 8-9; biotransformation
    of, 46-47, 225; bodily distribution of,
    45-46, 224; books for patients about,
    259-260; cellular-level effects of, 50-51;

child and adolescent use of, 233-237, 238; discontinuing, 215, 218; dosage adjustments to, 214; educating patients about, 176, 190, 199-200, 207-208, 258-260; effects of, 49; excretion of, 47-48; failure to respond to, 213-214; geriatric patients and, 231-233; interactions between, 49-50, 225-227, 239-246; length of treatment with, 219; managed care and, 11-12; meanings attributed to, 21-25; media attention on, 8-10; mood stabilizers, 181-191; pregnancy risks and, 229-231; psychotherapy vs., 8-9; receptor actions and, 51-53; side effects of, 49, 215, 216-217; signs of toxicity or overdose, 218; special populations and, 229-238; therapeutic index for, 227; trade vs. generic names of, 255-257; withdrawal symptoms from, 198-199. *See also* drugs; treatments
melatonin, 211
Mental Status Examination in Neurology, The (Strub and Black), 251
meprobamate, 7, 193
mescaline, 151
messenger molecules, 30-31
metabolic actions, 32
metabolic disorders, 17, 237
metabolic drug interactions, 49-50, 225-227, 239-246
metabolism of medications, 46-47, 225
metabolites, 46, 225
methadone, 150-151
methylphenidate: attention deficit disorder and, 156; controversy about, 8-9
methyprylon, 193
Michaels, Robert, 60
midazolam, 193
minor depressions, 76-77
mirtazapine, 166, 170
monoamine hypothesis of depression, 79-80, 81
monoamine oxidase (MAO), 163, 169
monoamine oxidase inhibitors (MAOIs), 163, 167, 169; anxiety disorders and, 105, 109, 110; atypical depression and, 74; development of, 163; dosages of, 171; drug interactions with, 242; seasonal affective disorder and, 77; self-injurious behavior and, 157; side effects of, 216
mood disorders. *See* depressive disorders
mood stabilizers, 181-191; anticonvulsants, 187-189; atypical antipsychotics, 189; blood level monitoring of, 183, 185, 186, 188; child and adolescent use of, 238; combinations of, 190; dosage guidelines for, 183, 188; educating patients about, 190; length of treatment with, 190; lithium, 182-187; mechanism of action for, 185-187; psychotherapy used with, 191; side effects of, 183-185, 187-189, 217;

treatment guidelines for, 182; trends in using, 181-182. *See also* bipolar disorders
morality issues, 22
"Mourning and Melancholia" (Freud), 69
MRI scans, 124

N
naltrexone, 148, 154, 157
narcissistic patients, 25
nefazodone, 167, 170, 246
Nemeroff, Charles, 134
nerve cells, 27-28
nervous system: autonomic, 39; conduction and transmission, 28-30; divisions of, 38; effects of receptor binding, 30; intercellular communication, 28; nerve cells, 27-28; neuronal malfunction, 33-34; parasympathetic, 39; peripheral, 39-40; receptors, 31-33; sympathetic, 38
neuroanatomy, 34-35
neurobiology, 27-41; brain structures and, 35-40; cellular nervous system and, 27-34; neuroanatomy and, 34-35; psychopathology and, 40-41
neurochemistry, 7, 67
neurocognitive mental status exam, 251-254
neuroendocrine pathways, 38, 102
neuro-imaging techniques, 11-12
neuroleptic malignant syndrome (NMS), 204
neurologic side effects, 183-184, 187
neuromuscular symptoms, 183-184
neurons, 27-28; malfunction of, 33-34; structure of, 28
neurophysiological models of schizophrenia, 126-127
neuroprotective proteins, 187
neurotic anxiety, 100, 106-107, 110
neurotransmitters, 27; effects on receptors, 30; neuronal malfunction and, 33-34; typology of, 30-31
nicotine, 62, 151
N-methyl-D-aspartate (NMDA) receptor, 126
nocturnal myoclonus, 158
noradrenergic hypothesis, 107
norepinephrine, 39; depressive disorders and, 79-80; lithium and, 186-187
norepinephrine reuptake inhibitors (NRIs), 163, 167; dosages of, 171; side effects of, 165, 167

O
obesity, 158
obsessive-compulsive disorder (OCD), 98, 113-117; behavioral techniques for, 115-116; books for patients about, 260; diagnosis of, 113-114; etiology of, 114-115; facts about, 114; length of treatment for, 219; medications for, 115-117; patients medicated for, 24; psychotherapy and, 115; quick reference to, 117; Tourette's syndrome and, 153; treatments for, 115-117

obsessive-compulsive personality disorder (OCP), 114
olanzapine, 125, 206
opiates, 150-151
organs: effects of nervous system activity on, 40; fetal development of, 230
orlistat, 158
overdose, 218
over-the-counter (OTC) products: antidepressants, 176-178; documented benefits of, 211; guidelines for therapists, 210; herbal remedies, 176-177, 209-212; need for research on, 212; problems with, 209-210, 212; side effects of, 211, 212
oxcarbazepine, 189

P
pain, chronic, 159
panic attacks: anxiety symptoms vs., 97-98; medications for, 110; stress-induced, 104
panic disorder, 100; biological factors in, 107, 108; length of treatment for, 219; treatments for, 110-111
paranoid patients, 24
paranoid schizophrenia, 122
parasympathetic nervous system, 39, 40
Parkinsonian side effects, 203, 248
paroxetine, 166, 170
pathophysiology, 58
patient compliance, 11, 208, 214
patient education: on antianxiety medications, 199-200; on antidepressant medications, 176; on antipsychotic medications, 207-208; books for, 259-260; on mood stabilizers, 190
PDR for Herbal Medicines, 211
pemoline, 156
peripheral nervous system, 39-40
personality traits: biochemical disorders and, 60, 61; psychological disorders and, 57-60
PET scans, 11, 18-19, 124
pharmacodynamics, 44
pharmacokinetics, 43-50, 223-227; absorption, 44-45, 223-224; distribution, 45-46, 224; drug interactions, 49-50, 225-227, 239-246; metabolism, 46-47, 225
pharmacological effect, 49
pharmacology, 43-53; age-specific, 232; cellular level effects and, 50-51; pharmacokinetic factors and, 43-50; receptor actions and, 51-52, 53
phencyclidine (PCP), 146, 151; model of schizophrenia, 126
phenelzine, 169
phenothiazines, 201
phentermine, 158
phobias, 99, 104, 109
physical illness. *See* medical disorders
postpartum depression, 78
postsynaptic neuron, 29
post-traumatic stress disorder (PTSD), 98, 131-138; diagnosis of, 133-134; etiology

of, 134-137; facts about, 134; length of treatment for, 219; medications for, 136, 137; psychotherapy for, 137; quick reference to, 138; stress response syndrome and, 131-132; symptoms of, 133; treatments for, 137
prefrontal cortex, 115, 116
pregnancy, 185, 229-231
premenstrual dysphoric disorder (PMDD), 77-78
presynaptic neuron, 28
primary psychoses, 121
primary sleep disorders, 157-158
propoxyphene, 150
propranolol, 109, 195
protein signaling network theory, 93
Prozac, 9-10, 166, 170
psilocybin, 151
psychiatric disorders: alcohol abuse and, 148; anxiety symptoms due to, 100, 105-106, 109-110; biological factors in, 40-41; differentiating drug side effects from, 247-249; medical disorders as cause of, 62-64; unexplained relapse of, 214
psychiatry: contemporary changes in, 3-4; history of biological psychiatry, 4-13
psychological factors: biology and, 16-20, 41; stressful life events, 40-41, 134-137
psychological masquerade, 62-63
psycho-neuro-immunology, 18
psychopathology, 40-41
psychopharmacology: history of, 4-13; managed care dilemma and, 11-12; reasons for learning about, 13-14
psychosomatic medicine, 17
psychostimulants: child and adolescent use of, 234; prescribing for depression, 169
psychosurgery, 5
psychotherapy: anxiety disorders and, 109, 110, 111; arguments in favor of, 9; bipolar disorders and, 94, 191; books for patients about, 260; brain functioning and, 18-19; depressive disorders and, 83, 175; managed care and, 11-12; medication vs., 8-9; obsessive-compulsive disorder and, 115; post-traumatic stress disorder and, 137; schizophrenia and, 208
psychotic depressions, 75
psychotic disorders, 120-129; anticholinergic effects vs., 248; books for patients about, 259; diagnosis of, 120-123; educating patients about, 207-208, 259; etiology of, 124-127; facts about, 120; length of treatment for, 207, 219; medical conditions as cause of, 119-120; medications for, 127-128, 201-208; primary psychoses, 121; psychotherapy for, 208; quick reference to, 129; schizophrenia, 121-123, 207, 208; symptoms of, 123; treatments for, 127-128, 201-208. *See also* antipsychotic medications

psychotropic medications: prescriptions written for, 11; side effects of, 216-217. *See also* medications
PTSD. *See* post-traumatic stress disorder
published resources for patients, 259-260

Q
quetiapine, 206
quezepam, 195
Quinlan, Karen Ann, 199

R
rapid cycling bipolar disorders, 91
rapid neuroleptization, 207
reactive-biological depressions, 74
reactive depressions, 71
reactive sadness, 69
reboxetine, 167, 170
receptors: binding of neurotransmitters to, 30; drug effects and, 51-53; impact of stress on, 32; intracellular actions and, 31-33; side effects and, 51-53
regulated systems, 32
relapse, 214
repetition compulsion, 135
resistance, 25
restless legs syndrome, 158
reuptake transporter pump, 30
risks of medication use: in children and adolescents, 233-237; in geriatric patients, 231-233; in patients with unusual metabolisms, 237; in pregnancy, 229-231
risperidone, 125, 206
Ritalin, 8-9, 156

S
sadness, reactive, 69
SAM-e, 177-178, 211
schizoaffective disorder, 121
schizophrenia, 121-123; diagnosis of, 121-123; dopamine model of, 124-126; educating patients about, 207-208; etiology of, 124-127; medications for, 127-128, 201-208; neurophysiological models of, 126-127; phencyclidine model of, 126; psychotherapy and, 208; quick reference to, 129; relapse and, 207; symptoms of, 123; treatments for, 127-128, 201-208; types of, 122
schizophreniform disorder, 121
schizotypal borderline personality, 140
seasonal affective disorder (SAD), 77
second messenger systems, 32, 33-34
secondary sleep disorders, 157
sedation side effects, 201, 205
seizures, 178, 204
selective serotonin reuptake inhibitors (SSRIs), 163, 166; aggressive behavior and, 159; anxiety disorders and, 104, 109, 110; atypical depression and, 74; dosages of, 171; drug interactions with, 241; eating disorders and, 154; obsessive-compulsive disorder and, 115;

premenstrual dysphoric disorder and, 78; seasonal affective disorder and, 77; self-injurious behavior and, 157; side effects of, 165, 166, 172, 216
selegiline, 169
self-mutilation, 156-157
separation anxiety, 103-104, 105
serotonin: anxiety disorders and, 103; atypical antipsychotics and, 205; depressive disorders and, 79-80; lithium and, 187; seasonal affective disorder and, 77; self-mutilation and, 157
serotonin and norepinephrine reuptake inhibitors (SNRIs), 163, 166; dosages of, 171; side effects of, 165, 166
sertraline, 166, 170
shell shock, 131
Sherrington, C. S., 7
sibutramine, 158
side effects, 216-217; of anticonvulsants, 187-189; of antidepressants, 164, 165, 166, 171-172; of antipsychotics, 203-205; differentiating from psychiatric symptoms, 247-249; geriatric patients and, 233; of lithium, 183-185, 186; medication effects and, 49; monitoring, 215; of OTC products, 211; patient compliance and, 11; receptor actions and, 51-53; summary table of, 216-217
signaling mechanisms, 32
sleep apnea, 157
sleep disorders, 157-158
SNRIs. *See* serotonin and norepinephrine reuptake inhibitors
social anxiety disorder, 99
social phobias, 99; biological factors in, 104-105; treatments for, 109
somatic therapies, 5-6
SPECT scans, 11
SSRIs. *See* selective serotonin reuptake inhibitors
St. John's Wort, 176-177, 210, 211
steady state, 47-48
stimulants: abuse of, 149-150; child and adolescent use of, 234; prescribing for depression, 169
stimulus-response specificity, 20-21
stress: acute reactions to, 131-132; anxiety associated with, 99, 109; biology altered by, 134-137; brain functioning and, 41; depression and, 79; impact on receptors, 32; psychopathology and, 40-41; relapse and, 214. *See also* post-traumatic stress disorder
stress response syndrome, 131-132
Stress Response Syndromes (Horowitz), 131
substance abuse, 145-152; alcoholism and, 147-148; anxiety from, 100, 105, 106, 109-110; diagnosis of, 60-62, 145-147; disorders mimicked by, 147; DSM-IV definition of, 146; facts about, 146; hallucinogens and, 151; medications for,

148, 150, 151; opiates and, 150-151; psychotic symptoms and, 120; quick reference on, 152; stimulants and, 149-150;
treatments for, 148, 150, 151
substance P, 30
suicide: borderline personality patients and,
142; major depression and, 71; Prozac
and, 9-10
sympathetic nervous system, 38, 39, 40
symptoms: of anxiety disorders, 98; of
benzodiazepine withdrawal, 198-199; of
bipolar disorders, 86; of borderline personality disorders, 140; of depressive disorders, 71, 73, 74, 76, 84; of
post-traumatic stress disorder, 133; of
psychotic disorders, 123; of schizophrenia, 123
synapse, 7, 28-29

T
tardive dyskinesia, 204, 205, 207, 248-249
target symptoms, 59
Taylor, Robert, 62
TCAs. *See* tricyclic antidepressants
teratogenesis, 185, 229, 230
terminal boutons, 27
Terr, Lenore, 134
therapeutic index, 227
therapeutic window, 183
Thorazine, 6, 201
thyroid function, 184
tiagabine, 189
Tofranil, 6, 163
tolerance, 146, 214
topiramate, 189
Tourette's syndrome, 153
toxicity, 46, 59, 218
trade names of medications, 255-257
tranquilizers, 10
transcranial magnetic stimulation (TMS), 175
transfer RNA (tRNA), 34
transmission, 29
tranylcypromine, 169
treatment-resistant depression (TRD),
174-175, 180
treatments: for aggression, 159; for alcohol-related disorders, 148; for anxiety

disorders, 107-111, 193-200; for attention
deficit disorder, 156; for bipolar disorders, 94, 181-191; for borderline personality disorders, 142; for chronic pain, 159;
for depressive disorders, 81-83; for eating
disorders, 154; for obesity, 158; for obsessive-compulsive disorder, 115-117; for
post-traumatic stress disorder, 137; for
psychotic disorders, 127-128, 201-208; for
schizophrenia, 127-128; for self-injurious
behavior, 157; for sleep disorders,
157-158; for substance abuse, 148, 150,
151. *See also* medications
triazolam, 193
tricyclic antidepressants (TCAs), 164-169;
dosages of, 171; drug interactions with,
240; side effects of, 164, 165, 172, 216
tyamine, 168
tybamate, 193

U
up-regulation, 32

V
vagal nerve stimulation (VNS), 175
valerian root, 212
Valium abuse, 198
van der Kolk, Bessel A., 134
venlafaxine, 159, 166, 170, 246
vesicles, 29

W
Ward, Nicholas, 76
weight gain, 185
Wellbutrin, 111n, 151, 167, 170, 245
Winter Blues (Rosenthal), 77
withdrawal symptoms, 146, 198-199

X
Xanax, 198

Y
yohimbine, 212

Z
zaleplon, 195
ziprasidone, 206
zolpidem, 195

John Preston, Psy.D., ABPP, is a licensed clinical psychologist and author of eleven books in the areas of neurobiology, psychopharmacology, and psychotherapy. He is on the faculty of Alliant International University's California School of Professional Psychology, Sacramento, and has served on the faculty of the University of California at Davis School of Medicine. He has lectured widely in the United States and abroad.

Mary C. Talaga, R.Ph., M.A., is Pharmacy Services Manager at the Kaiser South Sacramento Medical Center. She holds a B.S. in Pharmacy and a master's degree in Clinical Psychology with an emphasis in Organizational Development. She has been a pharmacist for 25 years, with specialization in psychiatric pharmacy. Ms. Talaga has held a number of management, patient care, and drug utilization positions throughout her career. Her current projects include development of collaborative care models for the treatment of depression in primary care. She frequently provides clinical in-service training to health professionals and general education to patients and consumers.

John H. O'Neal, M.D., has been a board-certified psychiatrist in private practice since 1977. Dr. O'Neal is a past chief of the Department of Psychiatry at Sutter Community Hospital in Sacramento. He is an associate clinical professor of psychiatry at the University of California at Davis School of Medicine and a Fellow of the American Psychiatric Association. He lectures on depression and psychopharmacology to mental health professionals, employee assistance programs, and the public. Dr. O'Neal received his EdM in clinical psychology from Harvard University.

Some Other
New Harbinger Titles

Surviving Your Borderline Parent, Item 3287 $14.95

When Anger Hurts, second edition, Item 3449 $16.95

Calming Your Anxious Mind, Item 3384 $12.95

Ending the Depression Cycle, Item 3333 $17.95

Your Surviving Spirit, Item 3570 $18.95

Coping with Anxiety, Item 3201 $10.95

The Agoraphobia Workbook, Item 3236 $19.95

Loving the Self-Absorbed, Item 3546 $14.95

Transforming Anger, Item 352X $10.95

Don't Let Your Emotions Run Your Life, Item EMOT $17.95

Why Can't I Ever Be Good Enough, Item WCIB $13.95

Your Depression Map, Item YDM $19.95

Successful Problem Solving, Item SPS $17.95

Working with the Self-Absorbed, Item WSAB $14.95

The Procrastination Workbook, Item PROW $17.95

Coping with Uncertainty, Item COPE $11.95

The BDD Workbook, Item BDDW $18.95

You, Your Relationship, and Your ADD, Item YYY $17.95

The Stop Walking on Eggshells Workbook, Item SWEW $18.95

Conquer Your Critical Inner Voice, Item CYIC $15.95

The PTSD Workbook, Item PWK $17.95

Hypnotize Yourself Out of Pain Now!, Item HYOP $14.95

The Depression Workbook, 2nd edition, Item DWR2 $19.95

Beating the Senior Blues, Item YCBS $17.95

Shared Confinement, Item SDCF $15.95

Call **toll free, 1-800-748-6273,** or log on to our online bookstore at **www.newharbinger.com** to order. Have your Visa or Mastercard number ready. Or send a check for the titles you want to New Harbinger Publications, Inc., 5674 Shattuck Ave., Oakland, CA 94609. Include $4.50 for the first book and 75¢ for each additional book, to cover shipping and handling. (California residents please include appropriate sales tax.) Allow two to five weeks for delivery.

Prices subject to change without notice.

Quick Reference to Psychotropic Medication®

To the best of our knowledge recommended doses and side effects listed below are accurate. However, this is meant as a general reference only, and should not serve as a guideline for prescribing of medications. Physicians, please check the manufacturer's product information sheet or the *PDR* for any changes in dosage schedule or contraindications. (Brand names are registered trademarks.) Note: Doses are for adults. Elderly patients generally require lower doses.

ANTIDEPRESSANTS

Names Generic	Brand	Usual Daily Dosage Range	Sedation	ACH[1]	Selective Action On Neurotransmitters[2] NE	5-HT
imipramine	Tofranil	150–300 mg	++	++	++	+++
desipramine	Norpramin	150–300 mg	+	+	+++++	0
amitriptyline	Elavil	150–300 mg	++++	++++	+	++++
nortriptyline	Aventyl, Pamelor	75–125 mg	++	++	+++	++
protriptyline	Vivactil	15–40 mg	++	++	++++	+
trimipramine	Surmontil[3]	100–300 mg	++++	+++	++	++
doxepin	Sinequan, Adapin[3]	150–300 mg	++++	++	+++	++
maprotiline	Ludiomil	150–225 mg	++	++	+++++	0
amoxapine	Asendin	150–400 mg	++	+	++++	+
trazodone	Desyrel	150–400 mg	++	0	0	+++++
fluoxetine	Prozac, Sarafem	20–80 mg	+	0	0	+++++
bupropion SR	Wellbutrin SR[4]	150–300 mg	+	0	++	0
sertraline	Zoloft	50–200 mg	+	0	0	+++++
paroxetine	Paxil	20–50 mg	+	+	+	+++++
venlafaxine XR	Effexor XR	75–350 mg	+	0	++	+++
nefazodone	Serzone	100–500 mg	++	0	+	++++
fluvoxamine	Luvox	50–300 mg	+	+	0	+++++
mirtazapine	Remeron	15–45 mg	++	++	+++	+++
citalopram	Celexa	10–60 mg	+	0	0	+++++
MAO INHIBITORS						
phenelzine	Nardil[5]	30–90 mg	+	0	+++	+++
tranylcypromine	Parnate[5]	20–60 mg	+	0	+++	+++
isocarboxazid	Marplan	10–40 mg	+	0	+++	+++

1 ACH: Anticholinergic Side Effects.
2 NE: norepinephrine; 5-HT: serotonin.
3 Uncertain, but likely effects.
4 Atypical antidepressant. Uncertain effects but likely to be a dopamine agonist, and indirect increase in norepinephrine.
5 MAO inhibitors operate via a different mechanism of action than other antidepressants, and increase NE. 5-HT, and dopamine.

ANTI-OBSESSIONAL

Names Generic	Brand	Dose Range[1]	Sedation	ACH Effects
clomipramine	Anafranil	150–250 mg	++++	++++
fluoxetine	Prozac[1]	20–80 mg	+	0
sertraline	Zoloft[1]	50–200 mg	+	0
paroxetine	Paxil[1]	20–60 mg	+	+
fluvoxamine	Luvox	50–300 mg	+	+
citalopram	Celexa	10–60 mg	+	0

1 Often higher doses are required to control obsessive-compulsive symptoms than the doses generally used to treat depression.

PSYCHO-STIMULANTS

Names Generic	Brand	Daily Doses[1]
methylphenidate	Ritalin	5–50 mg
methylphenidate	Concerta[2]	18–54 mg
methylphenidate	Metadate	5–50 mg
dextroamphetamine	Dexedrine	5–40 mg
pemoline	Cylert	37.5–112.5 mg
d- and l-amphetamine	Adderall	5–40 mg

1 *Note:* Adult doses.
2 Sustained release.

MOOD STABILIZERS

Names Generic	Brand	Daily Dosage Range	Serum[1] Level
lithium carbonate	Eskalith, Lithonate	600–2400	0.6–1.5
carbamazepine	Tegretol	600–1600	4–10+
divalproex	Depakote, Depakene	750–1500	50–100
gabapentin	Neurontin	300–1800	n/a
lamotrigine	Lamictal	50–500	n/a
topiramate	Topamax	50–300	n/a

1 Lithium levels are expressed in mEq/l; carbamazepine and valproic acid levels are expressed in mcg/ml.

HYPNOTICS[1]

Names Generic	Brand	Daily Doses
flurazepam	Dalmane	15–60 mg
temazepam	Restoril	15–30 mg
triazolam	Halcion	0.25–0.5 mg
estazolam	ProSom	1.0–2.0 mg
quazepam	Doral	7.5–30 mg
zolpidem	Ambien	5–10 mg
diphenhydramine	Benadryl	25–100 mg

1 To treat initial insomnia